Amazing
Iowa

★ ★ ★

Janice Beck Stock

Rutledge Hill Press®
Nashville, Tennessee

A Division of Thomas Nelson, Inc.
www.ThomasNelson.com

To my family, my friends, and all the wonderful people who call Iowa home

Published by Rutledge Hill Press, a Division of Thomas Nelson, Inc., P.O. Box 141000, Nashville, Tennessee 37214.

Library of Congress Cataloging-in-Publication Data

Stock, Janice Beck, 1954–
    Amazing Iowa / Janice Beck Stock.
      p. cm.
    Includes index.
    ISBN 1-55853-960-3 (pbk.)
    1. Iowa—Miscellanea. 2. Iowa—History—Miscellanea. I. Title.
F621.6.S76 2003
977.7—dc21   2003013076

Printed in the United States of America

03 04 05 06 07 — 5 4 3 2 1

CONTENTS

PREFACE

Anyone who knows me knows I love my home state—I'm proud to be an Iowan. As you read through these pages you'll come to realize why. Iowa is more than corn and hogs (although there's a lot of both, and, no, we don't grow potatoes—well—a few). Iowa is so much more.

I thoroughly enjoyed working on this book. It was a labor of love, though it took longer than I thought it would. There's always something more to discover. If you know of some great tales that I missed or just couldn't fit in (I ran out of time as well as space), let me know through my publisher, Rutledge Hill Press, a Division of Thomas Nelson, Inc., at *www.rutledgehillpress.com*.

This book is by no means a comprehensive history of the Hawkeye State. Some important stories, such as those about Herbert Hoover and the Henry Wallaces, are not given much space because their stories were covered in greater detail in an earlier Rutledge Hill book entitled *A Treasury of Iowa Tales,* which I helped research and review. The stories I chose to include were ones that are perhaps less well known or unique. Many that I included I found only in very old books, and they were important enough to be recorded again and not lost.

History is to each individual what he knows of the past and I hope, through this book, to help add to that knowledge. Official records and historical accounts often lack human interest, but I hope you won't find that true of this book. I want it to be read and enjoyed so that others might catch some of the enthusiasm I have for Iowa—for its past, its present, and its future. And whether you're from Iowa or just curious about it, I think you'll discover, too, that Iowa is so much more than you realized—truly amazing!

ACKNOWLEDGMENTS

I'd like to thank the personnel at the chambers of commerce and colleges throughout the state for the information they sent to me when I was working on another book, *Iowa Trivia,* which I wrote with the help of my cousin, Ken Beck, and my brother, Alan Beck. This material gave me a jump-start on stories for this book. I would also like to thank the historical societies in Iowa who sent their unusual and interesting tales for possible use—and a special thanks to those who took the time to talk to me on the phone and mail me (often at their personal expense) more detail on stories. Thanks to Dawn Lloyd, librarian at the Titonka Public Library, who e-mailed my plea for assistance to all the libraries in the state, and thanks to those librarians who replied.

I thank the people at Guinness for their help with world records from Iowa, and Pat Glynn at Wireless Flash News for some unique items. I really appreciated the advice and well wishes of Loren Horton, retired senior historian for the State Historical Society of Iowa.

I'm grateful to the Iowa Division of Tourism for allowing me to use some of its photographs, and for providing a wonderful website, *www.traveliowa.com,* which was invaluable in checking out sites throughout the state. Another invaluable tool was the "Famous Iowans" column by Tom Longden of the *Des Moines Register.* I appreciate the wonderful books written about the state and the authors who took the time to write them. I love history, I love reading and research, and I loved your books. (I feel like I've read them all, though I'm sure that can't be true.) I hope that *Amazing Iowa* contributes to this literature and helps to keep the stories of Iowa alive and interesting to the next generation of Iowans.

I wish to thank Larry Stone, my publisher at Rutledge Hill Press, for giving me the opportunity to do this book and for his faith in my ability, and Jennifer Greenstein, my wonderfully patient editor.

And, speaking of patience, I'd like to express my undying gratitude to my wonderful friends and family who offered encouragement when things started to slow me down. Thanks to my brother, mom, and dad for their photo-gathering trips, and especially to my daughters, Emily and Sally, and my husband, Jack, for putting up with many impromptu meals and slap-dash housework. I couldn't have done it without you.

1
The Land

A Place to Grow

The land brought people to Iowa and the land made most of them prosper and stay. Known for its fertile soil and agricultural prowess, Iowa leads the nation in production of

★ Pork

★ Corn for grain

★ Soybeans

★ Eggs

Ninety-one percent of the land area in the state is agricultural—the highest percentage of cultivated acres in the country.

But the first settlers were uncertain of the productivity of the wide-open prairie with its howling winds and fires. Even Father Jacques Marquette—he and Louis Joliet were the first white men known to step foot on what became Iowa soil—admitted as much. He wrote, "At first when we were told of these treeless lands, I imagined that it was a country ravaged by fire, where the soil was so poor that it could produce nothing." But those who followed quickly realized otherwise. Marquette went on to write, "But we have certainly observed the contrary; and no better soil can be found either for corn, or for vines, or for any other fruit whatever."

Legal settlement began in Iowa in 1833 and word spread quickly about the agricultural richness that lay beneath the head-high grasses and wild-flowers. Thirty million acres of prairie were broken by the plow and Iowa became an agricultural promised land. And small pockets of the virgin prairie have been protected, so that future generations can see how it all began. Iowans have become good stewards of the land, for no one knows better than an Iowan the treasure upon which he stands.

Did You Know? Robert Frost once wrote about the soil of Iowa, "It looks good enough to eat without putting it through vegetables." And it's priced to match! The average price of Iowa farmland rose to $2,434 an acre in the year ending March 1, 2002.

As Good As Gold

The John Hugh Williams family immigrated to Homer, Iowa, in the 1850s. During the Panic of 1857, their eldest son, James, was sent to Georgia to work. The family's correspondence to James from late 1858 until the secession crisis of 1861 offers a wealth of information about the daily life of an ordinary family on the Iowa prairie.

In the book *This State of Wonders—Letters of an Iowa Frontier Family, 1858–1861,* from the University of Iowa Press, father J. H. Williams writes in March 1859 about gold fever from the discovery of that precious metal in the Pikes Peak area of Colorado. He wrote, "It is entirely over looked, by the excited I might add ignorant beings that are runing a way from this state, in quest of Gold; there is more gold, in the green carpet which covers these extended plains, than can be obtained from any mine in California, or Pikes P." As an aside, he accurately predicted that "California will no doubt make a fine state not so much because there is Gold, there as because a large portion of it is well suited to agriculture . . ."

Soil Not Ours to Sell

Black Hawk, the proud leader of a band of Sauk Indians, knew the value of the soil and refused to believe that land could be bought, as evidenced in this excerpt from *The Autobiography of Black Hawk,* published in 1834:

> *My reason teaches me that land cannot be sold. The Great Spirit gives it to his children to live upon, and cultivate, as far as it is necessary for their subsistence, and so long as they occupy and cultivate it, they have the right to the soil. . . . Nothing can be sold but such things as can be carried away.*

Where the Tall Corn Grows

Most people associate Iowa with farms, and the product that first comes to mind is corn. (This is assuming that they know Iowa well enough not to confuse it with Ohio or Idaho.) Iowa has been the top corn-producing state in the nation since 1983 and has been at or near the top since the late 1800s. It was once thought that the taller the corn, the better, and that the best-looking ears should be saved as seed for the next year. But hybrid corn changed all that.

Hybridization and mechanization increased corn yields from 26.4 bushels an acre in 1926 to *146 bushels* an acre in 2001. Hybrid corn resulted in more even stands with good ears, and mechanical harvesters could pick the corn faster with less manpower.

If you are in Iowa between June and September, the corn you're most likely to see is dent corn. Dent corn makes up the bulk of Iowa and U.S. production. Two other types of corn you might see are sweet corn and popcorn.

Here's how to prepare sweet corn. (Of course, to have the best sweet corn you must start with *Iowa* sweet corn.) Simply boil it in salted water for a couple of minutes and serve it with salt and butter or you can cook it in the microwave. There's nothing else like it!

No corn tastes better than Iowa sweet corn. (PHOTO BY AUTHOR)

Corn Isn't Just for Eating!

Although there's nothing like a fresh ear of corn, most of it *isn't* used for food for people. The biggest use for Iowa's most popular crop is feeding livestock. Over a billion bushels are fed to cattle, hogs, chickens, turkeys, and other livestock in Iowa and around the world.

The second major use is processing into sweeteners, starches, corn oil, feed products, and ethanol. Since 1985 Americans have relied on corn more than sugar for sweeteners in their foods and soft drinks. (Ask any person who is allergic to corn and he or she will tell you the difficulty in finding products that contain no corn.) Corn-based ingredients are used in cough syrups, antibiotics, IV solutions, aspirin, and vitamins.

One of the newest markets for corn is in the production of polyactic acid, or PLA. PLA polymers are made from corn sugars. They can be used to make fabric more stain- and wrinkle-resistant, increase the gloss and clarity of plastic packaging, and make patio furniture more resistant to sun damage. And PLA, unlike synthetic materials such as petroleum-based plastic, is biodegradable and produced from annually renewable resources.

Think about that the next time you crunch into an ear of corn!

Did You Know? A refined corn product, Steepwater, helped win World War II! It was used in the production of large amounts of penicillin.

The Fruited Plain

Phil Stong, famous for his novel *State Fair*, wrote the following observations about Iowa in his book *Hawkeyes*:

> It is a farm state; first in corn, first in hogs and first in the gizzards of its countrymen. . . . Something more than the world's popcorn center is certain to come out of one-fourth of all the best land in the United States. You cannot have so much manure behind you and not sprout some fruit. . . . The economic situation makes evident the fact that in order to make the farmers of America prosperous it is necessary only to shoot everyone in Iowa and forbid its resettlement.

Strange . . . but True

During the growing season, you can watch Iowa corn grow by visiting the website *www.iowafarmer.com/corncam/corn.html*. Every fifteen minutes a digital camera records the corn's progress.

Did You Know? An Iowan invented the word "tractor"—short for gasoline traction engine. The word was popularized in 1907 by W. H. Williams, the sales manager of the Hart-Parr Company of Charles City. He had been trying to think of a shorter word for an ad to describe the machines the company was producing.

Everything but the Oink!

Iowa accounts for nearly 25 percent of the nation's pork production. Hogs provide a wider range of products than any other animal, from meat to pharmaceutical and industrial by-products. Iowa pork producers and researchers have been in the forefront in producing pork that's low in fat and waste, and high in nutrition and taste. Iowa hogs also are used to make items that range from heart valves and insulin to bone china, pigskin garments, and glue. Iowa pork has become the standard for excellence in pork products worldwide.

Here's a wonderful recipe for pork chop marinade. Of course, the marinade is only as good as the meat it covers, so use pork from Iowa. A good choice is the Iowa-cut pork chop.

Marinade for Pork Chops

1½ cups oil

¾ cup soy sauce

¼ cup Worcestershire sauce

½ cup wine vinegar

⅓ cup lemon juice

2 tablespoons dry mustard

2½ teaspoons salt

1 tablespoon pepper

1½ teaspoons dry parsley

⅛ teaspoon garlic powder

Mix together all the ingredients. Marinate pork chops for at least 3 to 4 hours in the refrigerator. It's best if the meat is completely covered; if it isn't, turn it once while marinating. Grill over a slow fire. Makes 3⅓ cups of marinade, enough to cover 6 to 8 pork chops. (You can marinate more pork chops, if you turn them once during marinating.)

Strange . . . but True

Shipwreck Leads to Sioux City Meatpacking

James E. Booge, a Vermont native, used the money he made prospecting for gold in California to buy a boatload of apples, flour, and whiskey in St. Louis in 1858. He planned to sell these supplies as he made his way up the Missouri River, but when he arrived in Sioux City on October 11, he still had most of the cargo with him. So he and his brother, H. D. Booge, opened a wholesale grocery company.

About 1870 a steamboat filled with wheat sank in the Missouri near Sioux City and James bought the water-soaked wheat. The wheat was fit only to feed to hogs, so that's what James did. He purchased hogs just so he could make use of the damaged wheat. He found no market for live hogs, so he butchered them and shipped most of the meat upriver to U.S. Army posts. Demand increased, so James built a three-story brick slaughterhouse downtown at the corner of Fifth and Water Streets in 1873.

By this time he was slaughtering 123,000 hogs a year. As the complaints from downtown business owners increased, Booge was forced to move his meatpacking business to a ten-acre site in the swampy South Bottoms in 1881. By now his plant was slaughtering 1,600 hogs per day in the winter and 800 hogs per day in the summer and gaining attention nationally.

Soon national meatpacking companies moved to Sioux City. Cudahy was first, followed by Armour in 1901, and Swift & Company in 1924, making Sioux City the meatpacking center of the Northern Plains—and it all started by accident!

Two of Iowa's Most Famous Pigs

At least two of Iowa's pigs have quite a claim to fame: Blue Boy, a fictional pig that appeared in a novel, movies, and a musical; and Floyd of Rosedale, who symbolized the football competition between the University of Iowa and the University of Minnesota.

Blue Boy was a Hampshire boar owned by Abel Frake in the 1932 best-selling novel, *State Fair*, written by *Des Moines Register* reporter and editorial writer Phil Stong. In the story, Blue Boy wins the Iowa State Fair grand championship. *State Fair* was made into three movies, in 1933, 1945, and 1962 (the last one, unfortunately, set in Texas). In 1995 Blue Boy hit the stage when the 1945 version became a stage musical, premiering in Des Moines at the Civic Center during State Fair time. It toured the United States before opening on Broadway in 1996.

Floyd of Rosedale is now a pig trophy that goes each year to the winner of the University of Iowa vs. University of Minnesota football game—but one year there was a real live Floyd. In 1938 Fort Dodge Creamery marketed milk and ice cream under the brand name Rosedale. Floyd Olson, governor of Minnesota, and Clyde Herring, governor of Iowa, had made a bet on the game for "the fanciest hog" each state had to offer. Iowa lost, and the manager of Fort Dodge Creamery, who also raised Hampshire hogs, supplied a hog for the Minnesota governor. (This pig was a half-brother of the pig that played Blue Boy in the 1933 movie *State Fair*.) The dairy named the pig "Floyd of Rosedale" after the governor, and shipped it

RODGERS & HAMMERSTEIN'S

Civic Center of Greater Des Moines
August 12-20, 1995

In 1995 State Fair *became a stage musical, premiering in Des Moines at the Civic Center during State Fair time.*

to St. Paul. The publicity generated convinced the Hampshire hog association to have a statue made of Floyd, which is passed back and forth to this day.

Calling All Hogs!

In 1926 the Swine Growers of America adopted rules to govern the hog-calling contest at the Iowa State Fair. These were the hog-calling criteria:

1. Carrying quality

2. Hog appeal

3. Variety

4. Musical appeal

5. Distinctness

"Carrying quality" brought the most points. Judges had to decide how the different calls affected the hogs, and which music most stirred the hogs (John Philip Sousa was one of the judges the first year!) Milford Beeghly in 1926 explained that he started with *Who-ee,* repeated it once in the tenor pitch, and then went *Pig-eee,* getting higher all the time and ending with a trill. This must have been effective, for Beeghly won that year.

Soybeans: Food, Fuel, and Truck Bed Liner

The soybean (*Glycine max*) has been called the miracle crop because it is the world's largest provider of protein and oil. The United States grows more soybeans than anywhere else in the world and Iowa is the national leader. Thanks to Iowa State University graduate George Washington Carver, people began to see that the soybean was more than just a forage crop. His studies, begun at Tuskegee, Alabama, in 1904, proved that soybeans provided valuable protein and oil.

Today, besides being used as feed and for its protein and oil, soybeans are used in concrete sealers, crayons, ink, lubricants, wax, and truck bed liners. (In 1940, Henry Ford axed a car trunk made with soybean plastic to demonstrate its durability.)

One of the most recent important uses of soybeans is as an alternative fuel called biodiesel. Biodiesel can decrease maintenance costs and reduce engine wear, and is the only alternative fuel that can be used in existing engines. This means that an entire fleet could immediately and seamlessly make the transition to this cleaner-burning alternative fuel.

More than forty fleets nationwide are using B20, a blend of 20 percent biodiesel and 80 percent petroleum diesel. They include the U.S. Postal Service; the U.S.D.A.; the U.S. Forest Service; the U.S. Army; the state governments of Iowa, New Jersey, Ohio, and Virginia; and the public utility companies Omaha Public Power, Commonwealth Edison, and Georgia Power. Biodiesel reduces air toxins by up to 90 percent, is ten times less toxic than table salt, and biodegrades as fast as sugar. And when it burns it smells like French fries!

Let There Be Peace

Norman Borlaug, who grew up on a farm near Protivin, won the Nobel Peace Prize for helping to feed people. Borlaug, the only agricultural scientist ever to win the prize, was honored in 1970 for his research in wheat genetics and for creating and implementing "Green Revolution" programs to share that knowledge with underdeveloped countries throughout the world. Borlaug is credited with saving millions of people from starvation, particularly in India and Pakistan in the 1960s.

The State of Iowa named October 16, 2002, the first Norman Borlaug–World Food Prize Day. He is the first person so honored by the State Legislature. After unsuccessfully trying to persuade the Nobel Prize committee to award a Nobel Prize for food and agriculture, Borlaug created the World Food Prize, which is awarded each year to people who have increased the quantity and quality of food in the world.

Borlaug said, "I realize how fortunate I was to have been born, to have grown to manhood, and to have received my early education in rural Iowa. That heritage provided me with a set of values that has been an invaluable guide to me in my work around the world. . . .These values . . . have been of great strength in times of despair in my struggle to assist in improving the standards of living of rural people everywhere."

Hybrid Corn Thaws the Cold War

In 1959 Roswell (Bob) Garst of Coon Rapids believed that "hungry people were dangerous people and that the world would be a safer place if Americans were talking to the Russians, rather than having an arms race." So he invited Soviet Premier Nikita Khrushchev to his farm to observe America's farming methods.

Bob Garst was born in 1898 and began to farm in 1917. But from 1926 to 1930 he worked in real estate in Des Moines, where he met geneticist Henry A. Wallace. He was excited by Wallace's ideas for hybrid seed corn, so in 1930 he went back to Coon Rapids and with his friend, Charles Thomas, started the Garst and Thomas Hybrid Corn Company. They became the Midwest marketers of Wallace's Pioneer Hi-Bred brand corn. Garst, a wonderful salesman, became wealthy.

When Khrushchev accepted his invitation and toured the Garst farm on September 23, 1959, Garst became a famous Iowan and brought a little warmth to the Cold War. He died in 1977.

The Garst family opened their farm facilities, a half mile east of Coon Rapids, as a resort in 1997. Garst Family Resorts has everything from bed-and-breakfast accommodations to private cottages, and activities that include horseback riding, fishing, canoeing, carriage rides, all-terrain vehicles, hiking, farm tours, astronomy programs, and a history lesson on the Cold War!

Strange . . . but True

The Quaker Oats Company plant in Cedar Rapids is said to be the largest cereal plant in the world, and Quaker Oats products are known just about everywhere. An Iowan, visiting Scotland, which is famous for its oatmeal, was so delighted with his breakfast of Scottish oatmeal that he ordered a barrel of the same oatmeal to be sent to his home in Iowa. The barrel arrived from Scotland bearing the label: "The Quaker Oats Company, made in Cedar Rapids, Iowa."

Every oatmeal lover is familiar with the Quaker Oats logo. (THE QUAKER OATS COMPANY, CEDAR RAPIDS, IOWA)

This Cereal Company Started Many Things

The Quaker Oats Company was responsible for many innovations in the food industry. They were the first to

★ Irradiate foods for vitamin enrichment

★ Nationally market a breakfast cereal

★ Manufacture ready-mix foods

★ Register a cereal trademark

★ Promote a food by national advertising ("Nothing is better for thee, than me!")

It Turned Out to Be Delicious!

Quaker William Hiatt owned a farm and orchard in Randolph County, Indiana. He was known locally as an authority on fruit, having developed some apple varieties of his own. His youngest son, Jesse, grew up acquiring the knowledge of planting, pruning, and grafting. In 1855 Jesse, his wife, Rebecca, and their five children moved to Madison County, Iowa, settling near Jesse's brother, Aaron. Farming and running a flour mill kept Jesse busy, but like his father, he loved to garden and soon had produced apple varieties of his own—the Hiatt Sweet and the Hiatt Black.

In 1872 he discovered a strange seedling growing between rows of another variety and he cut it down. It grew back the next year and Jesse, impressed with its hardiness, decided to let it grow. The apple world has never been the same, because that seedling produced the apple the world came to know as "Delicious." But Jesse had to nurture that seedling for ten years before it produced an apple—"the best tastin' apple in the whole world," he thought. He named it "Hawkeye" in honor of his home state. Finally, eleven years later, after Jesse had taken his apple to fair after fair, C. M. Stark of Stark Brothers Nursery in Louisiana, Missouri, tasted the Hawkeye apple and agreed that the apple was delicious. In 1894 Stark purchased the propagation rights from Jesse and renamed it "Delicious."

To introduce the Delicious to other parts of the country, Stark sent a few free Delicious trees with other orders. Because of its vigor, adaptability, and exceptional quality, it didn't take long for the rest of the country to agree with Stark and Jesse—this was a great apple. Besides its beautiful color—

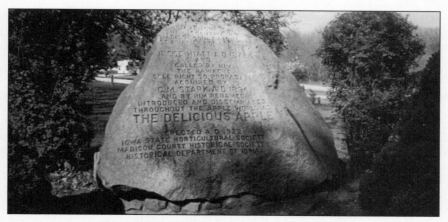

A memorial boulder in Winterset honors Jesse Hiatt's propagation of the Delicious apple (he called it the Hawkeye) in 1872.

striped with bright and dark red—and its unique shape—round and tapering with five distinct knobs on the blossom end—the apple was delicious: mild, not too sweet, and very crisp. The Delicious became the most popular apple in America and continues to hold that position. Iowa and apple lovers the world over are grateful that Jesse Hiatt was a patient man.

Did You Know? Every year Atlantic High School has a Tractor Day when FFA (Future Farmers of America) members drive their tractors to school and the teachers and students honor farming. The student council puts up a sign in the lunchroom saluting the FFA boys and girls as "Iowa's Agri-Future."

Reaching Out, Reaching Youth

Two Iowa county school superintendents were pioneers in the 4-H program and were instrumental in its success: Oscar (O. H.) Benson of Wright County and Jessie Field of Page County. Both became county school superintendents in 1906 and both encouraged teachers to correlate class work with work of the farm and home. Both, knowing the importance of agriculture to our nation, wanted to bring dignity to farming and emphasize the advantages of rural life, in order to encourage farm youth to remain on the farm.

Wright County claims to be the birthplace of the 4-H emblem, saying that Benson originated the idea after receiving a bouquet of 4-leaf clovers from country school children in 1906. The four-leaf clover could represent the message of a "four-square" education: educational development, fellowship development, physical development, and moral development. A three-leaf clover with an "H" on each leaf (Head, Heart, and Hand) was used as the membership emblem of the Wright County schools, and the four-leaf clover was used with a fourth "H" (Health) to show achievement in finished projects.

At the same time, Jessie Field is said to have designed the same three-leaf clover, with an "H" on each leaf, a kernel of corn in the center with the word

"Page," and the word "Iowa" on the stem. When a fourth "H" was added, she said it stood for "Home."

Whoever originally designed it, the clover became the official emblem of the organized clubs in 1911, with the fourth "H" representing health. This led to the organization formally adopting the name "4-H" in 1924.

O. H. Benson worked in Washington, D.C., as national director of boys' and girls' club work in the United States. Jessie Field Shambaugh (she married Ira W. Shambaugh in 1917) will forever be known as "the mother of 4-H" because she was the first woman to actively pursue her interest in the agricultural education of youth. Although the first clubs emphasized skills

Did You Know? In 1954 sixteen-year-old Janice Hullinger of Manly won the grand championship at Chicago's International Livestock Exposition with her calf, Shorty. Fifteen-year-old Barbara Clausen from Spencer was reserve grand champion. For the first time in the Expo's fifty-five-year history, girls, both 4-H members, beat out the older breeders to take the top two awards. Janice and her steer, which sold for $16,000, were flown to New York to appear on the *Ed Sullivan Show*. When Janice said she wanted inside plumbing for her family's home, the Crane Company of Chicago announced it would supply all the needed equipment for free.

Sixteen-year-old Janice Hullinger of Manly appeared with her grand champion 4-H calf, Shorty, on The Ed Sullivan Show *in 1954.* (NATIONAL 4-H ARCHIVES, WASHINGTON, D.C.)

needed for farming and homemaking, 4-H, which now operates under the extension service of the U.S. Department of Agriculture, has adopted broader opportunities for training and is active today in urban as well as rural areas.

The goal of 4-H is to help members develop to their fullest potential so they can become the leaders of tomorrow. The 4-H member pledges "my Head to clearer thinking, my Heart to greater loyalty, my Hands to larger service, and my Health to better living, for my Club, my Community, my Country, and my World."

The Iowa State Fair: An American Classic

The Iowa State Fair, held annually in August, celebrates Iowa's livelihood—farming. Besides being one of the oldest and largest agricultural expositions in the United States, the Iowa State Fair is a salute to the state's best in industry, entertainment, and achievement.

Since the first Iowa State Fair was held in Fairfield in 1854, the fair has attracted people from all over the state and the Midwest. More than a million people attended the 144th fair in 2002. The fair was canceled only in 1898, because the World's Fair was in Omaha, and during the World War II years of 1942 to 1945.

The fair has been held in Des Moines since 1880 and at East 30th and University since 1886, and the four-hundred-acre setting is listed on the National Register of Historic Places.

The late historian Sidney A. Foster said, "In all that is good, Iowa affords the best." To experience the most of Iowa in a short time and a grand sampling of individual achievement and Midwestern culture, lifestyle, and values, visit during the twelve-day run of the Iowa State Fair in August. There you can compete in contests such as

★ Rolling pin throwing

★ Hog calling

★ Husband calling

★ Beard growing

★ Nail driving

★ Horseshoe pitching

★ Yodeling

★ Whistling

★ Fiddling

There's always plenty to see at the fair. About 15,000 people enter more than 55,000 items in various categories of contests, from cows to quilts, to compete for fun and for ribbons. You'll find exhibits and shows to satisfy every taste:

★ Jumbo vegetables

★ Flowers (roses, gladioli, dahlias, etc.)

★ Art (biggest show in the state)

★ Auto and horse races

★ Livestock (including Biggest Boar, Super Bull, and Enormous Equine, as well as sheep shearing and baby pigs being born)

★ Truck and tractor pulls

★ Superstar stage shows and fireworks

★ Free entertainment on five stages ($350,000 worth)

★ And, of course, farm machinery

Getting hungry? Here's just a small sampling of things to eat. There are 150 food stands to choose from at the fair:

★ Funnel cakes, cinnamon rolls, and Dutch letters

★ Beef, pork, lamb, chicken, and turkey (specifically, turkey legs)

★ Ice cream (a favorite at the Dairy Barn booth or quick-frozen with liquid nitrogen by Iowa State University students)

★ Any cuisine you desire—American, Greek, Italian, German, Chinese, etc.

★ Twenty different items you can eat on a stick, from pickles to pork chops (so you can walk and eat at the same time)

See you at the fair! For more information visit *www.iowastatefair.org.*

The ten-acre midway is a big attraction at the Iowa State Fair. (COURTESY IOWA TOURISM OFFICE)

Did You Know?
Bill Riley, born in Iowa Falls in 1920, is known as "Mr. State Fair." Among other things, Riley initiated the Iowa State Fair Talent Search in 1960 and estimates that over the years he has introduced more than one hundred thousand young performers ages two to twenty-one. The Plaza Stage at the fairgrounds was renamed in Riley's honor in 1993. He retired as host of the Talent Search in 1996, turning it over to his son, Bill Jr., and Terry Rich. But Riley still comes to applaud the young talent from Iowa, as he's been doing for more than half a century.

Strange . . . but True

Gerry (age ten) and Kent (age eleven) Vandervelde rowed almost two hundred miles down the Des Moines River from Emmetsburg to attend the Iowa State Fair in 1950. Upon their arrival the first thing they did was take a boat ride at Ye Old Mill, the oldest amusement ride at the fair. Guess they hadn't had enough boating! Built in 1912, the ride was completely rebuilt in 1996.

It's All in the Name

Where did the name "Iowa" come from?

The expression "Iowa District," applied to the land that eventually was included in the state of Iowa, was popularized in a small book published in 1836, *Notes on the Wisconsin Territory; Particularly with Reference to the Iowa District, or Black Hawk Purchase,* by Lieutenant Albert M. Lea.

Maps of the western country show that for a century before Lea published his map, a river running through the country between the Mississippi and Des Moines rivers was generally indicated by the name "Ioway" or "Iowa"—the name the Sioux had given to the Native American tribe living near the river.

"Iowa" has been translated many different ways, including "dusty faces," "drowsy ones," "here is the place," and "beautiful land." Various spellings have included Ayavois, Ay-u-ou-ez, Aiaoua, Ioway, and Ayoouois. Lea must have pronounced it with a long "a," because when the organization of the Territory was proposed, he wrote to George W. Jones, delegate to Congress, urging that the spelling be "put back" to "Ioway," as "it ought to have been." But Lea had used "Iowa" in his book and thus it stayed. Lea declared in 1890 that Congress "stuck to my error."

Did You Know? Iowa is the only state in the nation that begins with two vowels.

However You Sing It . . .

Meredith Willson (from Mason City, of *Music Man* fame) was proud of Iowa. He wrote the following song for the state's centennial and to point out the correct pronunciation of the state's name. Unfortunately, a popular singer of the time, Rudy Vallee, introduced it by singing, "Io*way*, it's a beautiful name when you say it like we say it back home," which is just like we don't say it here!

Willson attempted to emphasize the correct pronunciation again, years later, by composing a number called "Iowuh!" for *The Music Man*. It was sung like an Indian war-chant, and there was no way to mispronounce the state name, but after surviving nine years of development on the show and most of thirty-eight rewrites, the song was cut two weeks before opening night.

Here are the lyrics to Meredith's first song:

Iowa
(Centennial song for the state in 1946)

Chorus:

IOWA, it's a beautiful name when you say it like we say it back home,

It's the robin in the willows, it's the postmaster's friendly hello.

IOWA, it's a beautiful name, you'll remember it wherever you roam;

It's the sumac in September, it's the squeak of your shoes in the snow.

It's the Sunday school and the old river bend, songs on the porch after dark;

It's the corner store and a penny to spend, you and your girl in the park.

IOWA, it's a beautiful name when you say it like we say it back home,

It's a promise of tomorrow and a memory of long ago.

IOWA, what a beautiful name when you say it like we say it back home.

—"IOWA" BY MEREDITH WILLSON.

Did You Know? Burlington attorney David Rorer convinced James Edwards, editor of the *Fort Madison Patriot,* to encourage the use of the nickname "Hawkeye" when referring to Iowa and Iowans. At the time, around 1840, Illinois was known as the "Sucker State" and Rorer didn't want Iowa to get a worse nickname. He felt a nickname commemorating Chief Black Hawk was a worthy one. Edwards promoted the nickname, and when he moved his newspaper to Burlington he changed its name to the *Burlington Hawk-Eye.* (The *Hawk-Eye,* by the way, is the oldest newspaper published in Iowa.)

THE LAND TRIVIA

Q. What Iowa county has the highest percentage of grade-A topsoil in the nation?

A. Wright.

Q. What is Iowa's chief fruit crop?

A. Apples.

Q. What is the state rock?

A. Geode.

Q. What year saw record low yields in corn, hay, oats, rye, and soybeans?

A. 1934.

Q. The average Iowa dairy cow produces how many gallons of milk a day?

A. Six. The best produce sixteen.

Q. Using the fruits, vegetables, and blossoms of rhubarb, dandelion, red clover, and cherry, what is produced in Amana?

A. Wine.

Q. What was the price of admission to the first Iowa State Fair?

A. Twenty-five cents.

Q. What part of the state is known as the Nursery Capital of the World?

A. Southwest Iowa (largely because nursery founders Henry Field and Earl May are located in Shenandoah).

Q. *New Virginia claims to be the birthplace of what breed of cattle?*

A. *Polled Hereford. The breed was developed in 1901 by Warren Gammon of Des Moines on a rental farm between St. Mary's and New Virginia.* (COURTESY AMERICAN HEREFORD ASSOCIATION)

Q. Iowa ranked first nationally in the production of what two crops in 1900?

A. Corn and oats.

Q. The Pleasant Creek Recreation Area has the most northerly stand in the Western Hemisphere of what kind of tree?

A. Pecan.

Q. What is the state tree?

A. Oak.

Q. Iowa has what percentage of first-class farmland in the United States?

A. Twenty-five percent.

2
Planes, Trains, and Automobiles

Ten Cents per Mile, Plus a Fence Rail

Before railroads, stagecoaches carried mail, freight, and passengers in Iowa. In 1838 the first regular stagecoach line in Iowa began operation. It ran twice a week from Burlington through Fort Madison and Montrose to St. Francesville, Missouri. This forty-five-mile trip took eighteen hours and the normal fare was "ten cents per mile and a fence rail." Male passengers used the fence rails for dislodging coaches that became stuck.

When the roads were impassable, postriders carried the mail on horseback. To deliver a letter weighing a half ounce, or a single folded sheet, more than four hundred miles cost twenty-five cents. The receiver often paid this postage because of the uncertainty of the letter reaching its destination.

How Furrow Is It?

The establishment of the first "official" road in the territory of Iowa, connecting Keokuk and Iowa City, was required by a law approved on December 14, 1838. The U.S. Congress passed a bill appropriating $20,000 for Iowa's first "military" road on December 31, 1838. Designation as a military road meant an increase in funding and allowed Iowa's first road to be extended from Iowa City to Dubuque.

To serve as a guide for road builders, Lyman Dillon, a Dubuque merchant, was hired to plow as straight a furrow as possible from Iowa City to Dubuque, a distance of 100 miles. He used five oxen.

Similarly, in the spring of 1856, the federal government employed Alex McCready to plow a trail from Fort Dodge to Sioux City. He and his son used a huge breaking plow drawn by six span of oxen to plow two furrows about sixty feet apart. Travelers who stayed between the two deep furrows would not get lost. It was known as "The Great Road" and at 130 miles was referred to as "the longest furrow in history."

Main Street of America

The Lincoln Highway across the state was America's first transcontinental highway. Established in 1913, it was a 3,389-mile collection of existing roads from New York's Time Square to Lincoln Park in San Francisco. Billed as the "Main Street of America," it went right through the middle of Iowa, crossing through thirteen Iowa counties.

As early as 1902 the American Automobile Association (AAA) thought a

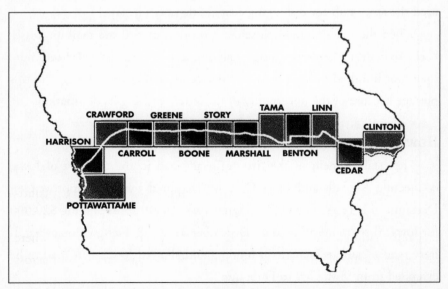

The Lincoln Highway crossed through thirteen Iowa counties. (COURTESY PAUL WALKER, STATE DIRECTOR, IOWA LINCOLN HIGHWAY ASSOCIATION)

coast-to-coast road was a good idea, but Carl Fisher, cofounder of the Indianapolis Motor Speedway, first got public support for the idea. Henry B. Joy, president of Packard, suggested naming it after Abraham Lincoln and proceeded to find the shortest and best route for the new highway.

When the uniform highway numbering system began in 1926, the Lincoln Highway became U.S. 30 between Philadelphia and western Wyoming, including the route across Iowa.

Lincoln Highway is rich in historical structures from gas stations to bridges. You can visit the 1920s George Preston gas station in Belle Plaine or the Youngville station at the junction of U.S. 30 and U.S. 218 in Benton County. Also in Belle Plaine are the Lincoln Café and what was once the Herring Hotel, both popular stops on the highway. In Tama on East 5th Street is a unique Lincoln Highway bridge. The side railings of the cement bridge—the only working original Lincoln Highway bridge of its kind in the United States—spell out the words "Lincoln Highway."

Did You Know? The government land surveys conducted in Iowa from 1836 to 1859 began in the southeast corner of the state and proceeded to the northwest corner. This system established the six-mile-square townships and the one-mile grid system of roads.

Let's Go through Iowa!

Abraham Lincoln figured prominently both times Iowa was chosen as a coast-to-coast route. The Lincoln Highway was named after him, and Lincoln chose Council Bluffs as the eastern junction of the first transcontinental railroad on November 17, 1863.

Construction began on the railroad in December 1863, starting where the Union Pacific rail line ended in Council Bluffs and running west across the plains and over the Rocky Mountains.

General Grenville Mellen Dodge resigned his military commission in

1866 to serve as chief engineer for the Union Pacific Railway. On May 10, 1869, the Union Pacific Railway and the Central Pacific Railroad (built east from Sacramento, California) met at Promontory Point, Utah.

Complete rail service across the country, however, could not begin until 1872 when the first railroad bridge was built across the Missouri River between Council Bluffs and Omaha. Before that, freight and passengers were ferried across the river.

When Railway Men Named Towns

Railroads contributed significantly to the development of communities in Iowa. Towns sprang up or thrived because the railroad came through—or dwindled and sometimes died because the railroad took a different route. By 1860 Iowa had 655 miles of railroad tracks, and in 1867 the first railroad that traversed the state from river to river was completed. Because of the railroad, Iowa's economy began to focus on commercial farming rather than subsistence farming.

Towns sprang up as the railroad was built, and railroad officials chose many town names. One of the most prolific railroad builders and town namers of Iowa was John Insley Blair, a fifty-eight-year-old businessman from New Jersey. He had attended the Republican Party National Convention in Chicago in 1860, where he accepted the invitation for an excursion into Iowa.

By 1862 Blair was ready to start building railroads across Iowa and the Midwest. His railroad, later renamed the Chicago & Northwestern, was the first to cross the state in 1867, bringing the first train into Council Bluffs on January 22 to connect with the Union Pacific. Blair had his hand in organizing the Sioux City and Pacific Railroad and the Iowa Falls and Sioux City Railroad Company. He also helped organize the Iowa Rail Road Land Company to handle the large tracts of land that were given to railroad companies at the time, and the Blair Town Lot and Land Company, which took over unsold town lots and land along the Cedar Rapids and Missouri River Railroad.

Many of the towns between Iowa Falls and Sioux City owe their existence to John I. Blair and, of course, they all had to have names. Blair didn't back down on this job either. Iowa has a Blairsburg and a Blairstown. Towns were named for

★ Marcus—his son

★ Aurelia—his daughter

★ C. E. Vail—his nephew

★ Oakes Ames—his partner

★ W. W. Walker—his business associate

★ William B. Ogden—his business associate

★ George W. and Selden R. Scranton—his business associates

When the Sioux City railroad, later part of the Illinois Central, was completed to a certain point, he allowed the ladies of the excursion party to name the new town site. The six ladies used their initials to name the town LeMars. At least twenty Iowa towns owe their names to Blair.

Blair is said to have built 803 miles of railroads in Iowa and laid out more than eighty town sites. He organized the company that built the bridge across the Missouri River from Missouri Valley, Iowa, to Blair, Nebraska. But he always returned to his hometown, Blairstown, New Jersey, where he died on December 2, 1899. The man who had been a storekeeper, postmaster, miller, banker, iron manufacturer, railway promoter, and namer of towns died a millionaire, with an estate valued at $70 million.

Fewer Coffins for Lorenzo

Lorenzo Coffin, a successful farmer and preacher, was appointed to the State Railroad Commission in 1883. Alarmed over the number of railroad brakemen who were falling to their deaths, he was successful in getting laws passed requiring the installation of automatic brakes and couplers on railroad cars.

So a Coffin was instrumental in helping to prevent early deaths of railroad workers!

Did You Know? The first electric streetcars in the state were put into service on December 20, 1888, on Locust Street and Grand Avenue in Des Moines. Introduced by the Broad Gauge Railway Company, this electric railway was the second in the United States. By the 1920s this mode of transportation had ended, however, because automobiles were taking over.

Just Say, "Charge It"

In 1887 William Morrison of Des Moines built the first successful "electric buggy" in the world in order to showcase his batteries. It was first exhibited in the Seni Om Sed (*Des Moines* spelled backward) parade in September 1888 or 1890. It had three seats, could seat twelve, and could attain a speed of twenty miles an hour on twenty-four storage battery cells located under the seats. The motor was four horsepower, and each battery weighed thirty-two pounds and required ten hours to charge.

William Morrison built his first-of-its-kind electric car to show off the batteries he made and drove it through the streets of Des Moines in 1887. (STATE HISTORICAL SOCIETY OF IOWA)

Morrision patented his buggy in 1891, sold the patent rights to the J. B. McDonald Company of Chicago, and sold his invention to Chicago businessman Harold Sturgis, who exhibited it at the 1893 Chicago's World Columbian Exposition as the "Sturgis electric." Fairgoers loved it but car buyers didn't, because it was slow and required recharging every fifty miles. However, in a twenty-two-mile race in Chicago in 1895 between gas-powered automobiles and horseless carriages, only two cars completed the course, and Morrison's electric car won—averaging more than fifteen miles per hour!

Other Iowa Horseless Carriage Pioneers

★ **J. C. Duncan:** The Davenport inventor was one of the first Americans to build and produce a successful automobile. In 1892 he drove his "steam wagon" from Davenport to Bettendorf.

★ **Fred S. and August Duesenberg:** These German-born brothers who grew up in Rockford, Iowa, first owned bicycle shops—August in Garner and Fred in Rockford. They designed and built their first car, the Marvel, in Des Moines in 1902. In Indianapolis in 1921 they established the Duesenberg Automobile and Motor Company. At that time, Duesenberg autos were the most expensive cars in the world, and considered to be the finest. They were status symbols for stars Greta Garbo, Gary Cooper, and Clark Gable. Duesenberg vehicles competed in twenty Indianapolis 500 races and won in 1924, 1925, and 1927. In the 1922 race Duesenbergs took seven of the first ten places.

★ **William Colby:** This Mason City businessman organized the Colby Motor Company, building a factory in 1911. This factory produced four cars per day. Competition from Detroit caused the company to fold in 1914. The only Colby auto known to remain today, a 1914 Model D Semi-racer, is on display at the Kinney Pioneer Museum in Mason City.

★ **Fred L. Maytag and Edward B. Mason:** These two financed the manufacture of the Maytag automobile line, making an estimated fifteen hundred cars in Waterloo by 1911. An original Maytag-Mason auto is displayed at the Grout Museum of History & Science in Waterloo.

The Maytag-Mason auto climbed the steps of the capitol in Des Moines in 1908. No other car could ascend such a steep grade. (STATE HISTORICAL SOCIETY OF IOWA)

Strange . . . but True

War hero Eddie Rickenbacker won a $10,000, 300-mile auto race in Sioux City in 1913 while wearing a bat's heart tied to his middle finger with red silk thread for good luck. He wore this on his mother's recommendation after he had asked her to consult a book on Swiss lore. Later, in his autobiography, he recalled: "Not being up on bat anatomy, I may have removed the gizzard rather than its heart, but whatever it was, I tied it to my middle finger."

Old, but Still Chugging Along

William Swartout of Mahaska County bought a Chalmers automobile in 1909. In 1934 he drove it all the way to Des Moines, which caused quite a stir. Passing motorists slowed to gawk at the old-fashioned car, and when he stopped at a filling station, a crowd gathered around him. He was asked how fast it would go and with pride replied, "They tell me she'll do forty. 'Course you'd have to take her top down."

Did You Know? Henry Ford had a Ford assembly plant in Des Moines at 18th and Grand that operated from 1920 to 1932.

This Iowan Found Cars Really Unlucky

John Motz, from Guthrie Center, had two unpleasant encounters with cars—they struck him on two different occasions. This increased his dislike for the machine. So when his wife died in 1931, he insisted that she be carried to her grave in a horse-drawn hearse. In December 1934 Motz had his final encounter with an automobile—he was struck again, and this time it was fatal. He died two weeks later. Fortunately, the same horse-drawn hearse that had borne his wife was available to take him to his final resting place.

Did You Know? Orville and Wilbur Wright lived in Cedar Rapids from 1878 to 1881. The year they arrived in Iowa, their father gave them a helicopter-type toy operated by a rubber band. This toy fascinated them and they successfully replicated it a number of times. Thus began their obsession with flight!

Strange . . . but True

Flights of Fancy

Is it a bird? Is it a plane? No, it's Roland Kumzak of Milford.

At the Clay County Fair in 1935, Clem Sohn of Lansing, Michigan, jumped from an airplane wearing a suit with webbing between the legs and canvas wings. His 175-mile-per-hour "flight" toward earth was slowed to less than 60 miles per hour by a parachute about three-fourths of the way down.

When the Jaycees of Spencer sponsored an Air Show in October 1935, Roland Kumzak of Milford offered to do what Sohn had done for

fifty dollars. Initially accepting his offer, the Jaycees withdrew from the contract because of community protest. They would, however, allow him to jump on his own, and ten thousand people showed up to see him do that.

The "flight" was spectacular and Kumzak thrilled many crowds after that. He eventually retired after a bad fall in Des Moines and went to California, where he earned a living inspecting parachutes.

Roland Kumzak of Milford spreads his "wings" in his webbed flying suit, circa 1935. (DON BUCHAN, POTPOURRI [ALBERT CITY: THE APPEAL PUBLISHING CO., 1977])

Did You Know? Twenty-three aviators made forty-six flights over various cities in Iowa between 1910 and 1911.

Other Early Iowa Flyers

★ **Arthur J. Hartman:** In 1910 Hartman piloted Iowa's first "aeroplane" flight on the fairway of the old Burlington Country Club. After rising ten feet in the air, the plane came down so hard it damaged the undercarriage. A road near the Burlington airport is named Art Hartman Drive in his honor.

★ **William (Billy) C. Robinson:** In 1914 this Grinnell resident broke the American distance record for a nonstop flight. Sponsored by the *Des Moines Capital* and the *Chicago Tribune*, the mail flight was cut short by weather conditions and a fuel shortage. But Robinson flew 300 miles between Des Moines and Chicago, exceeding the U.S. record by 125 miles. Robinson later crashed and died while attempting to break the altitude record. You can see his ill-fated plane's engine in the museum at Grinnell College.

★ **Clyde Vernon Cessna:** Cessna was born in Hawthorne, Iowa, in December 1879, and his family moved to Kansas late in 1880. Cessna was fascinated with machinery and became adept at repairing farm machinery and early automobiles. He began to build his first airplane in 1911 and in the late 1920s formed Cessna Aircraft Company of Wichita, Kansas, which eventually led the private plane market. Clyde Cessna died in 1954, and was inducted into the National Aviation Hall of Fame in 1978.

★ **John Percy Woodward:** In 1920 he became the first Iowan to fly mail on a scheduled route. He crashed on November 7, 1920, in a snowstorm near Cheyenne, Wyoming. Woodward Airport of Salt Lake City, Utah, was named in his honor.

★ **Clarence Duncan Chamberlain:** Chamberlain, born in Denison in 1893, gained worldwide fame by breaking the nonstop, long-distance record in 1927 by flying from New York to Berlin. He stayed in the air fifty-one hours and eleven minutes in his Bellanca monoplane, breaking the world's record by six hours (ten hours longer than Charles Lindbergh's historic flight to Paris). Chamberlain was the first pilot to fly a paying passenger across the Atlantic Ocean and was inducted into the National Aviation Hall of Fame in 1976, the same year he died.

★ **Glen Luther Martin:** Born in Macksburg, Iowa, in 1886, Martin was one of America's pioneer aircraft builders. He developed the Martin MB-1 bomber in 1918, the B-10 bomber in the 1930s, and the Marauder B-26 in 1940. The B-26 played an important role in the Allied victory in World War II. Martin died in 1955 and was inducted into the National Aviation Hall of Fame in 1966.

★ **Enola Gay Haggard:** The B-29 plane, *Enola Gay*, that dropped the atomic bomb on Hiroshima, helping to end World War II, was named after Glidden native Enola Gay Haggard. She was the mother of the pilot, Colonel Paul W. Tibbets.

Colonel Paul Tibbets piloted the B-29 plane Enola Gay, *which dropped the atomic bomb on Hiroshima in World War II. The plane was named after his mother who lived in Glidden.* (COURTESY www.theenolagay.com)

Did You Know? Amelia Mary Earhart (born in 1897 and presumed dead in 1937) lived in Des Moines from 1908 to 1914. As a young girl she saw her first airplane at the Iowa State Fair and later, while living in California, took her first flying lessons from Neta Snook from Ames, Iowa.

Did You Know? When the *Des Moines Register & Tribune* purchased a five-person Fairchild Cabin monoplane in 1928, it became the first newspaper in the country to own and operate an airplane with a pilot on full-time pay. It was also the first privately owned plane of its class in the United States. The plane, named *Good News* after a state-wide contest, not only got photographs and stories to readers quickly, but promoted aviation and airports in Iowa.

Other Transportation Firsts

★ **First airline stewardess:** Ellen Church of Cresco, born in 1904, became the first airline stewardess in the United States after approaching the traffic manager of Boeing Air Transport (United Air Lines) with the idea of hiring nurses to serve passengers. Church, hired as the chief stewardess, then hired seven more nurses ("Sky Girls") and helped design their uniforms. They began work on May 15, 1930.

★ **First slip form paver:** Iowa Highway Commission lab chief James Johnson developed the world's first slip form paver in 1947. This paver placed concrete slabs without the use of side forms or supports and made it possible to place and finish more than one mile of concrete highway per day.

★ **First aluminum girder highway bridge:** The world's first aluminum girder highway bridge was constructed over Interstate 35/80 in Urbandale in 1958. It was replaced in the early 1990s when the interchange was reconfigured.

★ **No Passing sign:** The Iowa State Highway Commission created the No Passing pennant sign in 1959, which was adopted and included in the national *Manual on Uniform Traffic Control Devices for Streets and Highways.*

★ **First recycled concrete pavement:** The Iowa Department of Transportation's Highway Division began research in 1976 that led to the country's first recycled portland cement concrete pavement.

Did You Know? Beginning in 1926 Iowa painted a center black line on every mile of primary road pavement to reduce head-on collisions. This continuous black center line was replaced with a dashed, white reflectorized line and yellow no-passing lines on all major roads in 1954.

The Sailing Pidgeon

Harry Pidgeon, who was born in Henry County, farmed until he was twenty-seven years old, then decided to try something different. He went to Alaska, where he collected specimens for American museums and dreamed of visiting the South Sea Islands. After returning to the States (Alaska wasn't one yet), he built a small flatboat and floated down the Mississippi. He then went to Los Angeles and became a photographer. In 1917 in Los Angeles he built a thirty-four-foot, V-bottomed yawl he called the *Islander*. This yawl became his home for three decades. He figured it had cost him a thousand dollars and a year and a half of work.

When he started sailing, he had no intention of going around the world, but he did want to make it to the South Seas that he had dreamed about while in Alaska. After he reached Samoa, halfway across the South Pacific, he decided to keep heading west. When he dropped anchor again in Los Angeles Harbor on October 31, 1925, he had crossed the South Pacific and Indian Ocean, gone around the Cape, across the South Atlantic, and through the Panama Canal. The trip had taken him just two weeks shy of four years to complete. He had stayed as long as he wanted, wherever he wanted, and had made friends everywhere. He not only had stories to tell, but photographs to show.

By 1937 when he was sixty-nine, he had circumnavigated the world in *Islander* again, this time sailing into Long Island and becoming the only man to have circled the world twice. He once wrote, "There is great satisfaction in accomplishing something by one's own effort." He proved he believed that by how he lived: sailing around the world—twice!

Unique Transportation Museums

★ **Iowa Aviation Hall of Fame:** This museum in the Greenfield Municipal Airport includes rare examples of early flying machines from the 1920s, 1930s, and 1940s.

★ **Antique Airfield and Airpower Museum:** Located near Blakesburg, the museum is the home of the Antique Airplane Association and the APM (Airpower Museum) Library of Flight. You can see aircraft, engines, and memorabilia, including a working model of a "ground effect" plane that rides on a cushion of air. Planes are flown regularly and runways are grass.

★ **Mid America Air Museum:** This Sioux City museum features a collection of full-size aircraft including a British Argosy AW650 four-engine transport, a German Messerschmitt ME 208, an A-7D Corsair, a Beech Queen II, and a Huey helicopter, plus ultralights and gliders.

★ **National Balloon Museum:** Located in Indianola, the museum covers more than two hundred years of ballooning history, both hot air and gas. The collection is on permanent loan from the Balloon Federation of America and is housed in a building that resembles the gondola of a hot air balloon.

★ **National Sprint Car Hall of Fame and Museum:** At the Knoxville Raceway in Marion County is the world's only museum dedicated to preserving the history of "big car" and sprint car racing. It displays more than twenty-five authentically restored sprint cars.

★ **National Motorcycle Museum and Hall of Fame:** This Anamosa museum houses more than sixty vintage and antique motorcycles from around the world, dating from 1908.

★ **Vinton Railroad Depot and Museum:** This Vinton museum features displays on the BCRN (Burlington, Cedar Rapids, and Northern) and Rock Island railroads.

★ **Hub City Heritage Railway Museum:** In Oelwein, the museum includes a railroad express building and yard office with refurbished cabooses and engines.

★ **Milwaukee Railroad Roundhouse Historic Site:** Located in Sioux City, the museum traces the history of northwest Iowa's railroad industry and includes a large HO scale model. (HO is a scale of 3.5 millimeters to 1 foot, or 1/87, used especially for model toys.)

★ **RailsWest Railroad Museum and HO Model Railroad:** An 1899 Rock Island depot in Council Bluffs houses a model railroad and dining car memorabilia and uniforms. Also on display are two steam engines, a 1917 waycar, a club car, a railway post office car, and a caboose.

★ **Union Pacific Railroad Musuem:** This Council Bluffs museum is the only one in North America that is associated with an active railroad company. It features displays on the region's railroad, transportation, and communication history, including covered wagons, the Pony Express, train robberies, and the telegraph. An interactive exhibit gives an idea of what it's like to be in a moving locomotive.

★ **Moravia Wabash Depot Museum:** This museum north of Centerville has an early 1900s rural combination depot, a model train, and a railroad section car.

★ **Iowa Railway Museum:** Ride the rails in Boone on a restored dining or observation car on the Boone & Scenic Valley Railroad. The museum features historic railroad items and equipment, and hosts "Pufferbilly Days" in early September, celebrating Boone's railroad heritage. (A pufferbilly was a little steam engine used in coal mines.)

★ **Kate Shelley Railroad Museum and Park:** In Moingona, this site features a video presentation of heroine Kate Shelley's dramatic story. Read in Chapter

7, "Heroes, the Law, and the Lawless," about how she averted a railroad tragedy in 1881.

★ **Iowa Great Lakes Maritime Museum:** In the Okoboji Spirit Center, in Okoboji, you'll find a fully restored boathouse, twenty-five classic wooden runabouts, period swimsuits, and recreational fishing and hunting articles. The museum has an Antique and Classic Wooden Boat Show in Arnold's Park each July.

 # TRANSPORTATION TRIVIA

Q. What job did Richard W. Sears, founder of Sears and Roebuck, hold while a resident of Lake Mills?

A. Railroad depot agent.

Q. What steamboat that sank in the Missouri River in 1866 was raised from the mud in 1965 with much of its cargo preserved?

A. The *Bertrand* (two hundred thousand preserved Civil War artifacts can be seen at the DeSoto National Wildlife Refuge Visitor Center, Missouri Valley).

Q. The first elevated railroad in the West, a prototype of Chicago's "El," was erected in what city in 1891?

A. Sioux City (the third such railroad in the nation).

Q. Before being designated U.S. Highway 65 in 1965, the road that runs two thousand miles from New Orleans to Winnipeg and crosses Iowa was known by what name?

A. The Pine to Palm Highway (also the Jefferson Highway).

Q. One of the founders of a bus line, Helen Schultz was known nationally as "Iowa's Bus Queen" when she established what company in 1922?

A. Red Ball Transportation Company (sold to the Minnesota-based Jefferson Highway Transportation Company in 1930).

Q. Where is the runway for the Laurens Airport?

A. The fairway of the Golf and Country Club.

Q. Railroad owner and avid hunter Charles Whitehead named what three towns along his railway for three of his favorite prey?

A. Mallard, Plover, and Curlew.

Q. Why is the interstate highway being built across eastern Iowa called "Avenue of the Saints"?

A. It will eventually link St. Paul, Minnesota, and St. Louis, Missouri.

3
Utopian Communities and Ethnic Settlements

Colony of Infidels

Two miles south of Farmington there was once a town called Salubria, founded by Abner Kneeland of New England in 1839. Kneeland, at one time a Baptist minister, became a Universalist minister and then came to believe in pantheism (that God is in everything). Convicted of blasphemy for an article he wrote and imprisoned for sixty days, he counted Ralph Waldo Emerson and Bronson Alcott among his supporters.

About a year after his prison term, he brought some followers to Iowa and established a colony where he could obtain what he called "freedom of inquiry." For five years he lectured in Iowa about his pantheistic beliefs, but his neighbors did not take kindly to this, calling Salubria the "infidel colony." Kneeland died in 1844, the colony disbanded, and the "infidels" joined neighboring churches. Abner Kneeland is buried in Farmington.

Romantic but Not Real

A group of Hungarian exiles led by Count Ladislaus Ujhazy came to Decatur County, Iowa, in 1850 and tried communal living. The count, who in Hungary had been known as the Count of Comorn, and the men who came with him had fought with Louis Kossuth in the Hungarian insurrection

(1848–1849) to free their country from Austria. Defeated, they fled to Europe and some continued on to America.

On the open prairie they dreamed of building a New Buda, named after the Hungarian capital, Budapest, complete with castles on great estates and city parks. But unfortunately, initially, that is all they did—dream.

Within five years the count and some of his followers moved on to Texas. In 1867 Austria issued a decree allowing the exiles to return. The count ordered his people to return, but would not go himself, fearing that Austria would not welcome him back. Since his people would not return without him, Ujhazy took his own life at the age of eighty-three, and the Hungarians returned to their homeland.

Those who remained in Iowa labored and prospered as members of other Iowa communities. New Buda, however, lives only in the name of a Decatur County township.

Did You Know? Iowa's county with the largest land area is named after Lajos (Louis) Kossuth, the Hungarian patriot and statesman who headed the Hungarian insurrection beginning in 1848. He was so admired by Iowans that in 1850 they named their new county after him. In 2001, as part of the county's sesquicentennial celebration, a statue of Louis Kossuth was dedicated. It stands in front of the Kossuth County Courthouse in Algona.

The statue of Hungarian patriot Louis Kossuth stands on the courthouse grounds in Algona, the county seat of Kossuth County, Iowa. (PHOTO BY AUTHOR)

Not Quite Perfect

In 1848 a Frenchman named Etienne Cabet—who had written a book about his dream of the perfect community—brought that dream to America. Some who had read his book followed him to Nauvoo, Illinois, which the Mormons had been forced by intolerant neighbors to abandon. But dissension plagued their ideal community and after Cabet's death in 1856, they split up. Many of them went to Texas, but a few came to Iowa in 1858, and bought 3,115 acres of land near Corning in Adams County on the Nodaway River.

They established the city of Icaria and practiced communal living. It was a socialistic group interested in economic and political reform. Their differences continued to divide them, however, and their children grew up and left the community. On February 16, 1895, the colony, consisting of only twenty-one members, disbanded.

Did You Know? Icaria had the theme "All for each, and each for all" and was the longest existing secular group in American history that strictly held to the communal principle of holding everything in common. One of the Icarians, A. H. Picquenard, became an architect and with John C. Cochrane designed the beautiful gold-domed Iowa State Capitol.

The Successful Amana Colonies

The Community of True Inspirationists originally came from Germany in 1842 and formed the Ebenezer Society near Buffalo, New York. As the city expanded and encroached upon their tract of five thousand acres, the elders decided to relocate. They purchased eighteen thousand acres along the Iowa River in Iowa County, and laid out the village of Amana, meaning "believe faithfully," in the summer of 1855.

Five more villages with the name Amana were established: West, South,

High, East, and Middle Amana. Deciding a better railroad was needed to prosper, the Amana Society bought the town of Homestead to the south, the only one of the seven villages not containing the name Amana.

The Inspirationist pattern of living was controlled by religion. In 1846 the Society's constitution had set up the principle that all property should be owned in common. This was based upon Acts 2:44–45: "And all those who had believed were together, and had all things in common; and they began selling their property and possessions, and were sharing them with all, as anyone might have need."

Believing that communal living would simplify life so that the members might have more free time to serve the Lord, all meals were served in community kitchen houses and men and women worked at the trades for which

The ambiance of Old Germany is still evident in many parts of the Amana Colonies, Iowa's biggest tourist attraction. One million people visit every year. (COURTESY IOWA TOURISM OFFICE)

they were best qualified. Some farmed the land or built furniture; others baked bread or prepared sausage; some operated looms in the woolen mills. And at the center of all activity was the church—usually with eleven services a week.

Strong worldly influences forced a change in this pattern and on June 1, 1932, the old order came to an end. A new Amana Society was formed and all former members were issued shares of stock in the common property. The new Amana Society was a business corporation operated for profit and paying salaries to its workers. But the religious unity remained unchanged. Throughout the twentieth century and into the twenty-first, the Amana Church Society has preserved the religious traditions of the founders and has protected the colony from major disruption.

Today the Amana Colonies are the number one tourist attraction in Iowa, with about one million visitors a year. When you visit, you can purchase antiques, furniture, baskets, clocks, woolen goods, and local wine and beer, or eat hearty family-style cooking. For more information visit *www.amanacolonies.com*.

Old-World Germany in Present-Day Iowa

Like the True Inspirationists of the Amana Society, the Amish were German settlers who fled to America because of religious persecution. But unlike the Amana colonists, the Amish continue to resist the "progress" of the world.

Wearing unadorned clothing from head to foot, the Amish have no electricity, telephones, or motorized machinery. Coming to Iowa in 1839, this branch of the Mennonites settled mostly in western Buchanan County and eastern Black Hawk County and remain there to this day.

The sight of a horse and buggy driven by a bearded man in a broad-brimmed hat and his wife in plain dress and bonnet are a reminder to us of what life was like in the past. This simple life is their way of keeping close to the Word of God.

Separatists Find Refuge

The creation of a state church by William I of Holland resulted not only in a loss of religious freedom but also in a gain in economic opportunity. By

1834 many people, called Separatists, withdrew from the church and formed their own small societies of the Dutch Reformed Church. One of the excommunicated ministers was Henry Peter Scholte.

Aided by emigrant associations, in October 1846, Scholte led thirty people to America to find a new home. More than eight hundred Hollanders followed in April 1847. A committee of five, headed by Scholte, secured title to eighteen thousand acres in northeastern Marion County, Iowa.

They laid out a town called Pella, meaning "city of refuge." Twenty-two years later the elders decided to buy land farther west to accommodate their grown children and their families. Thirty-eight sections of land were bought in Sioux County, and in the spring of 1870 they began the move to a new town they named Orange City in honor of the Prince of Orange in Holland.

Today both of these thriving communities contain a well-respected college associated with the Reformed Church of America: Central College in Pella and Northwestern College in Orange City. And they each continue to celebrate their Dutch heritage every spring with a Tulip Festival. Pella's annual celebration, Tulip Time, began in 1935 as an operetta produced by

Orange City celebrates its Dutch heritage every year in May with the Tulip Festival.
(COURTESY IOWA TOURISM OFFICE)

Pella High School students. The Holland Flower Bulb Growers Association gave Pella's Formal Tulip Gardens its first twenty-five thousand bulbs.

Pella also has completed a canal and windmill known as Molengracht, meaning "mill canal" or "windmill by the canal." The full-sized replica of an 1850 Dutch windmill, the nation's tallest working windmill, was constructed in Holland. Visitors can ride an elevator up four stories to the windmill's outdoor stage.

For information on Pella visit *www.pella.org* and for more about Orange City visit *www.orangecityiowa.com*.

Did You Know? Pella was long known as "Strawtown" because during their first winter in Iowa, most of the Hollanders lived in improvised houses made entirely of straw or in dugouts covered with straw or hay.

Going Dutch

The sharp lines and precision moves of the marching band from MOC (Maurice-Orange City)/Floyd Valley in field competition are impressive. But when it comes to the street parade competition, your eyes are immediately drawn to what you hear, and it's not the horn music or even the drums. It is wooden shoes—more than 170 pairs!

Klompen is the Dutch word for shoes and that's descriptive of the sound these shoes make marching down a paved street. The marchers wear four pairs of socks with a pad on top of the instep. A few blisters may form, but by the time they are seniors they will have marched some thirty-five miles in their wooden shoes, so they become accustomed to it.

The shoes are from basswood made in Holland and cost the band $4,000 to $5,000 a year. Carl Hoon, the band director in 1960, started the tradition to make his band unique. Not only do the band members wear wooden shoes, but their uniforms are also styled after the traditional folk costume of Holland's Vollendam province.

Their Dutch heritage is evident before they play one note. All it takes is one or two steps!

A Close Encounter

When Englishman William Close visited the Philadelphia World's Fair in 1876, he met a Mr. Paullin, who had recently returned from a trip through northwestern Iowa. Paullin told Close about the wonderful land around LeMars. When Close returned to England with the news, a group of English noblemen formed the Iowa Land Company in London with a capital of $25 million, and soon an English group of colonists was on its way across the Atlantic.

Acting on behalf of the Iowa Land Company, Close had purchased thirty thousand acres of Plymouth County. Headquarters were set up four miles north of LeMars and a thousand-acre "training" farm was established two miles north of that. Here the new colonists—most of whom were young dukes and lords and graduates of Oxford and Cambridge—were trained in the art of farming by Captain Reynolds Moreton.

These gentlemen farmers imported horses and dogs, constructed a race-track, and formed a polo team. Their fox hunts and steeplechases entertained the countryside. They opened their own taverns and clubs (House of Lords and Prairie Club) and their own hotel (The Albion House).

Unfortunately, many of the English were unable to take the harsh realities of the prairie. Enthusiasm waned and by 1900 the colony had disintegrated and most of its residents had returned to England. But their brief stay left lasting impressions. Descendants of the Shropshire and Southdown sheep that Moreton imported from Sussex can be found throughout the great sheep-raising ranches of the western plains. Moreton also imported Yorkshire hogs; specialized in the best breeds of cattle and horses; and encouraged the planting of elms, spruce, evergreen, walnut, and many types of fruit trees that remain in evidence today.

For the English, it was "fun while it lasted"—but Iowans continue to reap the benefits of their presence.

Visit the Past at Vesterheim

Vesterheim means "western home" in Norwegian and this museum in Decorah is the largest and oldest ethnic museum in the United States, and was the first open-air museum in this nation.

The idea of a Norwegian-American Museum began to take shape in 1895 at a meeting of Luther College Alumni. The pioneer Norwegians of northeastern Iowa wanted to display Norwegian-American relics in a "folk museum" representing the life and culture of common people. Starting with a pioneer log cabin moved to the Luther College campus, the collection grew to include another log house; schoolhouse; blacksmith shop; stone mill; and *stabbur*, or Norwegian storage building. These buildings, along with a house and grist mill from Valdres, Norway, and an early Decorah house of stove-wood construction, are now located on the Vesterheim museum grounds in downtown Decorah.

The museum's main building was built in 1877 as an elegant hotel and houses Norwegian textiles and traditional dress, items featuring Norwegian decorative painting, furniture and housewares, tools, machinery, and a three-story ship gallery. Vesterheim also owns the Washington Prairie Methodist Church and the Jacobson Farmstead outside Decorah.

The museum is dedicated to nurturing a living folk heritage. Each year more than fifty courses are offered in traditional Norwegian crafts through the Handwork School and Academy. Vesterheim holds national juried exhibitions in traditional knife making, *rosemaling*, rug hooking, weaving, and woodcarving during Nordic Fest, held in Decorah the last full weekend of July each year. (*Roselmaling* is a Scandinavian style of carved or painted decoration, consisting of floral motifs.)

It also sponsors Syttende Mai (Norwegian Independence Day) on May 17, Back Home on the Farm on the first Saturday in June, Scandinavian Food Fest on the first Saturday in October, and Norwegian Christmas on the first full weekend in December.

For more information visit *www.vesterheim.org*.

Unique Ethnic Museums

★ **The Danish Immigrant Museum:** This Elk Horn museum features Danish half-timbered architecture, and future structures will be connected around a central courtyard, typical of farms in Denmark. It showcases artifacts of Danish culture and traditions, exhibits about Danish immigration, and a Wall of Honor recognizing many of the approximately 360,000 Danes who immigrated to America. One of them, Victor Borge, gave his first piano, "the dearest of my personal possessions," to the museum, which also includes a Family History and Genealogy Center. The museum also operates Bedstemor's (Grandmother's) House, built in 1908 and containing authentic furnishings from 1910 to 1920. For more information visit *www.dkmuseum.org*.

★ **National Czech and Slovak Museum and Library:** Located in Czech Village in Cedar Rapids, the museum preserves the cultural traditions of the Czech

The National Czech and Slovak Museum and Library is located in Cedar Rapids. In attendance at its dedication in 1996 were the presidents of the United States, the Czech Republic, and Slovakia—this was the first time three heads of state have met in the state of Iowa. (COURTESY IOWA TOURISM OFFICE)

and Slovak farmers who were some of the first immigrants to the Cedar Rapids area. It has an extensive collection of *kroje* (folk costumes) from Bohemia, Moravia, and Slovakia. At the Museum and Library dedication in October 1996, Cedar Rapids hosted President Bill Clinton, the Czech Republic's Vaclav Havel, and Slovakia's Michal Kovac—the only time three heads of state had met in the state of Iowa.

★ **Manning Hausbarn:** This thatch-roofed *hausbarn,* originally built in the middle 1600s, is the only one brought to the United States from Germany and could be the oldest structure in the country. This 350-year-old, forty-foot structure from Offenseth in Schleswig-Holstein, Germany, was reassembled in Heritage Park east of Manning in 1999 under the supervision of master carpenter Martin Hansen from Germany, with a grand opening in the summer of 2000. In Germany it would be called *bauernhaus,* or "farmer house." And that is exactly what it was, a home for the farm family and its livestock. Heritage Park also is the home of the restored 1915 Leet/Hassler home and farmstead, listed on the National Register of Historic Places.

★ **Swedish American Museum:** This museum in Swedesburg, in southeast Iowa, features a library, coffee shop, gift shop, country store, huckster building, and *stuga* (Swedish cottage).

★ **Swedish Heritage and Cultural Center:** Located in Stanton, in southwest Iowa, the center features artifacts, documents, and photos depicting the journey of Swedish immigrants to the United States and southwest Iowa. Five exhibit rooms portray life in the Swedish settlement.

Did You Know? Stanton is known as "The Little White City" because every house is painted predominantly white.

Stran©e . . . but True

Stanton gets its water from a coffeepot—at least what looks like one. The Stanton water tower was converted to the world's largest Swedish coffeepot in 1971 in honor of native Virginia Christine who

became famous as "Mrs. Olson" in the Folgers coffee commercials. The "pot" holds 640,000 cups or 40,000 gallons, and is 36 feet high and 20 feet wide. The spout is 10 feet high and 6 feet deep, and the handle is 15 feet high.

To complement the coffeepot water tower, on June 22, 2001, Stanton dedicated another water tower shaped like a coffee cup!

A water tower shaped like a Swedish coffeepot graces the skyline of Stanton, the home of Virginia Christine, who portrayed "Mrs. Olson" in the Folgers coffee commercials. (COURTESY SWEDISH HERITAGE MUSEUM, STANTON)

Ethnic Events and Festivals

You can find events and festivals celebrating many ethnic groups in Iowa:

★ Cinco de Mayo Mexican Festival, Belmond

★ Greek Food Fair, Des Moines and Mason City

★ St. Patrick's Celebration, Emmetsburg

★ Italian-American Heritage Day, Oelwein

★ National Luxembourg Day, St. Donatus

★ Scandinavian Days, Story City

★ Meskwaki Pow Wow, Tama

Did You Know? The Danish villages of Elk Horn and Kimballton are the largest rural Danish settlements in the United States. Elk Horn is home of the Danish Immigrant Museum and the only authentic working Danish windmill in the United States. Built in 1848 in Norre Snede, Denmark, the windmill was dismantled and shipped to Elk Horn in 1976. More than three hundred volunteers reassembled the windmill. The Elk Horn Danish Windmill is one of Iowa's most popular tourist attractions and is an official Iowa Welcome Center, open every day except Christmas and New Year's Day. Visit the website at *www.danishwindmill.com.*

The windmill in Elk Horn was shipped from Denmark and rebuilt in 1979—it is the only authentic working Danish windmill in the United States. (COURTESY IOWA TOURISM OFFICE)

ETHNIC TRIVIA

Q. During World War I the town of Germania changed its name to what?

A. Lakota.

Q. Dublin, Ireland, is the sister city to what Iowa town?

A. Emmetsburg.

Q. The name of what Native American tribe of Iowa means "people of the red earth"?

A. Mesquakie.

Q. Families from what country were the first white settlers in Lyon County, settling near the Big Sioux River?

A. Norway.

Q. What community hosts the Croatian Fest?

A. Centerville.

Q. What was the original name of Madrid in Boone County?

A. Swede Point.

Q. Where can you find the sculpture *The Promise of America*, which honors Norwegian-American immigrants?

A. Lake Mills.

Q. What Native American tribe is thought to be the only one to cede land to Americans and then buy back part of it for a permanent home?

A. Mesquakie (Tama).

4

Palaces, Landmarks, and Other Unique Structures

The Edible Edifice

In Iowa, in many respects, corn is king. And when you have a king, you usually have a palace. That's exactly what Sioux City built in 1887—a corn palace.

A group of businessmen and citizens of Sioux City met to discuss ways of expressing their gratitude for a bountiful harvest and the growth of their city. They discussed putting piles of corn at intersections and decorating the courthouse with corn, which led to deciding to build an actual palace of corn.

On August 21, 1887, the *Sioux City Daily Journal* reported: "St. Paul and Montreal can have their ice palaces, which melt at the first approach of spring, but Sioux City is going to build a palace of the product of the soil that is making it the great pork-packing center of the Northwest."

The ten-thousand-square-foot, two-story wooden structure included eighteen thousand square feet of floor space and was covered with corn and grain, including sorghum, oats, millet, and cattails. The women of Sioux City supplied decorations, including a U.S. map made of grain and seeds with each state a different color, a stairway of corn, and a spider made of carrots hanging in a web of corn silk.

The corn craze caught on. Great arches were built at major intersections in town lit by more than seven thousand gaslights covered with various colored glass globes. Businesses decorated storefronts and displayed corn and other produce in windows. The ladies held corn parties and wore corn "bead" necklaces, while the men wore cornhusk hats and ties and smoked corncob pipes. The paper in Red Oak reported that in Sioux City during the jubilee "there will be no higher rank recognized than Kernels." The Corn Palace Board of Control formed a corporation, Sioux City Corn Palace Exposition Company.

The festival officially opened on October 3, 1887, and nearly 140,000 people attended the week-long celebration, including Cornelius Vanderbilt. The day after it closed President Grover Cleveland, on his tour of the country, came by special train to see the Corn Palace, declaring, "It is the only new and different thing I have seen in the entire trip."

The Sioux City Corn Palace, 1890, featured a two-hundred-foot main tower and six one-hundred-foot towers. (COURTESY DOWNTOWN PARTNERS SIOUX CITY)

For five years Sioux City was the Corn Palace City of the World, building a new and more magnificent palace each year through 1891.

In 1888 attendance was estimated at 350,000 people. In 1889 officials sponsored a special train, the Corn Palace Train, to tour the eastern United States and help attract attention to Sioux City. The train left in the spring and the 135 passengers attended the inauguration of President Benjamin Harrison, who, along with members of his cabinet, came on board to see the train. This publicity helped to make the 1889 festival the biggest so far. The next year, the Corn Palace included a miniature valley with a stream of water falling into a lake and a "Corn Palace Hymn" was composed for the celebration.

Although the 1891 Corn Palace and festival lasted three weeks, the weather was the worst. The palace was unheated, so cold, drizzly days kept attendance down. Not enough money was generated to tear the palace down, so an auction was held and H. H. Buckwalter bought a corn palace for $1,200. It was discovered that sheep would eat the corn and avoid the nails, so the corn was used for feed and the lumber, nails, and bunting were salvaged.

Plans were made for an 1892 festival but in May the Floyd River flooded Sioux City. Ten people died and around four hundred homes and businesses were damaged or destroyed. The festival was put on hold until 1893.

In 1893 a financial panic swept the country. In April two Sioux City banks failed and more than two dozen businesses folded. This financial hardship, along with the fact that Mitchell, South Dakota, had built a corn palace in 1892 when they realized that Sioux City would not have one, meant the golden days of the Sioux City corn palace were over. But it was grand while it lasted.

Other Products Given Palatial Prominence

Other Iowa towns built "palaces" to display their products. Forest City built a Flax Palace, Creston a Bluegrass Palace, and in 1890 Ottumwa built a Coal Palace.

Inside and out the Coal Palace served for two seasons as an exhibit hall of southeastern Iowa products. The 230-by-130-foot building with a 200-foot central tower cost $40,000 to build and included a working coal mine that was reached by an elevator underneath the structure. Visitors included President Benjamin Harrison and U.S. Congressman (later President) William McKinley. The Coal Palace was taken down after the 1891 season.

An eight-by-four-by-six-foot replica of the Coal Palace, built in 1998, can be seen in Ottumwa at the Wapello County Historical Museum.

The House That Powder Built

Carl Weeks of Des Moines created a mixture of face powder and cold cream, one of the first foundation makeups for women. The success of the company he founded, Armand Cosmetics, made it possible for him and his wife, Edith, to build Salisbury House on the west side of Des Moines in 1923.

This 22,500-square-foot Tudor-style manor with forty-two rooms on four floors was a recreation of the 500-year-old Old King's House that the couple had seen while traveling in Salisbury, England.

In 1953 Weeks wrote: "Salisbury House was built by face powder and was the result of a chain of events that started with my interest in a certain young lady, Miss Edith Van Slyke, whom I happened to meet on a Sunday morning in 1904 in a drugstore. She was going to Europe for a year of travel and study, and I promised to meet her there for a visit. I sold all that I possessed and bought a round trip ticket by way of Azores, Italy . . . and up to Dresden, where I met the young lady before Raphael's 'Madonna.' Then I went to Paris and there I stopped before a window display of face powder in the Rue de la Paix—and a sudden inspiration came to me. I took out my notebook and wrote out a formula that I would use if ever I tried it again. And that eventually was the powder that built Salisbury House."

Weeks, who earned a pharmacy degree from Hyland Park College in Des Moines at age seventeen, was a stickler for detail and accuracy. The design included all three historical periods that had been represented in the original English house: flint and stone from Tudor times (1484–1603), a Gothic porch from the reign of King John (1167–1216), and a brick portion from the time of Charles I (1625–1649). Even the forty-five thousand nails needed were individually handcrafted.

Five years later, in 1928, the project was complete: house, garage, and cottage, inside and out. It had taken two architects, hundreds of craftsmen, and $3 million. And as intended, it looked a hundred years old. But the inside had every modern convenience of the day: an elevator, a huge gas clothes dryer, a water softener, a telephone, and a security switch at Carl's bedside that controlled all the lights.

Over the years, because of their love for art, the Weekses collected art-work from all over the world. Practically every country and culture was represented in their collection, from a 1500 B.C. pottery vase from Cyprus to Navajo rugs, from Chinese statues to Russian icons. In 1934, during the height of the Depression, the Weekses gave the house to Drake University, for a future school of fine arts. They retained the art collection and remained in the house for a nominal rent. The plans for a fine arts school did not work out and in 1954 Drake sold the house and grounds, and the Weekses sold their art collection to the Iowa State Education Association.

Carl Weeks had written to a friend, "Salisbury House was something that had to be, and it had to be correct in every respect."

The House That Roared (and Barked!)

Three prominent Cedar Rapids families—and their pets—have lived at Brucemore, a Queen Anne–style mansion with twenty-one rooms and three stories, built in 1886. Located on twenty-six acres, the property includes a formal garden, a 1915 Lord and Burnham greenhouse, a 1927 swimming pool, and a duck pond. It became a National Trust Historic Site in 1981.

Thomas McElderry Sinclair and Caroline Soutter Sinclair moved to Cedar Rapids from New York in 1871. T. M. Sinclair and Company, a meat-packing plant, rapidly became an important Cedar Rapids business. In 1881 Thomas fell to his death at the plant, and Caroline became a widow with six children at age thirty-three. She built a mansion with a great hall, grand staircase, eight bathrooms, nine bedrooms, fourteen fireplaces, and a conservatory—at a cost of $50,000. By 1906, with her children grown, she traded homes with George Bruce Douglas and his wife, Irene.

George Douglas Sr. had cofounded the Quaker Oats Company, and his sons George and Walter founded the Douglas Starch Works in 1903. George and Irene renamed the mansion Brucemore after George's middle name and his family's ties to the Scottish moors. Their $30,000 in renovations included increasing the property and adding a sleeping porch, a garden house, a servants' duplex, a greenhouse, a carriage house, a squash and tennis court, a duck pond, formal vegetable and cutting gardens, and a swimming pool.

George died in 1923 and Irene in 1937, and she left the estate to the eldest of their three daughters, Margaret Douglas Hall. Margaret had married Howard Hall in 1924, and they had lived in the garden house.

Margaret and Howard Hall loved animals. Mrs. Hall had an exotic bird collection and there were always two German shepherds running around the estate. Howard—who was president of the Iowa Steel and Iron Works, established the Iowa Manufacturing Company, was chairman of many banks and director of Amana Refrigeration and the Quaker Oats Company—often

Brucemore in Cedar Rapids, complete with swimming pool, greenhouse, duck pond, and pet cemetery, is now used as a community cultural center and historic site. (COURTESY IOWA TOURISM OFFICE)

went to California on business. There he met Billy Richards, vice president of World Jungle Compound, the company that handled Jackie, the famous MGM lion. In 1937 the Halls acquired their own lion, a son of Jackie, whom they named Leo. Leo, who lived until 1951, appeared in many family photos and home movies and is buried along with twenty dogs in the pet cemetery on the estate.

Just as her parents had, Margaret and Howard gave extensively to numerous charities and organizations. They established the Hall Foundation, which funds educational and charitable causes in Cedar Rapids, and provided funding for the Margaret and Howard Hall Radiation Center and the Hallmar Convalescent Wing at Mercy Medical Center.

When Margaret died in 1981, ten years after Howard, she gave Brucemore to the National Trust for Historic Preservation for use as a historic site and community cultural center. For more information about the site, visit *www.brucemore.org*.

A Titanic Discovery

George Bruce Douglas's brother, Walter D. Douglas, perished in the sinking of the *Titanic* on April 15, 1912, at age fifty-one. Walter had been widowed at thirty-seven and had married Cedar Rapids native Mahala Dutton Benedict in 1906. He had retired in 1911 and moved to Minneapolis. Walter and his wife, Mahala, and their maid, Bertha, were returning from Europe on the *Titanic*. This trip to Europe had been partly to give them an opportunity to look for furnishings for their new house.

Walter, one of 1,513 people who died when the *Titanic* struck an iceberg and sank in the Atlantic, had refused to leave the ship early, reportedly saying, "I would be less than a man if I left before every woman was saved."

The lifeboat carrying Mahala and Bertha was recovered by the ocean liner *Carpathia*. Mahala said that at her last sight of her husband "he was turning to assist several women and children waiting to get into lifeboats."

In 1998 RMS Titanic, Inc., the company owning salvage rights to the vessel, raised a portion of the ship's structure that had broken off that fateful

April night. The large piece was identified as berth C-86 occupied by Walter and Mahala Douglas.

In August 1998 the Discovery Channel and *Dateline NBC* aired a prime time special featuring the story of this salvage operation and an interview at Brucemore with Borden Stevens, grandniece of Walter and Mahala Douglas. This portion of the Douglas's *Titanic* berth was part of "*Titanic*—The Exhibition," which toured the United States.

Walter D. Douglas is buried in Cedar Rapids.

The Palace of the Prairie

Benjamin Franklin Allen, Iowa's first millionaire, began construction on Terrace Hill in 1866. It was completed in 1869 at a cost of $250,000, which included the mansion, the carriage house, all of the furnishings, and about thirty acres of land.

It had the ultra-modern features of hot and cold running water, gas lights, a lift, and indoor bathrooms.

The Second Empire–style mansion (Italianate with a mansard roof) was designed by Chicago architect, William W. Boyington, who also designed the General Dodge House in Council Bluffs. The interior of the twenty-room rose-colored brick mansion includes walnut, butternut, oak, mahogany, and rosewood and was called "the Palace of the Prairie."

Allen, a banker, was hit hard by the financial panic in the 1870s and sold the property to Frederick Marion Hubbell, another early Des Moines settler, for $55,000. Hubbell was involved in the development of railroads, real estate, life insurance, and public utility companies. He came to love his new home and made several major improvements. Four generations of Hubbells called Terrace Hill home, over a period of nearly ninety years.

The Hubbell family gave Terrace Hill to the people of Iowa in 1971 to be used as the official residence of Iowa's governors. The first floor, restored to a nineteenth century appearance, is used for official state functions. The second floor provides offices for the governor and the governor's spouse, as well as a guest suite. The third floor serves as private quarters for the executive family.

Did You Know? B. F. and Arathusa Allen held a grand opening for Terrace Hill on January 29, 1869, their fifteenth wedding anniversary. John Wright, from the Opera House Restaurant in Chicago, prepared the food, which was served at 10 P.M. The menu included two twenty-five-pound fruitcakes, a twenty-five-pound lady cake, oysters, turkey in colored jellies, and ice cream molded in the figure of George Washington. Flowers were everywhere, and the floral centerpiece alone cost $700.

Covered with Gold, Yet Economical

The Capitol is an excellent example of nineteenth century Renaissance-style architecture, with five domes, including a large central gilded dome. The first cornerstone was laid on November 23, 1871, but had to be replaced because of an extremely harsh winter. The new cornerstone is dated 1873, the year the new foundation was completed, and, according to the directive from the General Assembly at the time, was to have only the word "Iowa" inscribed on it. But stonecutter J. G. Waers was so proud of his work that he added his own name into the letters of "Iowa."

When the Capitol was completed, the final report on June 29, 1886, stated that the cost had totaled $2,873,294.59. The audit showed that only $3.77 was unaccounted for in the fifteen years it had taken to complete the project. Governor Buren Sherman had said in 1884, "It is no doubt a fact that no other public building in the United States has been constructed with more rigid economy." Robert S. Finkbine, an Iowa City contractor, had been superintendent of construction. A fire in the north wing on January 4, 1904, required expenditures that raised the total cost to $3,296,256.

Some other Capitol facts:

★ Type of gold on the dome: 23 karat

★ Combined weight of gold: 100 troy ounces

★ Thickness of gold: 1/250,000 inch

★ Original cost of gilding the dome: $3,500

★ Cost of regilding the dome: $16,500 in 1927; $79,938 in 1965; and $400,000 in 1998

★ Weight of the four brass chandeliers in the Senate chamber: 2,000 pounds (500 pounds each)

★ Number of crystals in each of the four chandeliers in the House chamber: 5,600

The Capitol was completed in 1886. The golden central dome has been regilded four times, most recently in 1998 at a cost of $400,000. (COURTESY IOWA TOURISM OFFICE)

The Mansion Site Purchased for $105

Major Hoyt Sherman, a younger brother of General William T. Sherman, came to Des Moines in 1848 practically penniless, but died one of the richest men in Iowa in 1904.

Before the Civil War he and others organized the Iowa State Bank. After the war, he helped establish the Equitable Life Insurance Company of Iowa, of which he was president for fourteen years.

In *Pioneers of Polk County, Iowa, and Reminiscences of Early Days* (Des Moines: Baker-Trisler Co., 1908), L. F. Andrews reports that several years after

Hoyt Sherman arrived in Des Moines, he wanted to acquire five acres of the Pursley estate, which a local court had ordered to be subdivided and sold at auction. On auction day, Hoyt had only $100. He agreed to serve as clerk of the auction sale for a fee of five dollars When he was about to lose the five acres to a bidder who had offered $100, Hoyt added his five-dollar fee and nudged out the opposing bidder. Twenty-seven years later, in 1877, the imposing mansion known as the Hoyt Sherman Place arose on the five-acre tract.

The City Park Commission purchased the house and grounds in 1907 and then leased it to the Des Moines Women's Club. The club added an art gallery to the west side of the mansion and later a three-story auditorium on the east side.

Once a society showplace, then a civic meeting place, the mansion is now a museum of seventeenth century hand-carved furniture and nineteenth and twentieth century art, as well as a performing arts center. Listed on the National Register of Historic Places, the theater portion is set to undergo another restoration by late 2003, at a cost of $6.3 million. For more information on the mansion, visit *www.hoytsherman.org*.

Frank Lloyd Wright's Tadpole

Famous architect Frank Lloyd Wright designed nine residences in Iowa, including Cedar Rock, located on a limestone bluff overlooking the Wapsipinicon River near Quasqueton in Buchanan County.

Built for businessman Lowell Walter and his wife, Agnes, Cedar Rock was begun in 1948 and finished in 1950 in a style Wright called "Unisonian." The roof and floors are concrete and the walls are brick, glass, and walnut. The one-story, 150-foot-long house is built in the characteristic Wright "tadpole" form. The bedroom wing is the tail and the living and dining room, called "the Garden Room," form the head of the tadpole. The Garden Room has three glass walls with a fantastic view of the river and wooded valley, and every room has at least one clerestory window or skylight. (A clerestory window is on an outside wall that rises above an adjoining roof.)

Wright also designed the furniture, chose the carpets, and selected the draperies and accessories, including the dishes and knickknacks. Cedar Rock is one of only a few Wright houses with one of the architect's signature tiles embedded in an exterior brick wall.

The Walters were proud of their home and upon Lowell's death in August 1981, left it to the Iowa Conservation Commission and the Iowa people. The house, now open to the public, has changed little since it was built.

The Wright Stuff

Mason City claims the strongest Iowa connection to Frank Lloyd Wright. The Park Inn, in downtown Mason City, is the world's only remaining hotel designed by Wright. Next door is City National Bank, another Wright-designed building. Both opened in 1910.

While in Mason City, Wright was commissioned to design a house for George and Eleanor Stockman. An example of the Prairie School style of architecture developed by Wright, which emphasized low horizontal lines and open interior spaces, the two-story Stockman House was built in 1908 and is open for public tours today.

An entire neighborhood in Mason City, the Rock Crest/Rock Glen National Historic District, exhibits the Prairie School influence. Six houses were designed by Walter Burley Griffin and one by William Drummond, both of whom had worked in Frank Lloyd Wright's studio.

The other homes in Iowa designed by Wright in the 1940s and 1950s are in Cedar Rapids, Charles City, Oskaloosa (two), Monona, Marshalltown, and Johnston, but are not open to the public.

Skyscraper Penthouse—Iowa Style

In the mid-1970s, Arthur (Hap) Peterson of Titonka read an article in the magazine *The Furrow* about farm silos being converted into houses. It fascinated him, and he began to design his own silo house, with the help of his wife, Lois, for their 360-acre Titonka farm. The silo is 35 feet high and 20 feet in diameter. They used 30-inch-long cement staves that were 3½ inches thick for the outer shell. It has four levels, one main room per level, and a 25-foot octagonal "penthouse" on top. The penthouse is surrounded by a hundred feet of metal railing and was lifted into place by crane.

The silo house took three months and three weeks to build in 1983. The first floor has an office, laundry, and furnace room with a half bath. The second level has a family room with barrel-shaped furniture. The third level has a bedroom with bathroom, including closets and a circular bed. The fourth level is the kitchen, and finally, on top is a penthouse living room with seven triple-pane windows and a doorway for access to the wraparound deck. The stairway curves along the exterior wall on the inside with fifteen steps between floors.

The silo house in Titonka was built in 1983 specifically to be a house, from its first-floor office, laundry, and furnace room, to its penthouse living room four levels up. (COURTESY ARTHUR PETERSON, TITONKA)

From the top, with its panoramic view, Peterson can look down at the house he was born in, where his son now lives, look out across the neighboring fields, and be eye-level with the Titonka elevator and water tower. Hap Peterson's building fits right into the landscape, while adding its own unique variation to the Titonka skyline.

Did You Know? The Iowa Barn Foundation, established in 1997, is dedicated to preserving Iowa's rural buildings, symbols of Iowa's heritage. The primary mission of the nonprofit corporation is to educate the public about Iowa's vanishing barns and provide barn restoration matching grants to help property owners restore their barns. Property owners who use their own funds to restore barns that would otherwise qualify for a matching grant are eligible to receive an Iowa Barn Foundation Award of Distinction. For more information visit *www.iowabarnfoundation.org.*

We've Got You Covered

The bridges of Madison County, made famous by the book and movie of the same name, were originally covered to protect the flooring timber. These large pieces of lumber were more expensive to replace than the wood used on the sides and roof. Usually bridges were named after the closest resident.

Of the nineteen covered bridges that at one time existed in Madison County, five are still standing. A sixth, Cedar Bridge, was burned down by an arsonist on August 17, 2002. Pictured on the cover of Robert James Waller's novel, Cedar Bridge was built in 1883; it was 76 feet long and was the only bridge still open to vehicles before it was destroyed. Plans are under way to rebuild it.

The other five bridges are

★ **Roseman Bridge:** built in 1883, 107 feet long, southwest of Winterset

★ **Cutler-Donahoe Bridge:** built in 1870, 79 feet long, relocated to Winterset's City Park in 1970

★ **Holliwell Bridge:** built in 1880, the longest bridge at 122 feet, southeast of Winterset

★ **Hogback Bridge:** built in 1884, 97 feet long, northwest of Winterset

★ **Imes Bridge:** the oldest bridge, built in 1870, 81 feet long, moved twice, in 1887 and 1977; now east of St. Charles

The Covered Bridge Festival has been held for more than thirty years, long before the book or the movie came out. It is held the second full weekend in October and includes guided bus tours of some of the bridges, craft demonstrations, a Civil War reenactment, a car show and antique vehicle parade, music, and much more. For more information visit *www.madisoncounty.com*.

The Roseman Bridge Ghost

Legend has it that a posse cornered an outlaw who had escaped from jail in 1892 at Roseman Bridge. As the posse approached him from both sides, he rose through the roof and was never seen again. Some say you can hear his footsteps and laughter on the bridge.

Some say that the Roseman Bridge, southwest of Winterset, is haunted by an escaped outlaw. (COURTESY IOWA TOURISM OFFICE)

Did You Know? Winterset is home to one of only five stone outhouses listed on the National Register of Historic Places. This three-hole privy was built in 1856 and is located in the Madison County Historical Complex. The complex includes a brick mansion (built 1856), post office (used from 1870 to 1876), gas station (built 1934), and church (built 1881).

Three Stories Were Going Around

William H. Brown and Benjamin F. Haugh of Indianapolis, Indiana, designed the Squirrel Cage Jail in Council Bluffs. A patent they received on July 12, 1881, stated, "The object of our invention is to produce a jail in which prisoners can be controlled without the necessity of personal contact between them and the jailer." The structure was to provide "maximum security with minimum jailer attention."

The jail was built in 1885 at a cost of $30,000 ($8,000 for the outer building and $22,000 for the rotary jail cylinder in the center). It was used until

1969. It is the only three-story, rotary cell, "Lazy Susan"–type jail left in the U.S., and is one of only three such jails remaining.

Each floor had ten pie-shaped cells that revolved and were accessed by turning a hand crank until the cell lined up with a single door on each floor. The jail was built for sixty prisoners, but at one time in 1929 it held 165. There was a problem on hot days with the stench from the common waste receptacle running through the center of the cylinder of cells.

The front of the building had offices for the jailer, a kitchen, trustee cells, and quarters for women. J. M. Carter, the first superintendent, oversaw its construction and lived in an apartment on the fourth floor.

The Squirrel Cage Jail is on the National Register of Historic Places and is a historic museum open to the public, run by the Historical Society of Pottawattamie County.

The Squirrel Cage Jail in Council Bluffs is a three-story, "Lazy Susan"–type jail. Each floor has ten pie-shaped revolving cells. (COURTESY COUNCIL BLUFFS CONVENTION AND VISITORS BUREAU)

A Fort That Protected Indians

Usually forts were built to protect pioneer settlers from Native American tribes—but in Iowa, one fort was built to protect one Indian tribe from another.

Fort Atkinson, in what is now Winneshiek County, was built in 1840 to protect the Winnebago from the Sioux, Sauk, and Fox.

Fort Atkinson was built in the Neutral Ground, a strip of land forty miles wide in north Iowa, extending from the Mississippi River to the Des Moines River. The Neutral Ground was established in 1830 to separate the Sioux from the Saukc and Fox tribes. The fort was built to protect the displaced Wisconsin Winnebago Indians, who were moved into the Neutral Ground in 1837 as negotiated by the Treaty of 1830. A Winnebago farm, school, and mission, associated with the fort, were also established. Originally located on the Yellow River in Allamakee County, the school was moved in 1841 to the north end of what is now Auburn Township in Fayette County.

The fort is the only pioneer fortification in Iowa where the structures can be seen in their original location. Just a few pieces of the fort remain: foundations, one guardhouse, and one barracks that now houses a museum. The Fort Atkinson Rendezvous is held the last full weekend in September.

Fort Des Moines No. 3 Leads the Way in Racial and Gender Equality

There have been three Forts Des Moines. Fort Des Moines No. 1 was built at the head of the Des Moines River rapids near Montrose at the Mississippi in 1834, as a winter home for the three companies of dragoons stationed there. Fort Des Moines No. 2 was built on May 9, 1843, at the Raccoon Fork of the

Des Moines River in central Iowa, in what is now the capital city of Des Moines. It was designed as a place of defense against hostile Indians.

Fort Des Moines No. 3 was established by the U.S. government on the eve of World War I, four miles south of the second Fort Des Moines on Army Post Road. Here African Americans trained as candidates for the nation's first black officers. The first military training school of its kind in the United States, Fort Des Moines held its first graduation on October 15, 1917, with 639 candidates graduating as captains or lieutenants, including nine Iowans.

During World War II African Americans who volunteered to train as fighter pilots were sent here for basic training and then on to Tuskegee, Alabama. Several of the most prominent Tuskegee Airmen were from Iowa. Captain Luther Smith of Des Moines flew 133 combat missions against Nazi Germany and accompanied President Bill Clinton to Europe for the fiftieth anniversary of World War II. Captain Robert Williams from Ottumwa wrote the award-winning 1995 HBO film *The Tuskegee Airmen*.

Fort Des Moines, now designated a National Historic Site, was also home to another first. During World War II it hosted the formation of the first Women's Army Auxiliary Corps (WAAC), later called the Women's Army Corps (WAC). Between 1942 and 1945, seventy-two thousand troops were trained here and the first female officers for noncombat duty were commissioned.

A project is under way to establish the Fort Des Moines Memorial Park and Education Center here. Scheduled to open in the fall of 2003 with dedication planned for the summer of 2004, the site will celebrate how the Armed Forces contributed toward racial and gender equality. For more information visit *www.fortdesmoines.org*.

The Fort Burned By Its Own Troops

Built in 1808, Fort Madison was the first U.S. military post built in Iowa and was named to honor the new president. Sauk and Fox were regular visitors, trading furs and lead for knives, traps, blankets, and tools. In September 1812 hostile Sauk and Fox tribes attacked the fort. The siege continued off and on for a year, and the troops at the fort, facing a lack of supplies, set fire to it in September 1813 and escaped under cover of night through a trench leading to the Mississippi.

The Lone Chimney Memorial, on Highway 61 across from the Shaeffer Pen Company in Fort Madison, was built by the Daughters of the American Revolution and marks the site of Blockhouse No. 1 of the original Fort Madison. When the fort was burned in 1813, all that remained was a part of a blockhouse and a stone chimney. The chimney stood for years and was called "Po-to-wo-nook" by the Indians. When the city of Fort Madison celebrated its centennial in 1908, a reproduction of the chimney was built.

An accurate reconstruction of Old Fort Madison, including fire-stained foundation stones from the original site, can be seen in Riverview Park, Fort Madison. Authentically dressed interpreters describe the daily life of the soldiers and their families. Visitors can taste fresh-baked food, dip a candle, or hold a musket. A siege reenactment is held the weekend after Labor Day each year. For more information visit *www.fort-madison.net/oldfort*.

For the Birds (and the Bears): The First U.S. National Monument

Prehistoric mounds are common in the eastern half of the United States, but only Iowa had a culture that built ceremonial mounds in the shape of mammals, birds, or reptiles. The Winnebago, Iowa, and Otoe tribes are linked to these mounds.

Effigy Mounds National Monument, near Harper's Ferry in northeast Iowa, was established by presidential proclamation on October 25, 1949— making it the first national monument in the United States. The monument preserves prehistoric Native American mounds, wildlife, and other natural resources of the area.

The present visitor center was built in 1960. (A remodeled chicken coop served as the first visitor center.) Now 195 mounds are preserved, including 31 animal-shaped ones (24 are bear shapes and 7 are birds).

Effigy Mounds National Monument near Harper's Ferry was the first national monument in the United States. The white outline marks a Native American ceremonial effigy mound in the shape of a bear. (COURTESY IOWA TOURISM OFFICE)

In 2001 1,045 acres were added, connecting Effigy Mounds to Yellow River State Forest and expanding the park by more than 70 percent.

At Effigy Mounds National Monument you can learn about this fascinating prehistoric culture. For more information visit *www.nps.gov/efmo*.

 # UNIQUE STRUCTURES TRIVIA

Q. Because of a scarcity of timber, what substitute material was used for many pioneer homes in northwest Iowa?

A. Sod.

Q. The Morgan Manor Hunting Lodge of Massena, built in 1887, is celebrated for being used as what during World War II?

A. An obstetric hospital—and all 212 babies delivered there survived!

Q. The first religious services in George were held in what structure?

A. A train depot.

Q. What railroad builder, who was also a Civil War general and banker, built a Victorian mansion in Council Bluffs in 1869?

A. Grenville M. Dodge.

Q. The Eugene Closson Physical Education Center at Graceland College resembles what conveyance?

A. A covered wagon.

Q. In 1891 a large glacial boulder found in Black Hawk County was used to construct what building in Waterloo?

A. Boulder Church.

Q. What is the only school in the nation to have its entire campus listed in the National Register of Historic Places?

A. Cornell College in Mount Vernon, with forty-one buildings on 129 acres.

Q. In 1913 what was the first great hydroelectric project completed in the United States?

A. Keokuk Dam.

Q. What was built on the spot where Pope John Paul II gave an address and held a worship service in Iowa in 1979?

A. The Church of the Land, Living History Farms, Urbandale.

Q. For what is the Reverend John Todd House in Tabor famous?

A. It was a major station on the Underground Railroad.

5
Government and Politics

A Father's Devotion

Robert Cavalier de La Salle took possession of the "country of Louisiana" on April 9, 1682, for Louis XIV, king of France—and this area, which would eventually become the state of Iowa, continued under French rule for eighty years. In 1762, to keep Louisiana from falling into British hands, the province was ceded to Spain. In 1780 the province was ceded back to France, and in 1803 the whole tract sold to the United States for less than five cents an acre. The United States took possession on March 10, 1804.

From 1804 until 1821, Iowaland was first part of the District of Louisiana, then the Territory of Louisiana, and, finally, the Territory of Missouri. When Missouri became a state in 1821, the northern part of the Louisiana Purchase didn't have a government. In 1834 it became part of the Territory of Michigan and in 1836, part of the Wisconsin Territory.

By 1837 the Wisconsin Territory west of the Mississippi had grown to a population of about twenty thousand and the inhabitants desired a better government. On September 16, 1837, a territorial convention prepared a petition to Congress to consider organizing a new territory.

The Senate passed the bill "to establish the Territorial Government of Iowa" on June 1, 1838, but the House of Representatives was concerned that a new territory would destroy the balance of power between the slave and free states. The House voted 118 to 51 to create the Territory of Iowa, but with amendments to the bill that the Senate would have to approve. The senator from South Carolina, John C. Calhoun, opposed. The territorial delegate, George W. Jones, enlisted the help of Calhoun's daughter, Anna, to help change the senator's mind. Jones invited Anna to come to the Senate gallery when the Iowa bill was being debated and asked her to send for her father and take him into the library on his signal. She obliged and no sooner had Calhoun left the chamber with his daughter than the bill was brought up for final adoption. It passed, the Senate adjourned, and President Martin Van Buren signed the law. Iowa became a territory on July 4, 1838.

When Calhoun discovered what had happened he reportedly exclaimed, "Oh, Anna, you bad girl. You have prevented my making a speech to oppose the bill, as I would have done and done successfully, as the time for the consideration of territorial bills has expired."

Because of a daughter's interference, Iowa became a territory in its own right.

Did You Know? During the mid-1800s building a flagpole for your favorite candidate was a common practice—and the higher, the better. During Abraham Lincoln's bid for the presidency in 1860, a 100-foot pole was built for him in Henry County. One night some Democrat rivals chopped it down and the Republican pro-Lincoln forces were hopping mad. They built a new pole—120 feet high—and guarded it night and day. As we know, the Republicans got the last say, for Lincoln not only carried the state, but the nation.

To Be or Not to Be . . .

When a convention met at the capitol in Iowa City on Monday, October 7, 1844, to prepare a constitution for the future state of Iowa, one of the major issues was boundaries. Robert Lucas, governor of the Territory of Iowa, suggested the boundaries run from the Mississippi west to the Missouri, and from the state of Missouri north to the St. Peter's (now Minnesota) River. This would have given Iowa about sixty thousand square miles. The Lucas boundaries were adopted and the first constitution of Iowa was signed and sent to Congress, which accepted the new constitution on March 3, 1845, with one major change. The western boundary was moved east, making the proposed new state about two-thirds as large as originally proposed.

Iowa's delegate to Congress, Augustus Caesar Dodge, urged his constituents to accept Congress's proposal, because he felt they would never be able to obtain more. But Iowa residents, who had envisioned their state extending from river to river, were unwilling to accept the changes and rejected the constitution as amended.

Admission to the United States came on December 28, 1846, with the boundaries as they are today, not as far north as originally proposed, but extending east to west from river to river, as so many had hoped.

Did You Know? Enoch W. Eastman, one of the convention delegates who stumped the territory urging people to vote against ratification of the 1844 constitution because of the boundary amendment, supplied the phrase chosen for the state's inscription on its stone in the Washington Monument. His original phrase—"Iowa: the affections of her people, like the rivers of her borders, flow to an inseparable Union"—was shortened to "Iowa: Her affections, like the rivers of her borders, flow to an inseparable Union."

The Pig That Went to Vote

The state of Iowa had a governor before Iowa legally existed as a state. Governor Ansel Briggs was sworn into office on December 3, 1846, twenty-five days before President James K. Polk signed the bill of admission bringing the state into existence.

In October 1846 a heated political battle was being waged between the Democrats and Whigs. Besides electing officials for state offices, the state legislature would also elect two state senators and three supreme court justices. The Whigs knew they were the underdog, so a group of wealthy Whigs in Des Moines hired some Democrats to go into the wilderness and drive hogs for them. Twenty-four hours before the election, these Democrats found themselves in the middle of nowhere. One, realizing he had been duped and having found only one pig for his employer, traveled all night and through the next day, arriving at the polling place at dusk—carrying the pig as he cast his vote. His vote helped elect Democrat Ansel Briggs as Iowa's first governor.

Neither party won a majority in the legislature. A few Independents held the balance of power, and when one said the Democrats had offered him a bribe, an investigation took up the entire first session. So from late 1846 until 1848, Iowa had no senators in Washington, D.C. Finally, in 1848, George W. Jones and Augustus Caesar Dodge were elected.

Even in Iowa's first political election, hogs played a significant role!

Did You Know? In 1850 and 1855 Congress passed laws granting land bounties to those who had served in U.S. armies. Abraham Lincoln was granted three land warrants for his services as captain of the Illinois Volunteers in the Black Hawk War of 1832. He chose two of these land grants in Iowa: forty acres in Tama County, fourteen miles northwest of Toledo; and 120 acres in Crawford County, eight miles northwest of Denison. When Lincoln acquired the Tama County land it was worth ten dollars an acre. His heirs later sold both properties. (The Crawford County land was sold for $1,300 in 1892.)

Stran⊚e . . . but True

George W. and Sarah E. Wright of Tama County, Iowa, wrote to Abraham Lincoln on December 11, 1860, after he had been elected president, asking him to repay Mr. Wright fifty dollars. It seems George had been stumping for Lincoln and had bet a Democrat fifty dollars that Lincoln would win the election. When Lincoln won, the Democrat refused to pay up. Some words later, George knocked down the offender, who subsequently brought the law on George. It cost George fifty dollars to settle the lawsuit and he thought Lincoln, being indebted to him, should reimburse him for favors done.

One Man, One Vote

Former Iowa governor James Grimes of Burlington is not only known as the father of the Iowa Republican Party—but also for his refusal as a U.S. senator to vote to remove President Andrew Johnson from office in 1868 during his impeachment trial.

Though stricken with paralysis, Grimes had others carry him to the Senate floor to vote "not guilty." Most Republicans wanted to have Johnson removed, but seven did not. It would have taken only one more vote to oust him from office. Grimes felt strongly about not destroying the Constitution "for the sake of getting rid of an unacceptable president."

Republicans all over the country, even in Iowa, were livid. Because of this denunciation, despite faithful service to his state and country, Grimes resigned from the Senate the following year. He died in 1872 after a heart attack at the age of fifty-five.

Chief Justice Salmon P. Chase of the U.S. Supreme Court, who had presided over the Johnson Senate trial, respected the effort Grimes had made to cast his vote to protect the Constitution. Even now, more than a hundred years later, you have to admire a man who stood up for his own politically unpopular beliefs, even when he couldn't stand on his own power.

Did You Know? General Norton Parke Chipman, a lawyer from Washington, Iowa, was responsible for suggesting what we now know as Memorial Day. Chipman had served with distinction with the Second Iowa Infantry in the Civil War. In 1868, as adjutant general of the Grand Army of the Republic, Chipman wrote an order declaring that May 30 be set aside as Decoration Day to commemorate those who had died in the war, with flowers and appropriate services. The order was sent to John A. Logan, commander-in-chief, who added a few sentences and issued it. General Orders No. 1, issued on May 5, 1868, resulted in Memorial Day.

The Silver-Tongued Orator from Iowa

In 1885 Republican orator and future Iowa senator Jonathan P. Dolliver said in a speech: "Iowa will go Democratic when Hell goes Methodist"—this was how strongly Republican Iowa was.

Dolliver had come to be known as "the silver-tongued orator from Iowa" because of his knowledge, deep sense of honesty, and knack for public speaking. He and his brother, Robert, arrived in Fort Dodge from what became the state of West Virginia in 1878 to open a law practice. Jonathan lost his first law case involving a horse trade, but his eloquence attracted attention.

Jonathan Dolliver, Republican state senator and later U.S. representative, was known as "the silver-tongued orator from Iowa" and could have been president of the United States. (LIBRARY OF CONGRESS)

He served as the temporary chairman of the Republican State Convention in 1884 and 1888, and was elected to the U.S. House of Representatives, where he served for twelve years. The Republicans seriously considered him for the vice presidential nomination in 1900, but he declined when he heard that Theodore Roosevelt was willing to accept it. This deferral turned out to cost Dolliver nor only the vice presidency but also the presidency—as Roosevelt, of course, took over that office when President William McKinley died.

Strange . . . but True

Augustus Caesar Dodge of Burlington and his father, Henry Dodge of Wisconsin, made history by being the only father and son to simultaneously represent different states in the U.S. Senate. Augustus, elected in 1848, was one of Iowa's first two U.S. senators, along with George W. Jones, and served as U.S. minister to Spain from 1855 to 1859. Spain owned Cuba and while serving in Spain, Dodge tried unsuccessfully to buy Cuba for the United States. Just think how different things would be if Spain had been willing to accept his offer!

Iowa's First First Lady

Lou Henry became the first woman in America to earn a degree in geology, at Stanford in 1898. She was born in Iowa in 1874, and her family moved first to Whittier, then to Monterey, California, because of her mother's poor health. At Stanford, in the geology department, she met Herbert Hoover, who had been born in West Branch, Iowa.

Married in 1899, Lou and "Bert" went to China where he served as a mining consultant to the emperor. When the Boxer Rebellion broke out, they were caught in Tientsin and Lou attended to the wounded in hospitals, refusing to leave until the patients were also removed. During World War I, in London she organized the American Women's Committee for Economic Relief, to help get stranded Americans back home. In Belgium she established the American Women's Hospital and was later awarded the Cross of the

Chevalier, Order of Leopold, by King Albert. Working with Bert, she explored and lived in China, Burma, Tasmania, the Suez, Egypt, New Zealand, France, Italy, Japan, Australia, Russia, England, and Belgium.

In 1922 Lou was elected national president of the Girl Scouts, having been sworn in as a troop leader by founder Juliette Low in 1917. Lou said, "To me the outing part of scouting has always been the most important. The happiest part of my own very happy childhood and girlhood was without doubt the hours and days, the sometimes entire months, which I spent in pseudo-pioneering or scouting in our wonderful western mountains with my father in our vacation times. So I cannot but want every girl to have the same widening, simplifying, joy-getting influences in her own life." She also organized the women's division of the National Amateur Athletic Federation in the mid-1920s.

Lou Henry Hoover entered the White House as first lady on March 4, 1929, when Bert became the nation's thirty-first president, and from the outset she tried to make the White House more comfortable. All restoration projects were done at her expense and all guests were made to feel welcome, whether they were ambassadors or Girl Scouts. Her daily schedule was as full as the president's.

The Hoovers left Washington in 1933 for California and then moved to New York City so Bert could work on relief efforts with the Finnish Relief Fund—and, of course, Lou helped. She died of a heart attack on January 7, 1944, at sixty-nine years of age. She was an independent spirit and an exemplary public servant.

Lou Henry Hoover, wife of President Herbert Hoover, was born in Iowa in 1874 and became the first woman in America to earn a degree in geology. She was an exemplary humanitarian and public servant. (LIBRARY OF CONGRESS)

Did You Know? The second Iowa woman to become first lady of the nation was Mamie Doud Eisenhower, born in 1896 in Boone. You can visit her restored birthplace, which includes a museum and library. Also on display are her 1962 Plymouth Valiant and 1949 Chrysler Windsor autos.

Mamie Doud Eisenhower was the second Iowa woman to become first lady. (LIBRARY OF CONGRESS)

A Publisher and a Promise

Edwin Thomas Meredith was born December 23, 1876, in Avoca. After selling a small newspaper, *Farmers Tribune,* that he and his wife, Edna, had received as a wedding gift, they published their first issue of *Successful Farming* in October 1902. Thus began what would become a very successful publishing company—and it's still going strong today.

Realizing they were not reaching urban families, in September 1922 the Merediths printed the first edition of *Fruit, Garden and Home,* and in August 1924 they renamed the magazine *Better Homes and Gardens.*

Meredith also was a significant factor in the growth of the 4-H movement. And in between establishing *Successful Farming* and *Better Homes and Gardens,* Meredith served as secretary of agriculture under President Woodrow Wilson from 1913 to 1917. At the time of his death in 1928, he was being considered as the Democratic presidential candidate. Not bad for a boy from small-town Avoca!

Strange . . . but True

A Designer Health Plan

Vedic City, two miles north of Fairfield, was incorporated in July 2001. Built in conjunction with Maharishi University of Management in Fairfield, Vedic City is the first city in the modern world to be based entirely on the ancient principles of Maharishi Sthapatya Veda and other aspects of Maharishi Vedic Sciences. Veda is a design principle whereby things are built in accordance with natural law based on the Vedic Sciences, which acknowledge a cosmic creative intelligence. The city is "dedicated to creating maximum well-being for its citizens and visitors," achieved, purportedly, by the design itself, which promotes good health, clear thinking, happiness, and harmony.

Veda means knowledge in Sanskrit. The official language of Vedic City is Sanskrit and all buildings must face east to comply with Vedic architectural rules. In December 2002 the city passed the first reading of an ordinance that bans all nonorganic foods. The city has more than forty buildings, including a health spa, resort hotels, and homes. Plans are to build a theme park, observatory, and golf course.

GOVERNMENT AND POLITICS TRIVIA

Q. What salary did Herbert Hoover receive after being elected the first president born west of the Mississippi in 1928?

A. None (he wouldn't accept any).

Q. In what year was the state constitution changed to increase the governor's term from two to four years?

A. 1972.

Q. Who was offered the first governorship of the Territory of Iowa, but turned it down?

A. Henry Atkinson.

Q. Who was the only Iowa governor to serve two nonconsecutive terms?

A. Samuel J. Kirkwood, from 1860 to 1864, and from 1876 to 1877. (He became a U.S. senator for the second time in 1877, and in 1881 he became U.S. secretary of the interior under James Garfield.)

Q. What Iowan was vice president, secretary of agriculture, and secretary of commerce under President Franklin D. Roosevelt?

A. Henry A. Wallace.

Q. What Sioux Citian, as head of the Works Progress Administration (WPA), spent more than $9 billion during the depression of the 1930s and lived in the White House from 1940 to 1942?

A. Harry Hopkins. He was chief foreign policy aide and advisor to President Franklin D. Roosevelt; when he became Roosevelt's special assistant, he moved into the White House.

Q. What Iowa governor served five terms?

A. Robert Ray.

Q. Who was the first native Iowan to be state governor?

A. Beryl F. Carroll from Bloomfield, from 1909 to 1913.

Q. Iowa began its tradition of holding the nation's earliest presidential caucuses in what year?

A. 1972.

Q. Abraham Lincoln appointed what Iowan to his cabinet as secretary of the interior?

A. James Harlan. (His daughter, Mary, married Lincoln's eldest son, Robert Todd, and they lived in the Harlan-Lincoln Home in Mount Pleasant.)

Q. What two presidents, although not born in Iowa, lived there for part of their adult lives?

A. Richard Nixon lived at Ottumwa Naval Air Station from 1942 to 1943, and Ronald Reagan was the radio sportscaster at WOC in Davenport in 1932 and then at WHO in Des Moines from 1933 to 1937.

Q. What two Iowans were appointed to the U.S. Supreme Court?

A. Samuel F. Miller from Keokuk, in 1862, and Wily Blount Rutledge Jr. from Iowa City, in 1943.

Q. What four Iowans have been U.S. secretary of agriculture?

A. James (Tama Jim) Wilson (from 1897 to 1932, through the administrations of

McKinley, Roosevelt, and Taft to become the longest-serving Cabinet member ever); E. T. Meredith (in 1920); Henry C. Wallace (from 1921 to 1924); and Henry A. Wallace (from 1932 to 1940).

Q. What national labor leader was born in 1880 in the coal-mining camp of Cleveland, a mile east of Lucas?

A. John L. Lewis.

Q. R. W. Cassaday, from Monona County, was the first woman to hold what state office, from 1923 to 1924?

A. Secretary of agriculture.

Q. What Bloomfield lawyer was a Civil War brigadier general, editor of the *Davis County Republican,* and twice a candidate for the U.S. presidency?

A. James B. Weaver.

Q. In 1998 Tom Vilsack became the first Democrat to be elected governor in how long a period of time?

A. Thirty-six years. The previous Democratic governor was Harold Hughes, from 1963 to 1969.

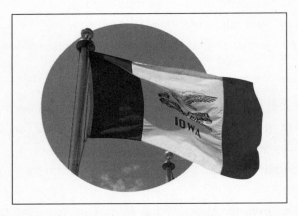

Q. What Knoxville resident designed the Iowa state flag?
A. Dixie Cornell Gebhardt. (COURTESY IOWA TOURISM OFFICE)

6
Wars and Rumors of Wars

Iowa's Only International Battle

The battle on Credit Island, near Davenport, was the only international conflict ever to occur in Iowa—over control of the fur trade on the upper Mississippi. It was fought August 21, 1814, between troops of Great Britain aided by the "British Band," a group of Indians led by Black Hawk, and U.S. troops. The British and Indian forces won, and it was the first battle Captain Zachary Taylor lost. You can find a Daughters of the American Revolution (DAR) marker commemorating the battle in Davenport on the southeast corner of Club and Credit Island Streets.

The Honey War

Almost as soon as Iowa became a territory, it became involved in a dispute with Missouri over just where the Missouri state line was located. In 1816 the U.S. government had sent J. C. Sullivan to survey the northern boundary of the land ceded to the U.S. government by the Osage Indians in 1808. He ran a line east from a point 100 miles due north of the intersection of the Kansas and Missouri Rivers to the Des Moines Rapids of the Mississippi.

When Missouri became a state in 1821, this Sullivan line was used as the northern boundary. As the northern part of Missouri and southeastern part of the Iowa Territory began to fill with settlers in 1837, the Missourians questioned the location of the boundary. The Missouri legislature sent a surveyor named Brown to determine the boundary according to the state constitution, which said it was a line west of the "Rapids of the river Des Moines." Brown went up the Des Moines River until he found a small rapids (near Keosauqua) and then ran a line due west from there. In 1838 Missouri passed a law claiming the Brown line as the state's northern boundary, thereby cutting off a 2,600-mile strip from the Iowa Territory, nine miles wide at the eastern end, and thirteen miles wide at the western end.

President Martin Van Buren sent Albert M. Lea as a commissioner to determine the correct line. His report stated that the Sullivan line was the correct one, but the trouble didn't end.

Within the disputed area were "bee trees," trees with natural hollow trunks that bees filled with wax comb and wild honey. The dispute became known as the "Honey War" and in the autumn of 1839, some Missourians cut down three of the trees and escaped with all the honey they could carry.

When a Missouri sheriff was arrested for trying to collect taxes a second time in Van Buren County in Iowa Territory, Missouri's Governor Lilburn W. Boggs called up troops. Iowa Territorial Governor Robert Lucas reciprocated and a militia of about twelve hundred men was ready to do war. The Iowa Legislative Assembly was not ready, however, and sent a commission to Missouri to confer on the matter. Both sides agreed to cease hostilities and allow the U.S. Supreme Court to determine the location of the boundary—and war was averted.

The Court decided in favor of Iowa ten years later, ruling that the original Sullivan Line that ended at the Des Moines Rapids in the Mississippi River was the correct line. By this time, Iowa had become a state and the boundary was marked with iron monuments at ten-mile intervals with wooden mileposts in between.

Thus the Honey War ended without a shot fired, and the only known fatalities were the three bee trees. But it did make for fine verses, both of which are sung to the tune of "Yankee Doodle."

Ye freemen of the happy land,
Which flows with milk and honey,
Arise! To arms! Your ponies mount!
Regard not blood or money.
Old Governor Lucas, tiger-like,
Is prowling round our borders,
But Governor Boggs is wide awake—
Just listen to his orders.

—JOHN I. CAMPBELL

Now, if the Governors want to fight,
Just let them meet in person.
And when noble Boggs old Lucas flogs,
'Twill teach the scamp a lesson.
Then let the victor cut the trees,
And have three-bits in money,
And wear a crown from town to town,
Anointed with pure honey.

—FROM A MISSOURI NEWSPAPER

Iowa Answers the Call, Over and Over and Over

On April 16, 1861, two days after the Union surrender of Fort Sumter, William Vandever, a member of Congress, hand delivered a telegram to Governor Samuel J. Kirkwood from the U.S. secretary of war. It read: "Call made on you by tonight's mail for one regiment of militia for immediate service."

Surprised, Kirkwood reportedly exclaimed, "The president wants a whole regiment of men! Do you suppose, Mr. Vandever, I can raise that many?"

It did not take long for him to receive an answer. Within ten days a regiment was ready, another had been accepted, and a third was waiting to be called. In all, in response to the president's calls for volunteers in 1861, Iowa supplied eighteen regiments of infantry, five regiments of cavalry, and three batteries of artillery.

By the end of the war, Iowa had sent about seventy-six thousand men to fight in the Union armies. This was more per capita than any other state, nearly half of Iowa's men of military age. All but about four thousand of the soldiers volunteered.

Revenge of the Red-Haired Warrior

An outlaw band of Sioux killed thirty-two settlers in 1857 in what became known as the Spirit Lake Massacre. The attack was led by Inkpaduta, whose name means "Scarlet Point." The warrior was more than six feet tall, with red hair and a face ravaged by smallpox.

The killing began on Sunday, March 8, at the Gardner cabin on West Lake Okoboji and ended on Friday, March 13, at the Marble cabin on Spirit Lake. Four women were taken captive: two were later killed and the other two were sold to Indians who were sent by Indian agent Charles E. Flandreau.

The last captive ransomed was fourteen-year-old Abbie Gardner. Her "price" was two horses, twelve blankets, two kegs of powder, twenty pounds of tobacco, thirty-two yards of blue cloth, thirty-seven and a half yards of calico, some ribbon, and other small articles. She had been captive for ninety-three days. In 1867 Abbie married Casville Sharp, and in 1883 she returned to the Okoboji region, bought the Gardner cabin, and made it her home. From here she sold souvenirs and a book she had written, *The History of the Spirit Lake Massacre and the Captivity of Miss Abbie Gardner.*

The reasons for the Spirit Lake Massacre are not known. Some believe it was an act of revenge for the killing of Sidominadota, who was from the same tribe as Inkpaduta and possibly related. He had been killed by Henry Lott, an unsavory character who had settled at the mouth of the Boone River in Webster County, in revenge for the death of his wife and son, caused by the activities of Sidominadota. But Sidominadota had been killed in late 1854, more than two years before this bloody rampage.

The winter was an unusually cold and snowy one and food was scarce. Perhaps hunger, the memory of the 1854 killing, and the constant reminder that the settlers were taking over the land combined to unleash the vengeance of Inkpaduta and his band. Fortunately, the Spirit Lake Massacre marked the end of Indian resistance on Iowa soil.

On Pillsbury Point, to the southeast of the Gardner cabin in Arnold's Park on West Okoboji, the state of Iowa built a monument in memory of those killed in the massacre. The names of the victims are carved into it.

Strange . . . but True

The Graybeard Regiment

By the autumn of 1862, the war was going badly for the Union and President Lincoln needed more men to strengthen the army. Iowans turned out in force for a regiment of more than one thousand older men—including one who was an octogenarian.

The thinking was that men over the normal age limit of forty-five could do guard duty and other jobs behind the lines to free up younger men for field action. Secretary of War Edwin Stanton commissioned George Kincaid, age fifty, of Muscatine, as a colonel and directed him to organize a regiment of older men. On December 15, 1862, the Thirty-Seventh Iowa Infantry Regiment was mustered into the Union Army at Camp Strong in Muscatine. The average age in the 1,041-strong "Graybeard Regiment" was fifty-seven. Most were over fifty, more than a hundred were in their sixties, many were over seventy, and one was eighty.

These men, who had 1,300 sons and grandsons fighting on the front lines, spent their service time guarding more than 160,000 Southern prisoners.

In 1865 the Graybeards were mustered out at Davenport. Iowa was the only state to have a Graybeard Regiment and that group of older patriots might be unique in all of history.

A Loyal Dunking

After Abraham Lincoln was shot in April 1865, Mary Rogan, employed at the Eureka House in Mason City and with Southern relatives and sympathies, was heard to say, "They say Lincoln has been shot. I hope to God it's true and I hope my brother shot him!"

In the North, in Iowa, in Mason City, that was considered treason. When President Lincoln had called for volunteers four years before, Mason City, a town of five or six hundred, had responded, as had all of Iowa.

According to the Mason City newspaper, the *Cerro Gordo Republican*, someone suggested, "Let's duck her!" The ladies approved the idea and they began to march toward Rogan's home, gaining recruits as they went. By the time they reached her home on the corner of Fifth Street and Delaware Avenue, there were fifteen to twenty women. They marched into the house, led Rogan out, and started down Main Street. The crowd of women grew larger, with the victim in the center. As reported in the newspaper, "She was being hurried off in the direction of Willow Creek, when the unsuspecting men in different parts of the town were apprised by her screams and vocifera-tions that something was in the wind, but starting for the 'front' they were informed that their presence was not needed."

Upstream from where Willow Creek crossed Main Street was a deep pool. Here, with practically everybody in town looking on, the women picked Mary up and threw her into the water. After they dunked her three times, Mary finally "begged pardon for what she had said and sacredly promised forever to be a good Union woman from that time forward, under all circumstances." They blacked her face, administered to her the oath of allegiance, and marched back up Main Street, singing. The men "joined in the procession and escorted them to McMillin's store, where candies were passed to the crowd."

Then W. E. Thompson spoke, referring to the death of the president and the nation's distress. From there the crowd proceeded to the Eureka House, "where they sang The Star-Spangled Banner and Rally 'Round the Flag, and then dispersed."

Mary Rogan kept her word. She later married a Union veteran, James Jenkinson, and grew to be well respected in the town that had given her a loyal dunking. Although this kind of intolerance for those expressing unpop-ular opinions would not be acceptable today, the outraged ladies of Mason

City apparently considered throwing water on the situation an appropriate way of cooling everybody off.

Did You Know? Robert E. Lee finished second in his 1829 class at West Point—behind Charles Mason, who became the first chief justice of Iowa. Mason was born in 1804 in New York and admitted to the New York Bar after graduating and teaching at West Point. President Martin Van Buren appointed him the first chief justice of Iowa when the Iowa Territory was organized in 1838. Mason served until resigning in 1847, after Iowa had become a state in December 1846. He died in Burlington thirty-five years later on February 22, 1882.

A Call for Arms

A group of mounted riflemen led by Lieutenant Colonel Cyrus Bussey routed Rebel militia from Missouri—preventing them from ever setting foot on Iowan soil. It was the closest Iowa would come to having a Civil War battle.

Governor Samuel J. Kirkwood had placed Bussey in control of the militia in southeastern Iowa. Bussey feared that the southern border counties were in peril; secessionists in northern Missouri had been organized into military companies under General Martin Green, so he organized companies of mounted riflemen in Lee, Davis, and Van Buren counties.

But the men had no rifles, and neither the governor nor General John C. Fremont, commander of the Department of the Missouri, could help. The general did, though, give him fifty thousand rounds of ammunition.

A spy Bussey had sent into northeastern Missouri warned him that Green and fifteen hundred Rebels were preparing to attack in Iowa within a day or two. Bussey had learned of a shipment of arms being sent by rail to General Grenville M. Dodge, commander of the Fourth Iowa at Council Bluffs. After writing out an unauthorized order for the guns to be delivered to his own regiment instead, Bussey intercepted the guns and armed his men.

He was none too soon, for on the morning of August 4, 1861, the Rebels were seen near Athens. Instead of taking the town by surprise, Green's men suddenly found themselves fired upon from all sides. They beat a hasty retreat, without ever touching Iowa soil.

Instead of a reprimand for taking arms in transit without authorization, Bussey received an appointment as a full colonel in the U.S. Army. It was a case of diverting munitions without permission resulting in a higher comissioned position!

Strange . . . but True

In a roadside park near Exira in Audubon County is a plow embedded in an oak tree, left by a farmer who went off to war. Frank Leffingwell had been plowing when Iowa soldiers marched by to do battle in the Civil War. Leffingwell decided to join them, unhitched his mules, and leaned his plow against a small bur oak in the grove. He never returned and the plow was forgotten. As the tree increased in size, it grew around the plow, lifting it off of the ground. The tree, still alive, covers all but the handles and part of the plow blade.

The Plow in the Oak is located one mile south of Exira. When the plow's owner went off to fight in the Civil War, the tree grew around his plow. (COURTESY AUDUBON COUNTY ECONOMIC DEVELOPMENT CORPORATION)

A Leg for a Song

For many months Union soldiers and officers had been imprisoned in Columbia, South Carolina, with Adjutant Samuel Hawkins Marshall (S. H. M.) Byers of the Fifth Iowa among them. As news of William T. Sherman's march through the South reached the prisoners, Byers wrote a poem and another prisoner set it to music. The camp reverberated with the song "Sherman's March to the Sea."

A Lieutenant Tower of Ottumwa, Iowa, who had lost a leg in the war, was exchanged for a Southern prisoner and set free. Before he left, his hollow false limb was stuffed with letters and papers from the prisoners, including the song.

When Columbia surrendered to the Union Army, the flags of both the Thirtieth Iowa and the Thirteenth Iowa flew over the city, one on the new state house and one on the old. As the escaped prisoners rushed out into the streets of Columbia, they heard the troops marching into town singing, "When Sherman marched down to the sea . . ." Iowa troops were singing an Iowan's song with flags of two Iowa regiments flying overhead.

Loyalty Inspires State Song

S. H. M. Byers wrote "Song of Iowa" in addition to "Sherman's March to the Sea." In his own words: "At the great battle of Lookout Mountain, I was captured in a charge, and taken to Libby Prison, Richmond, Virginia. I was there seven months in one room . . . The Rebel bands often passed the prison, and for our discomfiture, sometimes played the old German tune 'Der Tanenbaum' as 'My Maryland' set to Southern and bitter words. Hearing it once through our barred windows, I said to myself, 'I would like some day to put that tune to loyal words.'"

The "Song of Iowa" was written in 1897 and first performed by a French concert singer at the Foster Opera House in Des Moines the night after it was written. The song was an instant success, with the audience shouting "Encore!" again and again. It is now the official song of Iowa.

The Song of Iowa

You ask what land I love the best, Iowa, 'tis Iowa,
The fairest State of all the west, Iowa, O! Iowa.
From yonder Mississippi's stream
To where Missouri's waters gleam
O! fair it is as poet's dream, Iowa, in Iowa.

See yonder fields of tasseled corn, Iowa, in Iowa,
Where Plenty fills her golden horn, Iowa, in Iowa.
See how her wondrous prairies shine
To yonder sunset's purpling line,
O! happy land, O! land of mine, Iowa, O! Iowa.

And she has maids whose laughing eyes, Iowa, O! Iowa,
To him who loves were Paradise, Iowa, O! Iowa.
O! happiest fate that e'er was known,
Such eyes to shine for one alone,
To call such beauty all his own, Iowa, O! Iowa.

Go read the story of thy past. Iowa, O! Iowa
What glorious deeds, what fame thou hast! Iowa, O! Iowa
So long as time's great cycle runs,
Or nations weep their fallen ones,
Thou'lt not forget thy patriot sons, Iowa, O! Iowa.

—WORDS BY S. H. M. BYERS, TO THE
TUNE OF "O TANNENBAUM"

The Way to a Man's Heart . . .

"No soldier on the firing line gave more heroic service than she rendered," General Ulysses S. Grant said in reference to Annie Wittenmyer and her work in establishing dietary kitchens at military hospitals during the Civil War.

Annie Turner Wittenmyer was a blue-eyed, white-haired matron of

Keokuk. An educated woman, she was a writer of prose and verse and a devout Christian. She had recognized the need for diet kitchens while visiting her sixteen-year-old brother, David Turner, in a Union hospital in 1863 in Sedalia, Missouri, where he was suffering with typhoid fever and unable to stomach the fat-fried bacon offered as breakfast. Annie prepared his food herself, nursing him back to health, caring for other patients, and noting what they needed. She cooked what they could eat and many men recovered. Later that same year, she took her dietary kitchen plan to the Christian and Sanitary Commissions and the government agreed to adopt her plan if she would take charge.

And take charge she did, organizing a fully equipped dietary kitchen in every Union hospital. Thousands of lives were saved. Her idea has been used through all wars involving U.S. troops since then.

As the war drew to a close, Wittenmyer, entreated by ill soldiers to help their dependents, established children's homes in Iowa for those left orphaned by the war. When the Civil War ended, Camp Roberts in Davenport was abandoned and she raised money to care for and house soldiers' orphans there. This home became the prototype for such homes across the country. Originally Camp Roberts, later Camp Kinsman, it became the Iowa Soldiers' Orphans' Home in 1865 and was renamed Iowa Annie Wittenmyer Home in 1949. The complex, which has since been remodeled, remains to this day. Although its days as a children's home ended in 1975, the Annie Wittenmyer Complex now houses a branch of the Davenport Public Library and the Parks and Recreation Department, and has been headquarters for several children's organizations and programs.

Did You Know? Iowans took their place in history during the Civil War in a unique way—they were the first white soldiers in American history to fight side by side with African Americans, at the battle of Milliken's Bend in Louisiana in June 1863. More than eight hundred black Union soldiers from the Ninth Louisiana Infantry fought along with 160 white soldiers from the all-volunteer Twenty-Third Iowa Infantry.

Did You Know?

In Iowa you can find more than 290 monuments and memorials dedicated to the state's Civil War veterans, from bronze plaques on boulders to the 135-foot tall Iowa Soldiers' and Sailors' Monument on the grounds of the Iowa State Capitol. It was designed by Harriet A. Ketcham of Mt. Pleasant in 1888, but when she died of a stroke in 1890, Chicago sculptor Carl Rohl-Smith was commissioned to implement her design. The monument was finished in

The Soldiers' and Sailors' Monument, on the south side of the Iowa State Capitol grounds, was designed by Harriet A. Ketcham of Mt. Pleasant in 1888.
(PHOTO BY ALAN BECK)

1896 with Rohl-Smith's personal touches, but not formally dedicated until June 7, 1945. Restoration was completed in the summer of 1999.

Ike's Boss

General Hanford MacNider of Mason City once was the boss of a man who would become president—Dwight D. Eisenhower.

MacNider's actions and bravery in France during World War I earned him more military awards than any other American except for General John Pershing. As a brigadier general in World War II, MacNider was wounded eight times, and at age fifty-two he was awarded an oak-leaf cluster (instead of a third Distinguished Service Cross) for "extraordinary heroism" in action.

When was he Ike's boss? MacNider had been assistant secretary of war and acting secretary of war in Washington, D.C., from 1925 to 1928, and Dwight Eisenhower had been his assistant executive officer in the war department.

Stran©e . . . but True

After serving in the Union army for four years, Kendrick Wade Brown was mustered out as a captain. The night before he was discharged, his regiment camped overnight in front of a building in New York City that had the street address of 444 Broadway. A year later he moved to Ames, Iowa. While working as a traveling commercial salesman, he discovered that the clothing company he represented was based at 444 Broadway in New York City. When telephone service was installed in Ames, Brown requested "444" as his personal phone number. The number has become part of his family history—the last three digits of his grandson Farwell T. Brown's telephone number in Ames are 444.

Iowa Military Firsts

★ **First Iowan killed in World War I:** Merle Hay of Glidden was sent to France a month after he enlisted and was killed in his first battle, along with two other Americans. The three were buried in France. In 1921 Hay's body was returned to Glidden and in 1930 the state erected a monument at the cemetery. On Merle Hay Road in Des Moines you can find a plaque on a boulder where an American flag is raised each day to honor the first Iowan killed in World War I.

★ **First American woman to die in World War I:** Marion G. Crandell, a teacher at St. Katharine's School in Davenport, enlisted January 19, 1918, through the YMCA for canteen work. Two months later she was killed by a German bomb in Ste. Menehould, France. She was born in Cedar Rapids in 1872 and was buried in a French military cemetery in 1918, the only woman among six thousand soldiers.

★ **Most decorated American chaplain of World War II:** Father Albert John Hoffmann of Dubuque lost his left leg in Cassino, Italy, in 1943 when he stepped on a mine while going to help a German soldier, who was near death. By the time he was sent stateside he had earned a Purple Heart, a Silver Star, and a Distinguished Service Cross. When interviewed for the *Catholic Digest* in November 1944, he pointed out that it was his right leg that was stiff and caused him to limp, not his artificial leg. He commented, "As soon as my right leg gets a little better I'll go back to work. . . . I'll be assigned to some GI hospital in this country where amputees are quartered. When those boys see a one-legged chaplain getting around as spryly as I do, and better with an artificial leg than with the other, don't you think it'll give them hope? God let me lose a leg so I could help those boys. . . . Why, I've got it all over a two-legged priest in any amputee ward. So, in reality, I haven't lost a leg at all. I've gained one."

The Medal of Honor

Iowa U.S. Senator James Grimes came up with the idea of the Medal of Honor, America's highest military award in 1861, and it has been awarded to more than thirty-four hundred men and women who risked or gave up their lives in combat since 1863. And now, thanks to Bill Kendall, retired army first sergeant from Jefferson, there is a Medal of Honor flag. Kendall, who won the Silver Star, three Bronze Stars, and three Purple Hearts for service in Vietnam, designed the flag to look like the medal, with thirteen white stars on a field of light blue.

The flag's first ceremonial raising was Memorial Day, May 27, 2002, at the Jefferson Cemetery. Kendall hopes to see the flag designated by Congress as the official Medal of Honor flag to act as a reminder of the meaning of the Medal of Honor.

General Jack Pershing, the Fundraiser

Jack Pershing was born near the Adair County town of Fontanelle in April 1917. He helped the Red Cross raise money to aid U.S. troops during World War I. By the time he retired, before the war ended, he had traveled eight thousand miles and helped raise more than $40,000—not bad, considering that Jack was a rooster!

The stuffed remains of the rooster dubbed General Jack Pershing can be seen at the Iowa State Historical Building. When alive, the bird helped raise more than $40,000 for the Red Cross during World War I. That's something to crow about! (PHOTO BY JASON BECK)

The American Red Cross, always called upon in time of emergency, was looking for things to sell at auction to raise money. When Mark Dunkerson, a farmer from Fontanelle, was asked for a donation, the *Audobon County Journal* reported that he replied, "I don't have much to offer you, but there are a couple of roosters in that little flock of chickens. You could have one of them, if that would help any." No one would have ever guessed just how much that little black-brown rooster would come to mean to the Red Cross and the boys "over there."

When auctioneer David R. Jones of Casey held up the little scrub rooster in a yeast box, he received a feeble bid of fifty cents. "Sold," cried Jones. "Here's your bird. Come and get him."

"Aw, I don't want him. Sell him again," replied the buyer.

So he was sold again, and again, and again. It became a game with the rule that no purchaser could keep the fowl more than five minutes. At the end of the auction, the rooster had earned $292!

At a sale the next day in Canby, Jones and his partner, Ed Meinkey, let the rooster out of his cage. He raised $170. At this point, Jones decided to name the rooster General Jack Pershing and the show was on. Jack even seemed to know how important he had become. He would perch proudly on Jones's shoulder, cock his head, and crow lustily to the cheering crowd's delight.

Some of the amounts earned at his appearances were

★ Audubon, Iowa: $3,255

★ Exira, Iowa: $7,075 (the most earned in one day, on January 19, 1918)

★ Plankington, South Dakota: $2,636

★ White Lake, South Dakota: $3,102.50

★ Cumberland, Iowa: $3,004

★ Chamberlain, South Dakota: $4,221

★ Buckwana, South Dakota: $5,040

When fund drives for the war effort became more organized, Jones decided to retire Jack to private life with his own flock at Casey. When Jack died on March 22, 1919, taxidermist E. C. (Gene) Wilson of Exira mounted Jack without charge. He can be seen in the Historical Museum in Des Moines.

In his short lifetime, General Jack Pershing had traveled some eight thousand miles, been sold more than nine thousand times, and raised more than $40,000 for the American Red Cross—quite a war record.

Did You Know? Younkers Department Store in Des Moines designed and made a war stamp formal dress in 1942—with $1,500 worth of war stamps hand sewn between layers of netting. The dress was modeled to promote the sale of war bonds.

Iowa Gold Star Museum

Located in the former Iowa National Guard headquarters at Camp Dodge in Johnston, the Iowa Gold Star Museum's mission is to preserve and display the history of the Iowa-based military during war and peace, from 1846 to the present. Exhibits include military weapons from the Revolutionary War, a Medal of Honor from the Civil War, and an Iraqi tank.

The Five Sullivan Brothers—Together

Thomas F. and Alleta Sullivan of 98 Adams Street in Waterloo had five sons: George, Francis (Frank), Joseph (Red), Madison (Matt), and Albert (Al). There were only eight years between the oldest and the youngest, and the five brothers played, hunted, and fished together.

When they received word that their friend Bill Ball of Fredericksburg had died on the *Arizona* in the attack on Pearl Harbor on December 7, 1941, they decided to enlist in the navy and avenge his death together. (This was a reenlistment for George and Frank—they had each served previous four-year enlistments.) At the time, they were all working at the Rath Packing Company in Waterloo. Although assigning the brothers together was contrary to accepted policy, the navy relented and enlisted all five on January 3, 1942, and on February 15, after brief training at the Great Lakes Naval Training Center in Illinois, assigned them to the new light cruiser *Juneau*—together.

After its blockade duty in the Atlantic was over in August, the *Juneau* headed to the South Pacific. In the early morning hours of Friday, November 13, 1942, the *Juneau,* along with twelve other U.S. ships, was engaged in a close-range battle with Japanese ships—eleven destroyers, two battleships, and a cruiser—off the Solomon Islands near Guadalcanal. Within thirty minutes the engagement was essentially over, with the Japanese losing a battleship and two destroyers. Five of the thirteen U.S. ships had been sunk or heavily damaged. The *Juneau* had taken a torpedo hit on its port side and was listing severely. Later that morning, the *Juneau* and five other American ships were limping back to base when the Japanese submarine I-26 attacked. Aiming for the destroyer *San Francisco,* the torpedoes passed harmlessly in front of it and slammed into the *Juneau.* The *Juneau* exploded.

Between 80 and 140 men survived the explosion and made it to life rafts, but died from the heat, wounds, or sharks before being rescued by a Catalina seaplane three days later. Only ten men of seven hundred survived. Four of the Sullivan brothers went down with the ship. The eldest, George, made it to a life raft but then was lost to the sea. This tragedy ranks as the greatest single sacrifice by any one family in American naval history.

Condolences poured in, including two letters from President Franklin D. Roosevelt. Extra men were needed by the post office to handle the volume of mail arriving for the Sullivan family. Vice President Henry Wallace said, "It's the spirit of the Sullivans that will enable the United States to gain a complete victory." The Sullivan parents toured shipyards and munitions

The Sullivan brothers stand on the deck of the USS Juneau on February 14, 1942; from left to right, Joseph, Francis, Albert, Madison, and George. (COURTESY NAVAL HISTORICAL CENTER, WASHINGTON NAVY YARD, WASHINGTON, D.C.)

factories to urge workers toward greater production and a quicker end to the war. They were often joined by their only daughter, Genevieve, until she joined the WAVES (Women Appointed for Voluntary Emergency Service) on June 14, 1943.

On April 4, 1943, the navy honored the service and sacrifice of the five Sullivan brothers when their mother, known nationwide as "Mom Sullivan," christened the new naval destroyer, USS *The Sullivans*, in San Francisco. It is the only U.S. Navy ship ever named for more than one person. And when model ship–building kits became popular in the 1950s, *The Sullivans* was one of the first to be produced.

After being commissioned on September 30, 1943, *The Sullivans* saw action in every major phase of the Pacific campaign, returned to duty during the Korean War, and was decommissioned in January of 1965. Today it stands as a memorial in the Buffalo, New York, Naval and Servicemen's Park. A shamrock bronze plaque from the deck stands in Sullivan Memorial Park, which runs along the same Illinois Central Railroad line where Thomas Sullivan worked for thirty-nine years.

Hollywood rushed a film into production and on March 9, 1944, *The Fighting Sullivans* premiered in Waterloo. In 1951 Congress established a living memorial to the five Iowa brothers by planting a cluster of five apple trees on the Capitol Plaza in Washington, D.C.

The memorials continue. On Veteran's Day, November 11, 1988, the Conway Civic Center in Waterloo was renamed The Five Sullivan Brothers Convention Center. In August of 1995, Kelly Sullivan Loughren, granddaughter of the youngest of the five brothers, Al, christened the second ship named USS *The Sullivans* in Maine, an Arleigh Burke class guided missile destroyer.

And to continue the tradition, when James Sullivan, Al's son, turned seventeen in 1957, he enlisted in the navy like his father, his aunt, and his uncles before him.

Did You Know? There is a popular misconception that to prevent the tragedy of losing several family members at once, Congress passed the "Sullivan Law" preventing family members from serving on the same ship or in the same unit. However, no such law has ever been passed and no presidential executive order has been issued forbidding such assignments. The law was considered after the loss of the Sullivan brothers in 1942 but never passed.

WAVES at Cedar Falls

One thousand fifty young women from every state in the Union reported to the Naval Training School on the campus of Iowa State Teachers College in Cedar Falls in December 1942. This Iowa "boot" school for enlisted members of the Women Appointed for Voluntary Emergency Service (WAVES) was the nation's first. They were divided into two battalions of two companies, which were divided into four platoons.

Captain Ransom K. Davis, who had been on convoy duty in the Pacific, told these new recruits, "To the navy, each one of you represents a fighting man." Reportedly Davis, upon receiving his orders to report to Cedar Falls, had seen the word "Iowa" and had thought he was being assigned to the battleship. His initial disappointment, however, was short-lived and this first indoctrination class graduated on January 14, 1943. They graduated as seamen second class, with some going to specialized schools for training as hospital apprentices, machinist's mates, aviation metalsmiths, and aerographer's mates, and some to direct assignment as yeoman strikers (clerical workers).

The school was converted from indoctrination to yeoman training in April

Newly arrived recruits pose for a photograph in 1943 at the nation's first Navy WAVES training school, in Cedar Falls. Their uniforms hadn't arrived yet. (COURTESY NAVAL HISTORICAL CENTER, WASHINGTON NAVY YARD, WASHINGTON, D.C.)

1943. Eight- and twelve-week courses included shorthand, typing, naval forms, correspondence, filing, office procedures, physical education, military customs, and current events. The first yeoman class graduated on May 28, 1943, and twenty-five graduation exercises took place from 1943 to 1945.

On May 10, 1943, Davis turned over his command to Commander E. E. Pettee. In his farewell address Davis said, "I have seen the spirit with which class after class of trainees have responded to their training. I have come to realize how really capable, enthusiastic, loyal, and patriotic the WAVES are, and I hope to spread the good word about them wherever I may go." The May issue of the *Iowave* paper contained this pledge to Davis: "The WAVES will be the best, and the best of the WAVES will be IOWAVES."

The Iowa Navy: Who Needs an Ocean?

The Iowa Navy began in the minds of Ben Sanders and Herschel Hill, co-owners of the Okoboji passenger ship, the *Queen*. With a fine ship at their command, the formation of a navy seemed in order, so in 1954 they took their idea to the Spirit Lake Chamber of Commerce, which then took on the responsibility for this lighthearted way of promoting sea-less Iowa.

The Iowa Navy is a "backward navy," meaning the higher your commission, the lower your rank. The oath is taken and the salute given by raising your left hand. The highest commission is held by Ben Sanders, "Unable Seaman Ninth Class." He also has the distinction of being the only non-commissioned officer in the navy.

As part of its tongue-in-cheek effort to promote the landlocked state, the Iowa Navy issues Admiral Commissions, designations approved only by the Spirit Lake Chamber of Commerce, to people throughout the world who are outstanding in their particular field. Included among its thousands of "admirals" are presidents of the United States; governors of every state; famous people from the television, motion picture, and entertainment industry; foreign dignitaries; and highly regarded people in religion, business, and sports.

The *Queen* was named the flagship of the Iowa Navy on May 23, 1954. The waters of the navy are all those within and bordering Iowa, and the home port is in the Iowa "Great Lakes" of East and West Okoboji and Spirit Lake.

In 1955 the U.S. Navy accepted the proposal of the Iowa Navy that all U.S. naval recruits during May and June would be brought to Spirit Lake for two days of fun followed by a mass induction ceremony into the U.S. (and Iowa) Navy. The celebration included free rides at Arnold's Park, and the U.S. Navy band and dignitaries attended. That year 252 men were inducted.

In 1956, 341 men were inducted and in 1957, 369 young men were sworn in to the U.S. Navy in the largest peacetime induction ceremony in the history of our country.

The Iowa Navy was dry-docked in 1957 upon the withdrawal of the U.S. Navy from participation in Iowa Navy Days. In 1967 a new Iowa Navy was organized, but the *Queen* was decommissioned in 1973. On June 10, 1979, fifty naval recruits of the U.S. Navy were inducted into the Iowa Navy at the same time, and a new flagship was christened the SS *Empress*. The

Empress left service in 1983, but in the spring of 1986 the *Queen II,* a replica of the *Queen,* was launched as the new Iowa Navy flagship.

You can take a ride on the *Queen II* any day between Memorial Day and Labor Day. Her home port is the state pier in Arnold's Park on West Lake Okoboji.

Cresco Is Sea-Worthy

Despite being far from any seashore, Iowa has filled many ranks in the U.S. Navy—and the town of Cresco alone produced five admirals:

★ Arthur T. Moen, rear admiral, was born in Cresco in 1894, and graduated from Cresco High School in 1912 and from the Naval Academy in 1917. During World War II he was responsible for transporting three hundred thousand men without the loss of a ship. He died in 1962.

★ Frank J. Lowry, vice admiral, graduated from Cresco High School in 1907 and from the Naval Academy in 1911 and was part of the Atlantic patrol during World War I. He commanded the invasions of Salerno and Anzio, Italy, in World War II and also commanded Mare Island Naval Base in Vallejo, California. He died in 1955.

★ George E. Peckham, rear admiral, was born in Cresco, and graduated from Cresco High School in 1926 and from the Naval Academy in 1931. He played a major role in the battle of Komanorskie Islands and served in the European-African and Philippine liberation theaters. Peckham died on September 14, 1998.

★ Wallis F. Petersen, rear admiral, graduated from Cresco High School in 1918 and from the Naval Academy in 1924. He was an executive officer on board the USS *Elliot,* commander of the USS *Mustin,* and commander of the Fifth Naval District, Norfolk, Virginia. He died in 1988.

★ Michael J. Malanaphy, rear admiral, was born in Cresco, and graduated from Cresco High School in 1917 and from the Naval Academy in 1922. During

World War II he was Flotilla Commander in Taiwan, Guam, Iwo Jima, and Okinawa. He retired and returned to Cresco, where he died in 1989.

Did You Know? Iowa Governor Tom Turner called out nineteen hundred National Guardsmen to protect veterinarians testing cows for tuberculosis in 1931 in Tipton. Many farmers in Cedar County felt the law calling for compulsory testing of cattle for tuberculosis was unconstitutional, but the courts upheld the law, the testing continued, and the "cow war" ended.

The Oleo War (As the World Churns)

In 1943 O. H. Brownlee, an Iowa State research associate in economics, wrote the pamphlet *Putting Dairying on a War Footing.* This was in the midst of World War II and a world food shortage. In the pamphlet Brownlee claimed that drinking whole milk instead of eating butter would provide people with more food value for less work. With conservation in mind, Brownlee proposed that other animal or vegetable fats be used instead of butter.

Iowa's dairymen were "churning." Not only did the pamphlet state that oleomargarine "compares favorably with butter both in nutritive value and palatability," but the author was also an Iowa State man!

Thus began the margarine war. Iowa State president Charles Friley yielded to the pressure from the Iowa Farm Bureau and dairy farmers across the state, recalling the pamphlet and having it revised. This had some university faculty members crying "foul." But the new version stated that "fortified oleomargarine is nutritious and acceptable by many consumers as a spread." It did not directly compare margarine with butter.

Brownlee had unwittingly stirred up a lot of trouble, but he and others quickly discovered that for dairy farmers (and some cooks) there is no substitute—butter's always better.

WAR TRIVIA

Q. What Union officer from Burlington inspired the cry "hold the fort" during a battle at Alatoona, Georgia, in 1864?

A. John M. Corse.

Q. The use of what Davenport college facilities by the Navy during World War II kept that school open and its faculty employed?

A. Saint Ambrose.

Q. Who was the organizer of Company G, a military company for female college students, similar to ROTC?

A. Carrie Lane. (Her married name was Carrie Lane Chapman Catt.) She was also the only woman to graduate from Iowa State College in 1880.

Q. In 1942 an ordnance plant employing nineteen thousand workers was opened by the federal government in what Iowa town to manufacture ammunition?

A. Ankeny.

Q. The last battle in Iowa between Native American tribes took place in 1854 between the Sioux and Winnebago near what town?

A. Rolfe.

Q. After graduating from West Point in 1828, what Civil War figure operated a sawmill on the Yellow River while serving in the U.S. Army at Fort Crawford?

A. Jefferson Davis.

Q. The Mormon Battalion's two-thousand-mile infantry march, the longest known, began in Council Bluffs in July 1846 and ended six months later in San Diego for what war?

A. The Mexican War.

Q. What Iowa governor was in Ford's Theater with President Abraham Lincoln when Lincoln was shot?

A. William Milo Stone. He helped lift the wounded Lincoln from the floor and remained at his bedside until the president died.

7
Heroes, the Law, and the Lawless

Kate's Courageous Crawl

In 1881 fifteen-year-old Kate Shelley of Moingona crawled over a 673-foot Des Moines River bridge during a fierce storm to warn an eastbound Atlantic train about a damaged railroad trestle.

A terrific storm had hit the area on July 6, flooding Honey Creek and damaging the railroad trestle that crossed it. A locomotive sent from Moingona to test the track conditions safely crossed the Des Moines River bridge, but plunged into Honey Creek when trying to cross over the damaged trestle. Kate, her mother, brothers, and sisters had heard the engine fall into the flooded creek. (Three years before, Kate's father, a railroad section foreman, had been killed at work and her oldest brother had drowned before that.) Knowing that a passenger train was soon due from the west, Kate left in the storm for the Moingona depot to prevent another tragedy. On her way she shouted to the locomotive's engineer and fireman, Ed Wood and Adam Agar, that she was going for help. The two men were clinging to tree limbs over the rushing floodwaters, and their two companions that night, George Olmstead and Patrick Donahue, had already drowned.

Kate crawled over the Des Moines River bridge on her hands and knees in the storm, in the dark. She was cut and bleeding when she reached the

113

other side, but arrived in Moingona in time to warn the express about the washout. She then led the rescue party to the two marooned crewmen.

It took nearly three months for Kate to fully recover her health after the ordeal, but the news of her bravery spread around the world. Editorials, stories, and poems were written about her. A tribute by poet Eugene J. Hall closes with this verse:

> *Let the Nation be just and accord you its praise.*
> *Let your name, let your fame, and your courage declare*
> *What a woman can do and a woman can dare.*

The Iowa State Legislature awarded Kate $200 and a gold medal inscribed with the following words:

> *KATE SHELLEY*
> *—whom neither the terror of elements*
> *nor the fear of death could appall in*
> *her efforts to save human lives.*

The railroad company gave her $100 and a lifetime railroad pass. The railroad employees presented her with a gold watch and chain. The *Chicago Tribune* collected and sent enough money to pay off the mortgage on the Shelley home. Benefactors sent her to college, and she attended Simpson, where she received a teaching certificate. She taught school for a few years and in 1903, twenty-two years after her heroic act, accepted the position as Northwestern Railroad Station Manager at Moingona, where she worked until her death.

In 1926 the Kate Shelley Bridge, made of steel, was built across the Des Moines River near Moingona, west of Boone. It is the longest and highest double-tracked railroad bridge in the world.

You can see the lantern Kate started out with that night in 1881 in the State Historical Museum in Des Moines, broken glass and all. You can also visit the Kate Shelley Railroad Museum, built on the spot where the railroad depot stood in Moingona in 1881. The museum contains artifacts relating to Kate's life, a recreated nineteenth century railroad passenger station, a working telegraph system, railroad memorabilia, and a Rock Island passenger car used as a theater for a video presentation of the Kate Shelley story.

When Kate Shelley died of tuberculosis in 1912 at age forty-seven, the railroad company sent a special train for her funeral party. Her grave in Boone bears this plaque: "Hers is a deed bound for legend . . . a story to be told until the last order fades and the last rail rusts."

Kate Shelley prevented a railway tragedy at fifteen years of age when she crawled across a damaged railway trestle in a storm on July 6, 1881. This picture was taken shortly after her recovery from the incident. (COURTESY BOONE COUNTY HISTORICAL SOCIETY)

Did You Know? In August 2001 a German shepherd named Buddy was inducted into Iowa's Hall of Fame for Courageous Animals in the Hero Category. Buddy had distracted a fifteen-hundred-pound eland, an African antelope, that had escaped from a game farm, allowing his owner, Betty Kuhl of Thurman (population 236), time to reach her home in safety. Betty had just gotten home and was getting her mail when the eland charged toward her. She had not previously noticed the animal, but Buddy came to the rescue. He ran at the eland, circling it and holding its attention while Betty made it into the house.

Mother of the State Highway Patrol System

Viola Babcock Miller, the first woman ever elected Iowa secretary of state, also established the Iowa Highway Safety Patrol.

Viola (Ola) Babcock was born on a farm near Washington, Iowa, on March 1, 1871, to Nathan L. and Ophelia Smith Babcock. She was educated in the Washington public schools, at the Washington Academy, and at Iowa Wesleyan College in Mount Pleasant. She taught in Washington, where she was active in civic and club work and the woman's suffrage movement.

She married Alex Miller, editor of the *Washington Democrat*, in 1895 and they had three children: Joseph, who died in infancy, and Barbara and Ophelia. In 1926 Alex ran for governor of Iowa and Ola gained a great deal of political experience while working for him and the Democratic Party. Alex was not elected and early in 1927 he had a heart attack and died.

Ola was an active volunteer for Franklin D. Roosevelt in his campaign for the presidency in 1932. Just a few months before the election, she discovered that her own name had been placed on the Democratic ticket for Iowa secretary of state to honor her husband. Never dreaming that she would win, she campaigned energetically, relying on the experience she had gained over the years.

Ola won the election, beating her opponent by only three thousand votes. She was not only the first woman in Iowa ever to win a state office, but also the first Democrat in Iowa to be elected to high public office since the Civil War.

She threw herself into her job, reorganizing the department to improve its function. She quickly won over many who had been apprehensive as she proved herself a faithful servant of the people. Iowa traffic fatalities had concerned her for many years, so she instructed each of the fifteen license inspectors of the motor vehicle subdivision to cover six or seven counties and stop reckless drivers. It was a pilot program of highway patrolmen in civilian clothes, and motorists, fearing robbery, didn't like it. So she put the men in uniform.

Her premise was: "From now on, save lives first, money afterwards." And within the first year Iowa traffic accidents, injuries, and deaths decreased dramatically.

She easily won reelection in 1934 and soon after instituted testing for driver's licenses and inspections on roads to check for licenses. She and her men gave safety talks in schools and at meetings all across the state. Yellow lines, 700 feet long, were painted on all curves and hills, and two black lines, a foot apart, were painted in the center of all hard-surfaced state roads.

The success of these programs helped her to get a bill passed authorizing a force of fifty-five state uniformed highway patrolmen, and the purchase of thirty new cars and twelve motorcycles for the patrol. Governor Clyde L. Herring signed into law the Act of 1935, establishing the Iowa Highway Safety Patrol, on May 7, 1935. The patrolmen were trained at Camp Dodge and began duty on July 28, 1935.

Ola was reelected in 1936 by a landslide, but died of pneumonia on January 14, 1937. All fifty-five Iowa Highway Patrolmen attended her funeral at the Washington Methodist Church.

On the first anniversary of Ola's death, the entire Iowa Highway Patrol wore black armbands for only the second time in their history. The first had been after the death of Oran Pape, a Dubuque patrolman and former Iowa football star, killed by a highway bandit. Ola had called that tragedy "the darkest day of her career."

Ola Babcock Miller was inducted into the Iowa Women's Hall of Fame in 1975 and in 2001 the new state office building, which was the old Historical Building, was named in her honor.

Pioneer of the Public Opinion Poll

Ola Miller's son-in-law was George Gallup of Jefferson—who developed the Gallup Poll. George had married Ola's daughter Ophelia, and while helping his mother-in-law get elected in 1934, he came up with the idea of taking a national weekly poll of public opinion. Thus the Gallup Poll was born.

Gallup founded the American Institute of Public Opinion in Princeton, New Jersey. On October 20, 1935, the first release was printed dealing with the issue of government spending.

Strange . . . but True

In 1860 David Scott from Walnut Township in Appanoose County put a leather collar on a wolf cub he had trapped and chained it to a post. The next morning the cub and chain were gone. Two years later, the animal was captured again still wearing the chain. (In Iowa in 1880, a bounty of one dollar was paid for wolf scalps.)

Very Specific Rules for Fences!

The following law can be found in *A History of Polk County, Iowa—1880*, in the chapter on Iowa state laws, under the heading "Fences":

> *A lawful fence is fifty-four inches high, made of rails, wire or boards, with posts not more than ten feet apart where rails are used, and eight feet where boards are used, substantially built and kept in good repair; or any other fence, in the opinion of the fence viewers, shall be declared a lawful fence—provided the lower rail, wire or board be not more than twenty nor less than sixteen inches from the ground.*

Did You Know? The first murder trial and legal execution in Iowa was in 1834 in Dubuque. Patrick O'Connor admitted he had shot and killed his business partner, George O'Keaf. The accused chose the twelve jurors from twenty-four men selected by the prosecution and defense counsels. The jury returned a verdict of murder in the first degree and O'Connor was hanged at the corner of what are now White and 7th Streets.

Stran©e . . . but True

From the files of the *Red Oak Sun,* January 6, 1922:

> *Deputy Sheriff Art Baker . . . has worked out a novel sleuth in the shape of one of the spring pigs raised on the county farm, and expects to use it soon in detecting illicit stills in the rough parts of the country, or elsewhere. Art . . . feeds him regularly on mash . . . this would-be liquor . . . until Mr. Pig staggers around the little pen back of the jail. . . . This is a regular part of the pig's education. . . . The officers get word or surmise that there is a still being operated in a certain neighborhood. The pig detective is made to fast for a day, so that his hunger, thirst and scent are whetted to a keen edge. The pig is taken to the neighborhood where the still is thought to be in oper-ation, and his taste for the mash is so strong that he goes straight to the place where the "hootch" is being made. Art says his scent is as keen as that of a bloodhound, and that he is one of the most valuable and economical dry agents the county has ever employed.*

It's just one more way that hogs have played an important role in the history of Iowa!

The 1839 Bean Poll: When Outlaws' Fates Were Decided by Beans

In the late 1830s a band of outlaws led by hotel keeper William W. Brown of Bellevue terrorized this Jackson County town. Finally, in 1839, the townspeople had had enough. Sheriff Warren got a warrant for the arrest of Brown and his gang and authorized the formation of a posse of forty armed men. The sheriff and posse confronted the outlaws at the hotel and in the ensuing battle four citizens and three bandits were killed, seven bandits escaped, and thirteen bandits were captured.

A jury of eighty men was convened to determine the bandits' punishment. One by one, each juryman was handed a box containing red and white beans. They were to choose a bean—a red one for whipping, a white one for hanging—and put it in a second box.

The judge announced the verdict: "By a margin of three beans the jury has decided on whipping."

The thirteen prisoners were lashed on their bare backs, then placed in boats on the Mississippi with enough rations for three days and made to promise never to return.

It would be nice to report that this show of mercy led the criminals to reform—but three of the thirteen were implicated in the murder of Colonel George Davenport five years later.

Largest Embezzlement in History

A young woman in Sheldon single-handedly brought down one of the strongest banks in Iowa.

Bernice Iverson (also sometimes spelled Burnice) went to work in the bank her father owned, Sheldon National Bank, in Sheldon in 1922. Soon after, she discovered a shortage that she didn't know how to handle—so she just removed the account card.

Perhaps this made her realize how easy it would be to alter accounts, for over the next thirty-nine years she systematically changed as many as four hundred customer account cards, filing two sets of account cards in the bank basement. By the time bank examiners discovered the embezzlement on January 16, 1961, the total was $2,186,959—the largest embezzlement in history at the time!

This shook the town of Sheldon, population 4,251, and gained worldwide attention. No amount of insurance could cover this staggering loss. At the time the Federal Deposit Insurance Corporation's maximum coverage for each depositor was $10,000 (today it is $100,000). Sheldon National Bank had survived the Depression and was known as one of the soundest banks in the state, but now it was closed by the U.S. Federal Reserve.

Ralph Hollander, who had become a director at the bank by inheriting his father's bank stock, recalled having recently read an article in the business magazine *Fortune* listing identifying characteristics and peculiarities of embezzlers. He had read the list to his wife, who admitted it sounded like their longtime family friend Burnice, the wife of Ralph's cousin Wally Geiger. They had laughed, knowing that Burnice and her family had controlling interest in the bank, and believing that you can't steal from yourself. But no one was laughing that fateful January day in 1961.

Bernice Iverson Geiger of Sheldon embezzled over two million dollars from her father's bank over a thirty-nine-year period. (SHELDON'S MOST SHOCKING SCANDAL, BY RALPH HOLLANDER)

O'Brien County lost $87,364 and the Sheldon School District lost $58,000. Businesses with large accounts lost up to $400,000. The directors, not wanting to appear in Federal Court, split the heavy penalty among themselves.

For years the Federal Deposit Insurance Corporation (FDIC) used this embezzlement case in their teaching classes for new examiners. Bernice Iverson died on October 25, 1981, at age seventy-nine. She had returned to Sheldon after serving six years of a fifteen-year sentence in the Federal Reformatory for Women in Alderson, West Virginia.

Settling the Drake Estate

An enterprising fellow swindled Iowans out of thousands of dollars by convincing them he was the heir of Sir Francis Drake.

Oscar M. Hartzell claimed to be a baron and heir of the English lord who had died in 1696, and "sold" shares to get the estate settled. Maintaining that

$22 billion in gold bars had been shipped to the United States and that payment would be forthcoming, Hartzell took the money and fled to England in 1933. He was convicted and found to be a psychopath. He had run his scheme from 1924 to 1933, and had given many Iowans a head start into the Depression.

Did You Know? Gary Lewellyn, a Des Moines stockbroker, swindled his father's Humboldt bank out of nearly $17 million in 1982, the biggest white-collar crime in Iowa history.

World's First Moving Train Robbery

Jesse James and his gang perpetrated the world's first robbery of a moving train near Adair on the evening of July 21, 1873, derailing the train by dislodging a rail, roping it, and pulling it out of line. But instead of the $75,000 in gold they believed to be on board, the bandits got only about $2,000 in currency. The gold shipment on the recently completed Chicago, Rock Island, and Pacific railroad line had been delayed.

The book *A History of Polk County—1880* recorded the incident without identifying any of the seven or more robbers. According to that record, the men overpowered the train within twenty minutes. The engineer of the train died as the engine plunged into the ditch. A posse of several hundred people pursued the robbers, but they escaped into Missouri.

The site of the robbery is marked by a locomotive wheel along County Road G30.

The large photo of Jesse James was taken in 1875, just two years after his gang robbed a train near Adair. The inset photo was taken at his death on April 3, 1882.

Strange . . . but True

The Dillinger gang robbed the First National Bank of Mason City on March 13, 1934, using twelve hostages riding on the running boards of the getaway car as a human shield. The gang got away with more than $52,000—but left almost $250,000 behind. The gang members included John Dillinger, Eddie Green, John Hamilton, Tommy Carroll, Homer Van Meter, and George (Baby Face) Nelson.

"Jesse James Slept Here"

Many places in Iowa claim that Jesse James stopped there on his way to or from the Great Northfield, Minnesota, bank robbery—much as people in other areas may put up signs claiming "George Washington Slept Here."

Jesse James and his gang held up the bank in Northfield in September 1876. They killed the cashier, and Jesse and Frank James fled back to Missouri. It is likely that the James brothers came through Iowa, and they certainly must have stopped somewhere in the state—but surely not as often as is claimed.

One such claim from Plymouth County prompted a poem, "The Brave Cashier" by John Walsh, written around 1885. Walsh was twenty-five years old when he wrote the poem, but he was only sixteen when the Northfield robbery occurred. Here is an excerpt:

Across Iowa's fair prairies
Where scarce a wolf can hide
The Jameses took their trail for home,
Undaunted side by side.
In the prison yard at Stillwater
You can all see today,
Two members of this wretched band,
The rest have passed away.

While down in old Missouri
Near the city of St. Joe
They have made a grave,
And within its shade,
Their chief is lying low.

—FROM "THE BRAVE CASHIER" BY JOHN WALSH

Did You Know? The word "rogue" certainly applies to criminals such as the James gang—but can also be used to refer to corn. According to *Webster's New World Dictionary*, a rogue "varies markedly from the standard, especially an inferior one." In the cornfields "de-roguing" means stripping those inferior cornstalks that can spring up next to the main plant.

Bar Admits Belle—A National First

Arabella Mansfield, born Belle Aurelia Babb in 1846 at Sperry Station in Des Moines, was admitted to the Iowa bar in 1869, becoming the first woman lawyer in the United States.

When Belle was four, her father died in a mining accident while searching for gold in California. Her mother moved her and her brother, Washington, to Mount Pleasant in 1860. Belle graduated from Iowa Wesleyan in 1866, taught at Simpson College for a year, and then returned to Mount Pleasant in 1867 to study law with her brother.

In 1868 she married natural history professor John Mansfield, and they both passed the bar in 1869. They both became professors at Iowa Wesleyan and in 1876, at DePauw University in Greencastle, Indiana. At DePauw she served as dean of the School of Art (1893) and dean of the School of Music (1894).

In 1870 Arabella Mansfield chaired the Iowa Woman's Suffrage Convention. She and her husband studied in Germany in 1872 and she traveled to Japan in 1909. John died in 1894 and Arabella in 1911, and she is buried in Forest Home Cemetery in Mount Pleasant. She was inducted into the Iowa Women's Hall of Fame in 1980.

Quack! Quack!

Norman Baker of Muscatine managed to convince thousands of Iowans that he had a cure for cancer, until he was convicted of using the mails to defraud in 1940.

From 1929 until 1938 Baker injected a liquid into sufferer's muscles in Muscatine. He was continuously attacked by the American Medical Association and other doctors and newspapers and labeled a quack. Dr. Morris Fishbein of the AMA said, "Of all the ghouls who fed on the dead and dying, the cancer quacks are the most vicious and heartless. Most vicious of all is Norman Baker."

Baker didn't mind being called a quack. Over a door in his building in Muscatine it said, "A quack is one who thinks and does things others can't do."

Baker lacked not only a medical degree, but also a high school diploma. He had been a hypnotist, a tool and die maker, and a calliope maker before becoming a medical imposter who obtained a radio broadcasting license. The license for his KTNT radio station was revoked in 1931 because of the abusive language he used in his attacks on his foes.

In 1938 he moved his operation to Eureka Springs, Arkansas, because of lawsuits. Chemists revealed that his miracle cancer shot consisted of one-third alcohol, one-third carbolic acid, one-third glycerin, and a hint of peppermint. After being convicted, Baker spent 1941 to 1945 in the federal penitentiary at Leavenworth, Kansas.

Although reported to have raked in as much as $75,000 per month during his heyday, his estate totaled only $10,066 when he died on his houseboat at Miami, Florida, in 1958 at age seventy-four.

Anamosa State Penitentiary Museum

Housed in the prison's old cheese factory, the Anamosa State Penitentiary Museum opened on May 24, 2002, located just outside the north wall of the Anamosa State Penitentiary.

Once known as the "White Palace of the West" because of the limestone Fort Dodge inmates used to build it in 1872, the prison is Iowa's largest. In the late 1800s and early 1900s the Anamosa prison was one of Iowa's biggest tourist attractions. Tourists paid twenty-five cents to tour the prison. Tours are no longer offered, but the museum offers a glimpse of what life was like inside the prison.

On display are a bear trap, crudely fashioned weapons, and other contraband confiscated from inmates as well as photographs, postcards, stereoviews (double photos viewed through a stereoscope), and other souvenirs from the old tours. It has a reproduction of an 1881 four-by-nine-foot cell house, a video of prison life, and memorabilia from the movie *Penitentiary,* which was filmed at Anamosa in 1935.

Just up the street from the museum is the administration building, which was also built by inmates. It is an awesome structure, with marble floors and etched-glass windows. The prison warden used to live on the top three floors.

For more information visit *www.members.aol.com/aspmuseum.*

Villisca's Horrible Unsolved Mystery

On the evening of Sunday, June 9, 1912, the town of Villisca had no electricity because the city council and the power company had disagreed and the power had been shut off. Because of the darkness, most of the town's residents had gone to bed early. They awoke the next morning to discover that during the night somebody had axed eight people to death in the home of Josiah B. Moore.

Joe Moore's brother, Ross, and a family friend, Mary E. Peckham, discovered the bodies on the morning of June 10, when they came to see why Joe had not opened his farm implement store. The day before, Joe and his wife, Sarah, and their four children, ages five to eleven—Herman, Katherine, Boyd, and Paul—had attended a worship service where the Reverend Lyn George Jacklin Kelly had spoken. Kelly was a traveling preacher who had just recently settled in Macedonia with his wife.

After the service, Lena and Ina Stillinger, daughters of Joseph and Sarah Stillinger, came home with the Moores to spend the night. These two sisters and the entire Josiah Moore family never saw morning. The Stillinger girls were found in a downstairs bedroom. Upstairs, Mr. and Mrs. Moore were in one bedroom and their four children in another. There were no signs of struggle, and apparently all eight had died while they slept. Every mirror and window had been covered with black clothing and all the shades were pulled. All the bodies, including the faces, were neatly covered with bedding or clothing. Upstairs a chimney had been taken from one of the lamps and downstairs was a blood-stained ax.

It did not take long for rumors to run rampant through Villisca, to other towns and, within days, across the country. Suspects abounded but evidence was lacking.

Who did it? Was it State Senator F. F. Jones of Villisca, angry about Moore taking the John Deere dealership away from him and about an alleged affair between his daughter-in-law and Moore? Did he hire William

The Villisca house where eight people were axed to death in 1912 is now open to the public. (COURTESY VILLISCA AXE MURDER HOUSE/OLSON-LINN MUSEUM)

Mansfield of Blue Island, Illinois, to "take care of" Moore? Many believed Mansfield was responsible for the ax murders in Paola, Kansas, four days before those in Villisca and later for the ax murders of his wife, child, and father- and mother-in-law on July 5, 1914.

Or was it the traveling preacher, Kelly, who had been in Villisca on the night of the murders and had left in the early morning hours of June 10? Could it have been the itinerant jobber, Andy Sawyer, who had shown up early on June 10 in Creston at the Burlington railyards looking for work? Sawyer slept with an ax and often talked of the Villisca murders.

In 1911 the son of a prominent Villisca family had been killed in a race riot in Oklahoma and his widow shunned by his family. Had she sent an Indian to avenge the treatment she had received from her husband's family and had he gone to the wrong house? Or was the murderer Joe Risk, the half-demented man found in a rowboat seven miles south of Clarinda on the morning of June 12 with his shoes and overalls smeared with blood?

The mystery was never solved, and we may never know. Not until 1987 did the residents of Villisca decide to talk about this part of their past as part of their first Heritage Days celebration. The house where the murder occurred was added to the National Register of Historic Places in 1998 after being purchased and restored by a privately owned local museum in 1994.

If you want to try to solve this mystery yourself, you can pay a visit to *www.villiscaiowa.com*, where you will find the entire text of the evidence given at the coroner's inquest and a rundown of all the suspects at the time.

Did You Know? As a result of the public's frustration with law enforcement's inability to coordinate the Villisca investigation and convict a killer, the Iowa Bureau of Criminal Investigation was formed in 1921. It is now known as the Iowa Division of Criminal Investigation.

THE LAW AND THE LAWLESS TRIVIA

Q. In 1876 the Des Moines police force was established with how many men?

A. Eight.

Q. What duo robbed the Knierim bank of $272 in 1934?

A. Bonnie Parker and Clyde Barrow.

Q. In 1868 the first law school west of the Mississippi moved to the University of Iowa after being established three years earlier in what town?

A. Des Moines.

Q. The world's oldest lawyer, Cornelius Van de Steeg of Perry, practiced his profession up to what age?

A. 101 years, 11 months.

Q. Who were the plaintiffs in the Iowa Supreme Court case that established "fair comment and criticism" as an important principle of libel law?

A. The Cherry Sisters of Marion.

Q. Where was Iowa's first fire department organized?

A. Carroll.

Q. In what year was the state constitution changed to increase the governor's term from two to four years?

A. 1972.

Q. What famous western lawman lived in Pella from age two to sixteen?

A. Wyatt Earp.

8

Religion and Education

Hittin' the Sawdust Trail

William Ashley (Billy) Sunday transferred his energy from the baseball field, where he was the fastest base runner of his time, to the evangelism circuit and never looked back. He was born on November 19, 1862, in a log cabin in rural Nevada. When he was a month old, his bricklayer father died of pneumonia at an army camp in Patterson, Missouri, during the Civil War. When he was eleven, his mother sent him and his brother, George, to the soldiers' orphans' home at Glenwood near Council Bluffs, because she could not support them. Eventually the boys were sent on to the orphans' home at Davenport. After leaving the Davenport orphanage, Billy stayed with Senator John Scott of Nevada, graduating from Nevada High School in 1881 and gaining local fame for his baseball abilities.

He worked for a furniture maker in Marshalltown, served on the Marshalltown fire brigade, and played for the town baseball team, where Marshalltown's own Adrian (Cap) Anson noticed his outstanding athletic ability and speed. Anson, manager of the White Stockings (which became the Chicago Cubs), signed the twenty-year-old and took him to Chicago in 1883.

Sunday played centerfield for the Chicago team and became the first man in baseball to run the bases in fourteen seconds. He stole 258 bases during his career and ninety during a 116-game season. He struck out the first thirteen times at bat, and asserted that he invented the bunt.

On a Sunday afternoon in 1886, after having a few beers with his baseball buddies and sitting out on the curb, Billy heard a gospel mission band playing what he described as "the gospel hymns I used to hear my mother sing back in the log cabin in Iowa" (All quotations are from *Rogues and Heroes from Iowa's Amazing Past* by George Mills [Ames, Iowa: Iowa State University Press, 1972]). He left his buddies and went into the Pacific Garden Mission in Chicago where he became a born-again Christian. Billy continued to play major league baseball for five more years but never again on Sunday. Sundays he spent working for the Young Men's Christian Association. In one game, as a ball was hit over his head in the outfield, he said he prayed, "God, if you ever helped mortal man, help me get that ball and you haven't got much time to make up your mind either." Sunday leaped and caught the ball, making a spectacular play.

In 1891, despite being offered $400 a month by the Philadelphia Phillies and $500 a month by the Cincinnati Reds. Billy took a job as the secretary of the religious department at the Chicago YMCA at a monthly salary of $83.33.

In 1894 the Pittsburgh Pirates offered him $2,000 a month, but instead Sunday became the advance man for evangelist J. Wilbur Chapman for $40 dollars a week. When Chapman quit to take a church pulpit in 1896, Sunday was out of a job. At the time, Sunday, who had married Helen Amelia Thompson in 1888, had two children: Helen, born in 1889, and George, born in 1892. He later said, " I laid it before the Lord and in a short while there came a telegram from Garner, Iowa, asking me to come out and conduct some meetings. I didn't know anybody out there and I don't know yet why they ever asked me to hold a meeting, but I went."

In January 1897 Billy Sunday held his first revival meeting in Garner. Nearly one hundred people accepted Christ during the week of meetings and an evangelist was ignited. This debut started a career that made Billy Sunday the most famous preacher of his time. He was ordained by the Presbyterian

Church in 1903. A 1914 *American Magazine* poll ranked him the eighth greatest man in America.

When Billy Sunday preached he didn't just talk. He would pound the pulpit, sometimes even leaping over it, roll on the floor, and wrestle with a red kitchen chair to illustrate man's struggle with sin. One writer at the time observed, "It all seems natural. Like his speech, it is an integral part of the man. Every muscle of his body preaches in accord with his voice." Sunday was well known for chasing not only the devil but also "Demon Liquor," being a staunch supporter of Prohibition. Many times he said, "I'm going to make this place so dry they'll have to prime a man before he can spit." Billy and his wife, called "Ma," were in great demand. People would wait for hours to get seats in the frame tabernacles with the pine plank benches and sawdust on the floor. "Hittin' the sawdust trail," the words Sunday used to describe his evangelism efforts, soon became a part of the American vernacular.

Sunday's unusual style and sincere warmth reached thousands. He once said, "I know no more about theology than a rabbit does about Ping-Pong or golf. I want to preach the gospel so plainly that men can come from the factories and not have to bring along a dictionary." There is no doubt he succeeded. In 1914 Des Moines alone had 10,000 converts. In 1915 Sunday converted 40,000 people in Philadelphia, and in 1916 he converted 63,716 in Boston. The ten-week New York Campaign in 1917 resulted in a $100,000 offering to the Red Cross and other World War I charities, and more than 98,000 people coming forward to accept Christ.

Billy Sunday took his energy from the baseball field to the Christian field in 1891. Sunday, who later became a well-known evangelist, described his evangelism efforts as "hittin' the sawdust trail." (STATE HISTORICAL SOCIETY OF IOWA—DES MOINES)

Billy Sunday said of himself, "I was bred and born in old Iowa. I am a rube of the rubes. I am a hayseed of the hayseeds, and the malodors of the barnyard are on me yet; I have greased my hair with goose grease and blackened my boots with stove blacking. I have wiped my proboscis with a gunnysack towel; I have drunk coffee out of my saucer and I have eaten with my knife. I have said 'done it' when I should have said 'did it,' and I expect to go to heaven just the same."

He followed his vocation until the day he died. He preached his last sermon on October 27, 1935, and died from a heart attack on November 6 in Chicago, thirteen days shy of his seventy-third birthday. He had requested, "No sad stuff when I go. No black, no crepe, no tears. But have them sing the 'Glory Song.'"

They did, and here's a verse:

> *Oh, that will be glory for me,*
> *Glory for me, glory for me,*
> *When by His Grace I shall look on His face,*
> *That will be glory, be glory for me.*

Three "Fifteens" to Keep You Faithful

A story has been passed down that says that when Billy Sunday was converted, a Christian man put his arm on the twenty-three-year-old's shoulder and said, "William, there are three simple rules I can give to you, and if you will hold to them you will never write 'backslide' after your name. Take fifteen minutes each day to listen to God talking to you; take fifteen minutes each day to talk to God; take fifteen minutes each day to talk to others about God."

Impressed, Billy determined to make these the rules of his life. From that day on, for the rest of his life he spent the first moments of each day alone with God and God's Word, and before he did anything, he went first to the Bible.

The Miracle of the Little Brown Church

About two and a half miles east of Nashua stands a little church, world famous as "The Little Brown Church in the Vale" from a well-known song. Many do not realize that the songwriter only imagined the church—and that the church later just happened to be built in the exact spot and exact color that he envisioned!

In 1848 the village of Bradford was settled, and by 1855 the first members of the Puritan-Congregational Church had begun to hold meetings. By 1856 Bradford had five hundred residents.

William S. Pitts, a music teacher from Wisconsin, was on his way to visit his future wife in Fredericksburg in 1857 when the stagecoach stopped to change horses in Bradford. Pitts walked down Cedar Street until he came upon a lovely spot that inspired a poem in his head. Upon his return to Wisconsin he wrote the poem "The Church in the Wildwood" and later set it to music.

The villagers of Bradford, east of Nashua, completed building The Little Brown Church in 1862, with no knowledge of the song. The song was sung publicly for the first time at the church's dedication and the two have been inseparable since. (DUNN PHOTOGRAPHY, CHARLES CITY)

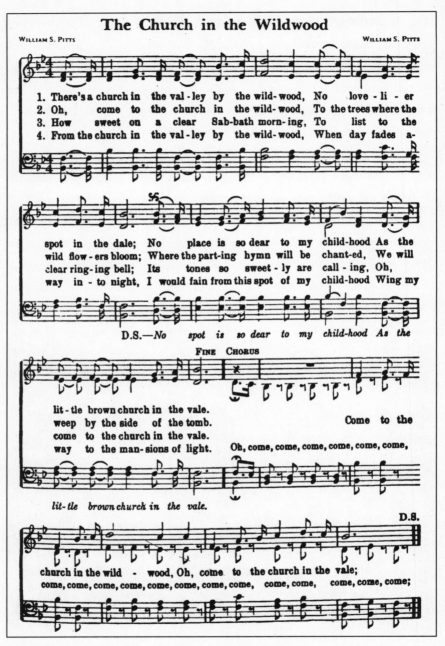

Dr. William S. Pitts wrote the hymn "The Church in the Wildwood" in 1857, seven years before the little brown church was built in the very spot he envisioned.

Afterward, when reflecting on this episode, he said, "As I pondered on this Iowa experience, I came to realize that what was needed to complete the picture was a little church, a little brown church in the wildwood—a church and a bell calling, come, come, come. Gradually words and music came to give form to my vision. They were written down and laid aside and I found that only then was I at peace with myself." Pitts put his song away and forgot about it.

Meanwhile the church members in Bradford wanted a church building. In 1860, with the help of pastor John K. Nutting, who had come to serve in 1859, and the donation of the property by a local family, the foundation was laid. Because of the financial panic of 1857 and the start of the Civil War, money was scarce but work on the church continued. Money was so tight that Reverend Nutting, whose salary was $500 a year, received only $4 in cash in 1859—with the rest in food, fuel, and services. By 1862 the building was completed. The cheapest paint to be found was brown Ohio Mineral Paint, so the church was painted brown. With help from friends in the east, a bell was obtained and the church building was finished in the summer of 1864.

In the meantime Pitts had married and remained in Wisconsin until 1862, when the couple moved to Fredericksburg to be near the wife's aging parents. Imagine his surprise when, after being hired to teach a singing class at the Bradford Academy in 1864, he found a little brown church in the very spot he had envisioned one seven years before! Fittingly, the first public rendition of the song the world knows as "The Little Brown Church in the Vale" was December 29, 1864, at the dedication of the church it immortalized.

How did the song come to be known throughout the world? Pitts sold the song to a Chicago music publisher in 1865, and in the 1920s and 1930s the Weatherwax Quartet traveled throughout Canada and the United States and used "The Church in the Wildwood" as its theme song. As highways improved after World War I, automobiles brought many sightseers and the church became almost as famous as the song.

Today around five hundred couples get married at The Little Brown Church every year. A Marriage Reunion is held the first Sunday of August, marking its fiftieth anniversary in 2002. And although the town of Bradford, once the county seat, no longer exists, the church remains an active Congregational Church and the song is still sung, usually at the end of each service. For more information visit *www.littlebrownchurch.org*.

Sometimes It's Hard to Tie the Knot

Getting hitched can be pretty difficult, as one young Iowa couple found out in 1915.

The couple's first wedding announcement appeared in the *Republican* in Decorah, Iowa, prior to the nuptials:

> *At the Lutheran Church at Calmar, Tuesday morning at 10:30 o'clock, by Rev. Paul Koren, Mr. F.R. Englehardt and Miss Helma Johnson. Mr. Englehardt is one of the prosperous young farmers living between Calmar and Fort Atkinson, where the newly married couple will make their future home. The bride is a sister of Marshall Johnson of Decorah.*

On November 25, the newspaper ran the following story:

PASTOR KOREN WAS LOST AND THE BRIDE AND GROOM HAD MUCH DIFFICULTY IN BEING MARRIED

> *Since writing the [previous wedding announcement], we learn that Mr. and Mrs. Englehardt had much trouble in getting their destinies united. They had made arrangements with Rev. Paul Koren to marry them and as he had married all of Mrs. Englehardt's sisters, he was desirous of officiating. He had to go to Dayton, Ohio on business, but promised to be back in time for the ceremony. He was expected on [train] No. 3, due at 10:25 A.M., but arrived on No. 1 at 4:05 A.M., and went to bed. They met No. 3 and not seeing Mr. Koren thought he had missed connections; so they took an automobile and went over to Frankville Township and found a minister, but he was officiating at a funeral and could not serve. They soon found another minister, but he had visitors from Missouri and could not tie the knot. They found another divine, but as he lived in Allamakee County he did not feel warranted in taking the*

responsibility. Finally, they located Rev. Anderson south of Ossian and were married. All of this time Rev. Koren was in the hotel waiting to be called. The wedding dinner was set for noon but it was nearer two o'clock before the bride and groom appeared and the dinner was eaten.

This Woman Reconsidered—Decades Later!

Norman Caskey proposed to Mildred Emmeck in 1933 when they were both teens in Glidden—but she didn't say yes until sixty-eight years later!

Back in 1933 Emmeck was teaching at a country school where married women were not allowed to teach, so she turned Caskey down. The two eventually married other people and raised families.

After Caskey's wife died in 1999, he decided to visit his first love, who had moved into a Rockwell City retirement home after her husband died in 1992. A short while later Emmeck joined Caskey at the Eastern Star Masonic Home in Boone. In 2001 Caskey proposed again and this time Emmeck said yes!

The Bell That Was Not a Hummer Dinger

When Michael Hummer was expelled from the Presbyterian ministry in 1848, he thought he should at least receive the church bell as back wages. He tried to get it, but he never did.

Michael Hummer, pastor at First Presbyterian Church in Iowa City since 1841, went east to raise money to build the church building. During his two and a half years back east, he not only collected money and a church bell (said to be the first church bell west of the Mississippi River), but also became captivated by Swedenborgianism, a doctrine of mysticism.

Back home, his congregation appreciated the money and the bell but not his new form of spiritualism. In 1848 the presbytery expelled him from the ministry. He felt the congregation still owed him back pay, however, so he decided to take the church bell.

Hummer had moved to Keokuk, followed by a friend, J. W. Margrave, a former church trustee, and they returned to Iowa City to take the bell.

Margrave helped lower the bell from the bell tower using a block and tackle, and left to get a wagon while Hummer was in the belfry taking down the block and tackle. A crowd had gathered during the proceedings, and while Margrave was gone, somebody moved Hummer's ladder and others took the bell, concealing it by sinking it in the Iowa River.

Margrave returned and helped the irate and helpless Hummer down from the belfry. But what about the bell? According to one story, two Mormons in Iowa City at the time knew where the bell had been sunk. They took it with them to Utah and sold it to Brigham Young. Twenty years later, in 1868, Young, having heard the story of the missing Iowa City bell, wrote to S. M. Osmond, the minister at Iowa City, that the bell "is still laying here idle, as it always has done, and is at your disposal on the same conditions, whenever you please to send for it, accompanied with sufficient evidence that you are authorized to receive it for the congregation for whom it was manufactured." But an attempt to raise funds for its return was unsuccessful and the bell remained in Utah.

Meanwhile, after lengthy litigation, the trustees settled with Hummer for $400 in cash, plus $100 to be paid over one year with interest and costs up to $50. And because they charged the missing bell against him, Hummer became the legal owner of the bell that had been taken from him. No one knows, with certainty, for whom the bell tolled after that mishap in 1848. But there is one thing for sure—it never was a Hummer dinger.

Stran©e . . . but True

Marva Drew of Waterloo spent six years typing the numbers 1 through 1,000,000 in order to secure a position in the *Guinness Book of World Records*. Unfortunately, she must not have had witnesses, because she did not make it into the book—the record in the book remains sixteen years for typing those numbers. Marva passed away in 2000 but her husband, Earl, says he'll sell the record-setting pages for $250,000. In the meantime they are tucked away in ten boxes in his attic.

Typos Seen Sooner Rather Than Later

Thanks to a Methodist pastor in Dyersville, Reverend Thomas Oliver, people could finally see what they were typing as they typed. He invented the first visible typewriter in 1894. Up until then, the only typewriter available was "invisible," meaning the typist could not see what was being printed on the paper in the machine until he was completely finished, making it difficult to correct typos. Soon after devising his new typewriter, Oliver took a pastoral position in Epworth and opened a typewriter factory across from his church—the first real typewriter factory in the world.

Oliver was more concerned with improving his typewriter than marketing it, but still word got out. The Oliver typewriter was the first typewriter to appear on stage, when twenty of them were used in the opening scene of the play *The Girl at the Helm* in 1905 at the La Salle Theater in Chicago. The play was successful, even playing in foreign countries, and the Oliver typewriters went along for the ride, generating considerable publicity.

Nine different models of the Oliver typewriter were made. Models No. 3, 5, and 9 are on display at the Dyer-Botsford Victorian House and Doll Museum in Dyersville.

The Grotto of the Redemption: A Promise Kept

When nineteen-year-old Paul Matthias Dobberstein came to America from Germany in 1892, America was in the midst of a financial crisis. After arriving in Naperville, Illinois, he heard an appeal from the bishop at Dubuque for German-speaking priests. Scholarship funds were available, so he attended Saint Francis Seminary near Milwaukee.

Only a month away from ordination, he became critically ill with pneumonia in May 1897. While fighting for his life he prayed to the Blessed Virgin Mary to help save him. He promised that if his life were spared he would build a shrine of precious stones to God's glory. His health slowly returned and he was ordained and spent one year recuperating while serving as a chaplain to the Sisters of Mercy at Mount Carmel Hospital in Dubuque.

By the spring of 1898, Dobberstein was ready for action. Bishop John

Hennessy sent him to the northwestern Iowa prairie frontier village of West Bend. When Dobberstein arrived in October 1898, he was welcomed by the Germans of St. Peter and Paul's Parish. In his first sermon he said, "All is to be done here, all take hold of the rope and pull ahead, and if there be anyone here who thinks he cannot afford to pull ahead, I shall ask only one favor of him, and that is to let go of the rope and not hold back those who wish to go ahead."

By the spring of 1899, they had begun to build a parochial school. It opened that fall under the direction of members of the Franciscan Sisters of Perpetual Adoration.

Now it was time for Dobberstein to start on his shrine. Backed by his congregation, he purchased a house north of the church and eight acres of land. For more than ten years he stockpiled rocks and precious stones. He took vacations in the Black Hills of South Dakota and in New Mexico near the Carlsbad Caverns, and returned with boxcar loads of rocks and crystals and petrified wood. Soon the farmers nearby were helping add to the collection by bringing him stones from their fields.

The first work on the grotto began in 1912 and from the beginning Dobberstein had only one goal in mind: to tell in stone the story of man's

The Grotto of the Redemption in West Bend, shown here in an aerial view, includes nine separate grottos portraying scenes from the life of Christ in rock and precious sones. (COURTESY IOWA TOURISM OFFICE)

fall and his redemption by Christ. He believed that others might see in the beauty of stones the beauty of the creator and then be drawn to God. In the words of Father Dobberstein, as reprinted in the booklet *An Explanation of the Grotto of the Redemption* (1994: West Bend, Iowa):

> *Spoken words are ephemeral; written words remain, but their durability depends upon the material upon which they are written; but if carved into bronze or sculptured into stone they are well nigh imperishable. This IMPER-ISHABLENESS is the outstanding feature of the Grotto.*
>
> *Thus the story of the REDEMPTION will continue to tell its edifying story long after the builder has laid down his trowel, and will be a silent sermon expressing in permanently enduring precious stones, the fundamental truths of Christianity.*

From the beginning people came to watch Father Dobberstein's vision become a reality. For forty-two years Dobberstein worked on the Grotto of the Redemption. He died in 1954, and the Grotto became the property of the Diocese of Sioux City, transferred from the parish of West Bend.

Father Louis Greving, who had been sent to West Bend in 1946, acquired an electric hoist, which was installed in 1947. Before that each stone had been carried and placed by hand. Matt Szerensce, who graduated from the parochial school in 1912 and shared his pastor's dream, worked on the Grotto for forty-seven years until he retired in 1959. Greving continued to build and care for the Grotto until he retired in 1996. Deacon Gerald Streit was appointed director of the Grotto in 1994 and oversees the maintenance and preservation of the Grotto today.

Some one hundred thousand people visit the Grotto each year, with an estimated six million visitors since 1912. Including nine separate grottos portraying scenes from the life of Christ, the Grotto is comprised of rocks and precious stones that have been obtained and donated from around the world; the estimated monetary value of the rocks and stones is $4,308,000. Sometimes called the Eighth Wonder of the World, the Grotto represents the largest collection of minerals and rocks concentrated in any one spot. The Grotto is lit every evening until 11 P.M. and visitors can come any day of the year. For more information visit *www.nw-cybermall.com/grotto.htm.*

Str∂n©e . . . but True

The name "Dobberstein" is a German word meaning "a dauber of stones, a white washer, or a plasterer of stones."

Tiny Chapel Stands on Sacred Promise

Known as "the smallest church in the world," St. Anthony of Padua chapel seats eight worshipers, two each on four pews. The church measures twelve feet by sixteen feet and contains an altar and four arched windows and has a spire. It is located at Festina, just north of West Union, and was built by Johann Gaertner, who fought under Napoleon Bonaparte at Moscow, Russia, and Waterloo.

According to legend Gaertner's mother, while praying for his safety during the march into Russia, promised God she would build a chapel if his life were spared. Gaertner survived, but his mother died before she could fulfill her promise. Her son, however, carried out her wishes. After coming to America in 1840, Gaertner settled in Iowa in 1851. In 1886 he built the chapel with the help of his son-in-law, Frank Joseph Huber. Gaertner was ninety-two years old at the time. The chapel was dedicated in 1886. Gaertner died on June 27, 1887, and Huber died on Novemver 25 of the same year.

The roadside chapel is privately owned and maintained by the living family members of Johann Gaertner and Frank Joseph Huber, but is open to the public. Each year, on the Sunday closest to June 13, the mass for the feast of St. Anthony of Padua is offered on its small altar.

The POW Nativity Scene

From 1943 to 1946, Camp Algona on the west side of Algona was the headquarters for thirty-four prisoner-of-war camps in Iowa and Minnesota.

Eduard Kaib, an architect and noncommissioned German Army officer, grew homesick while imprisoned there in 1944. He built a small crèche out of soil and baked and painted the figures.

Camp Commander Colonel A. T. Lobdell, impressed with Kaib's work, asked if he would build a larger one. Kaib and five other prisoners completed a Nativity scene in December 1945 with sixty figures made to scale at half life-size, fashioned of concrete over wire-and-wood frames and finished with hand carving in plaster.

When the camp disbanded in 1946 and the time for Kaib's repatriation neared, he agreed that the Nativity scene could become a permanent exhibit provided that it be open every Christmas, that admission never be charged, and that the scene never be sold.

Years later, in a letter sent from his home in Germany to school children in Bancroft, Kaib wrote, "I never intended to create a piece of art. The only intention was to help bring the joy of Christmas to our camp. And you can imagine that I am very glad the Nativity scene still after 40 years helps to heal the wounds of war." Kaib died on May 24, 1988, in Bielefield, Germany.

A building was constructed on the Kossuth County Fairgrounds to house the crèche and shelter the five thousand people who visit annually. The Men's Club of the First United Methodist Church in Algona has overseen it since December 1958, and it is maintained by donations. It is open daily every December.

Strange . . . but True

George Cubbage taught the first school in Dubuque in 1833. Captured by Indians during the Black Hawk War, Cubbage was supposedly traded by the Indians for five plugs of tobacco because, being bald, he could not be scalped. He later sued the government for $102 in damages incurred during the Indian raid and won.

The Little Sod Schoolhouse

A historic marker northeast of Algona, at 2407 River Road, locates the spot of an early educational structure, the first school "building" in Kossuth County. The structure, no longer there, was walled with logs, covered with sod, and built into the side of a hill. The tablet erected in 1937 by the Daughters of the American Revolution reads:

Site of Gopher College
1856–1858
First School in Kossuth County

The Unnatural "Natural Method"

In 1897 Henry and Henrietta Olerich of Lake City adopted eight-month-old Viola Rosalia from a Des Moines orphanage—for an experiment in education.

Olerich, who supported education reform, wrote: "Our chief object for adopting a child was to test, in a practical way, a new theory of education, which we believed to be much superior to any educational system which has heretofore been used." He also sought to demonstrate that a "woman-child can become as expert and reasoned as a man-child."

Olerich explained that "no attempt was made to select a particular child; on the contrary, we desired to get an average child, hence physical health was the only point of pedigree which we regarded of vital importance, and even of this we knew little or nothing."

He called his educational process the "Natural Method" and argued that any healthy child with average intelligence could be taught advanced skills by manipulating the environment. Attractive educational toys would ignite and sustain an interest in learning. Force, he noted "always kills interest," and his process would include only natural, voluntary play. Olerich had been an Iowa country teacher, principal, and superintendent of schools for more than twenty years and had never condoned the practice of "forced attendance, forced study and forced behavior."

His "Natural Method" included a system of rewards. Baby Viola was taught to spell by using hollow blocks to which printed words were attached. The blocks each contained a peanut. Viola was asked to get a block with a certain word on it. If she brought the correct block, she would spell the word by sight, then from memory, and often by sound. She then received the peanut as a reward.

Viola Olerich, "the Famous Baby Scholar," appears in a demonstration circa 1900, two years before she was forced to retire from the stage because of advanced age. (STATE HISTORICAL SOCIETY OF IOWA—IOWA CITY)

By the time she was twenty-one months old, Viola could locate by name all the states and territories of the United States. When she was two, her father began to exhibit her intellectual skills, and she was known as "the Famous Baby Scholar." She could name and locate the bones of the human body and twenty-two kinds of geometric lines and angles. She could identify the flags of twenty-five countries, the portraits of more than a hundred famous people, the currency of the Unites States, plus many leaves and seeds. She reportedly could also read fluently, even some simple passages in French and German.

Her first "performance" was in Odebolt on April 6, 1899, and she appeared all over the Midwest during the next several years. Olerich would talk for fifteen to twenty minutes, and then Viola would perform for about twenty minutes. He would afterwards give a brief summary. Mostly she would answer questions Olerich asked, and sometimes the audience would ask a question.

Many newspapers raved about Baby Viola's abilities, but not all of them. An editor in Carroll, Iowa, wrote in May 1899: "It certainly is a rare sight to see a little tot like that evince such mature mind. But we do not believe that this child or children in general will be benefited by hot-bed processes that force such mature development. Maturity does not belong to the embryonic stage of plant or animal mind or matter, and we should not overtax the infant forces to effect manifestations that in the natural evolution of child being should come later. So, what Henry Olerich calls the natural method, we believe to be an unnatural method, and we would not permit its application to our young son for any consideration."

Undaunted, Olerich gave Viola a Smith Premier typewriter on February 22, 1900. By the end of the year her typing speed and accuracy were so advanced that it was included in her repertoire.

Viola retired in 1902 at the age of five. Later, as recorded for "Viola R. Storms Oral History" (December 20, 1973), she recalled, "There comes a time . . . when the baby ceases to be cute, and it isn't particularly novel that the child of five should know these things [flags, currency, leaves, etc.], not the way it is with the child of two or three."

And Olerich had moved on to the next project. At age fifty he abandoned the academic life and became a machinist for the Union Pacific Railroad in Omaha, Nebraska. (The family had moved to Council Bluffs in 1899.) During his time with the railroad and after his retirement in 1910, he wrote books and essays supporting a form of cooperative socialism. In 1893 he had written a utopian novel entitled *A Cityless and Countryless World.*

Viola entered kindergarten at age six, advancing easily through public schools in Council Bluffs and Omaha. She left school after eighth grade because of the illness of her mother. In 1918 she married John Storms, an office employee of the Cudahy Packing Company in Omaha, and had three children.

And what about the impact of Olerich's educational experiment? Viola said, "You don't do (children) any favor by educating them beyond their age group. Little children are afraid of you because you know more than they do. And the older ones—some of them will make a big fuss over a little child that knows a great deal and others will consider you an unmitigated nuisance. You're ill at ease with all children after an experience like that."

Olerich's reasons for adopting Viola were questionable, but he certainly had some novel ideas about improving the quality of American education.

Just One Man, but Lots of Tests

E. F. Lindquist of Gowrie made the name of "Iowa" well known in schools across the nation, with the standardized tests he developed.

Lindquist, who lived from 1901 to 1978, created the Iowa Tests of Basic Skills (ITBS) and the Iowa Tests of Educational Development (ITED). The ITBS was introduced across Iowa at the junior high level in the fall of 1935. It soon caught the attention of educators across the nation. By 1940 the ITBS had been extended to grades three through five and was being published nationwide—and is still given in Iowa and throughout the United States.

But that's not all this Iowan did. He also founded the American College

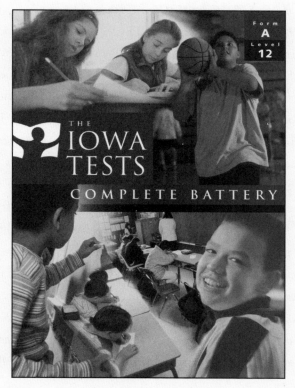

The Iowa Test of Basic Skills (ITBS), first introduced in 1935, is still given in Iowa and throughout the nation. (COPYRIGHT © 2001 BY THE UNIVERSITY OF IOWA. ALL RIGHTS RESERVED. NO PART OF THIS WORK MAY BE REPRODUCED WITHOUT PRIOR WRITTEN PERMISSION OF THE RIVERSIDE PUBLISHING COMPANY, ITASCA, ILLINOIS.)

Testing (ACT) program and directed development of the General Education Development (GED) tests for the U.S. Armed Forces Institute for service personnel who had not finished high school.

Lindquist received his undergraduate degree from Augustana College in 1922 and his Ph.D. from the University of Iowa in 1927. He was director of the College Entrance Examination Board (CEEB) and the ruling body for the Scholastic Aptitude Test (SAT); organized the Measurement Research Center, the world's largest processor of educational tests; and invented a high-speed test-scoring machine.

Schools today wouldn't be the same without him!

The Man Who Visited Every Town

In July 1987, after twenty years, Ray Beyer of Bettendorf completed his quest of visiting every single town and village in Iowa—all 1,168 of them.

Beyer had grown up in Blairsburg and while a student at Buena Vista in Storm Lake began to notice how many towns he had visited in his job delivering medicine to veterinarians throughout northwest Iowa. He became determined to visit every single one. He became a credit manager with John Deere, and had to speed up his quest when he learned of his impending transfer to Dallas—while he still had forty towns left.

He finished by visiting Hawkeye, then with a population of 512, which he had saved for last because of the name. The town welcomed him royally with a sign that read, "You've saved the best for last." Governor Terry Branstad gave him a letter of congratulations, two Hawkeye lapel pins, a huge town flag, a book of Hawkeye history, and mugs bearing the town name.

Beyer said, "I suppose this has been sort of a goofy thing to do. I can't imagine that there's ever been anyone else who's done it. I do want to say that even though my family will be living in Texas, our hearts will always be in Iowa."

With a Little Help from a Rhyme

Laura Portz of Bellevue memorized the ninety-nine counties of Iowa when she was in grade school in the early 1900s by setting them in rhyme:

Our home is in Iowa
Westward toward the setting sun,
Just between two mighty rivers,
Where their crystal waters run.
It has towns and it has cities,
It has many noble streams.
It has ninety-nine counties,
And we'll now repeat their names:

Lyon, Osceola, Dickinson,
Where Spirit Lake you see.
Emmet, Kossuth, Winnebago,
Worth is near Lake Albert Lea.

Mitchell, Howard, Winneshiek,
Allamakee, so fine.
Make eleven northern counties
On the Minnesota line.

Clayton, Dubuque, Jackson, Clinton,
Together with Scott and Muscatine.
Lee, Louisa, and Des Moines,
On the eastern side are seen.

Van Buren, Davis, Appanoose,
Decatur, Ringgold, Wayne, we spy.
Taylor, Page and Fremont
On the Missouri border lie.

Pottawattamie, Harrison, Mills,
Monona, Woodbury, Plymouth, Sioux
Are all the counties that around
The border of our state we view.

Next we name O'Brien,
Palo Alto, too and Clay
Hancock, Cerro Gordo, Floyd,
Then see Chickasaw, I pray.

Fayette, Bremer, Butler, Franklin,
Next upon the map we see,
Wright and Humboldt, Pocahontas,
Buena Vista, Cherokee.

Ida, Sac, Calhoun, and Webster,
Hamilton with a name so rare.
Next is Hardin, Grundy, Black Hawk,
Then Buchanan, Delaware.

Linn, Benton, Tama, Marshall,
Greene, Story, Crawford, Carroll, Boone.
Let not your patience weary,
We will have them all too soon.

Jones, Cedar, Johnson, Iowa,
Poweshiek, by the same.
Next is Jasper, Polk and Dallas,
Names of Presidential fame.

Guthrie, Audubon, Shelby,
Cass, Madison, Adair,
Warren, Marion, Mahaska, Jefferson,
And Keokuk, too are there.

Wapello, Monroe, Washington,
Henry, we have missed.
Lucas, Clarke, Union, Adams,
And Montgomery fills the list.

RELIGION AND EDUCATION TRIVIA

Q. The first missionaries to Iowa were of what faith?

A. Roman Catholic.

Q. The first wedding in Iowa, of William Ross and Matilda Morg, took place in what town?

A. Burlington.

Q. Where was the first Quaker church west of the Mississippi River founded?

A. Salem.

Q. What denomination built the first church in Iowa in 1834 in Dubuque?

A. Methodist.

Q. What is the largest religious denomination in Iowa?

A. Roman Catholic.

Q. Built in 1886, where is the oldest Lutheran church in continuous use west of the Mississippi?

A. St. Ansgar (First Lutheran Norwegian Church).

Q. Herbert Hoover was a lifelong member of what Christian sect?

A. Quaker (Society of Friends.)

Q. In what year did thirteen hundred European Mormon converts carry their possessions from Iowa City to Salt Lake City in handcarts?

A. 1856.

Q. What college in Epworth is the nation's only four-year Catholic seminary devoted exclusively to training young men for foreign missions?

A. Divine Word College.

Q. Abbot Bruno laid the foundation of what Trappist monastery near Dubuque in 1849?

A. New Melleray.

Q. Educational testing and speech pathology began at what institution?

A. The University of Iowa.

Q. In what year did Des Moines become the second city in the nation with kindergarten in public schools?

A. 1884.

Q. With what religious denomination was Central College affiliated when it opened in 1853?

A. Baptist.

Q. In 1872 what Davenport native became the nation's first woman high school principal?

A. Phoebe Sudlow.

Q. Where was Iowa's first public junior college established?

A. Mason City, in 1918.

Q. In 1839 the first free public school for physically handicapped children in the nation was opened in what city?

A. Des Moines.

Q. George Washington Carver taught what subject for two years at Iowa State?

A. Botany.

Q. In what year did Cornell College become the first U.S. college to elevate a woman to full professorship with a salary equal to her male colleagues?

A. 1871.

Q. Where was the first statistical laboratory in the nation?

A. Iowa State University. In 1933 an institute was established to develop statistical methodology to apply to other research efforts.

Q. In what year did a state law give all children the right to free high school?

A. 1911.

Q. Who was the first woman teacher in what became the state of Iowa?

A. Rebecca Palmer, in the winter of 1834–35.

Q. In what town did former governor William Larabee and his wife establish a school as their gift to the people?

A. Clermont.

9
Sports

When Keokuk was in the "National League"

Some Iowans like to remember when Keokuk was in the National League—although its baseball team actually belonged to the National Association of Professional Baseball Players, organized in 1871 (the National League came later).

The first baseball game between rival New York teams was on June 19, 1846. It didn't take long for baseball to become the national pastime and Iowa was right in there. The Keokuk Westerns applied to join the National Association and were accepted in 1875.

The Keokuk Western uniforms were white with blue stockings and trimmings, with a "K" on the front and one on each sleeve, and small-brimmed hats instead of caps. Keokuk's first professional game was at home on May 4, 1875, against the White Stockings of Chicago, who won, 15–1. The Keokuk team unfortunately lost most of the games that followed, and defeated only the Red Stockings of St. Louis, 15–2 on May 7.

On June 10 Keokuk played Boston at home, with Albert Goodwill Spalding pitching against them. (Later, in February 1876, Spalding founded a sporting goods company in Chicago.) Boston won, 6–4, but refused to play the second game and left for home, probably because of low attendance or low gate receipts. (Admission was fifty cents for adults and twenty-five cents for children.) The Westerns played one more game against the Mutuals of New York and lost 1–0 when the game was halted in the fifth inning because of rain.

On June 17 the Keokuk *Daily Gate City* newspaper announced that the Keokuk Westerns, who finished their only season with a 1–12 record, had been disbanded. The board of directors had been "convinced that the organization could not be permanently maintained for the reason that the population is not sufficient to furnish audiences." The Keokuk players moved on to other teams.

The other teams must not have felt that the Westerns poor showing was due to individual players, as they snatched them up right away.

And so the Keokuk Western uniforms were retired. They might not have tallied up many in the "win" column, but they sure looked good trying, small-brimmed hats and all.

From then on baseball fans of Iowa could talk about the glory days, "when Keokuk was in the National League."

Did You Know? As a minor league team in 1954, the Keokuk team, then called the Kernels, was affiliated with the Cleveland Indians. Their most notable player was Roger Maras, who went on to play for the New York Yankees in 1957 and changed the spelling of his name to Maris. He was the first player to beat Babe Ruth's record of most home runs in one season, hitting sixty-one home runs in 1961. Minor league baseball ended in Keokuk in 1962.

"If You Build It, They Will Come"

Yes, you can visit the famous Field of Dreams cornfield baseball diamond—in Iowa, of course.

In the 1989 movie *Field of Dreams*, one of the characters urges another to build a baseball diamond in his cornfield, and visitors mysteriously begin to show up. The same is true of the Dyersville cornfield where the baseball diamond was built—eight hundred thousand visitors have appeared since the movie was released.

In the movie Kevin Costner's character, Ray Kinsella, plows up a cornfield to build a baseball diamond. The ghosts of baseball legends, including Shoeless Joe Jackson, come to play. And for the past decade "the Ghost Players" have visited the baseball field the last Sunday of each month to entertain visitors. This unique group of ballplayers, nicknamed "the Harlem Globetrotters of baseball," has attended special events all over the world.

The movie is based on the book *Shoeless Joe* by W. P. Kinsella, a Canadian who studied at the University of Iowa's Writers' Workshop—yet another Iowan connection.

Most Iowans think the best line from the movie is when a young baseball player from the past emerges from between the cornstalks to ask Ray, "Is this heaven?" Ray replies, "It's Iowa."

The Field of Dreams is open daily from April to November. Visit *www.fieldofdreamsmoviesite.com* or *www.leftandcenterfod.com* for more information.

A visitor goes to bat on the Field of Dreams in Dyersville. (COURTESY IOWA TOURISM OFFICE)

Stran©e . . . but True

Donnie Lansing owns the farmhouse and most of the ball field (except left and center) where the movie *Field of Dreams* was shot. In 1987, long before Universal Studios contacted him about using his field for a movie, Lansing and his uncle Herb Kramer had just finished putting up hay on the farm and were standing in the driveway looking at the newly mown hay field. Kramer said, "Hey, you know what, Donnie? You ought to build a ball diamond out there. It'd be a nice place to have a game." The two men laughed.

That winter Donnie hurried over to his uncle's to tell him the news—a movie was going to be made at the farm with, believe it or not, a baseball diamond built in the very spot his uncle had imagined.

The High School Junior Who Pitched for the Cleveland Indians

William Feller also built a ball field on an Iowa farm—in 1931, on the family farm northeast of Van Meter, for his twelve-year-old son to practice on. It certainly paid off, as Robert William (Bob) Feller became one of baseball's best-ever pitchers.

Bob was born on that farm November 3, 1918, and his father spent hours, before school and after chores, teaching him to hit, catch, and throw. On cold and rainy days they played catch in the barn. Those hours of practice paid off: In 1935 when Bob was just fifteen, Cy Slapnicka saw him pitching for Farmers Union, a semiprofessional team in Des Moines, and illegally signed him to a Cleveland Indians contract—for one dollar and a ball autographed by the Cleveland Indians team. The summer before his senior year in high school, Bob Feller pitched for the Cleveland Indians.

He pitched his first professional game in July 1936 in an exhibition game against the St. Louis Cardinals and struck out eight batters in only three innings. In his first start, against the St. Louis Browns, on August 23, the Indians won 4–1 and Bob struck out fifteen batters. That same season he struck out seventeen Philadelphia Athletics and established a new American League record. He became widely known as "Rapid Robert" and went 5–3, with seventy-six strikeouts in sixty-two innings and a 3.34 earned-run average before returning to Iowa that year to complete high school.

He set a new major league record on October 2, 1938, when he struck out eighteen Detroit Tigers in a nine-inning game. He pitched his first of three no-hitters in Chicago against the White Sox on April 16, 1940—the only no-hitter in major league history pitched on opening day. That year he won a career-high twenty-seven games and the following year won twenty-five. He was the first pitcher in major league history to win twenty or more games in one season before age twenty-one, and had 107 major league victories before he was twenty-three. He was poised to rewrite the record books in lifetime strikeouts and wins when World War II broke out.

In December 1941 Feller joined the Navy and spent the next forty-four months as an anti-aircraft gunner aboard the USS *Alabama*. He won five campaign ribbons and eight battle stars in combat in the Pacific.

The years in the service may have harmed his sports records, but didn't hurt his ability to pitch. On April 30, two weeks into the 1946 season, Feller pitched his second no-hitter against the Yankees in Yankee Stadium. By the end of that season he had won twenty-six games and stuck out 348 batters, another major league

Bob "Rapid Robert" Feller grins from a postcard—memorabilia from the career of the greatest pitcher in Cleveland Indians history can be seen at the Bob Feller Hometown Exhibit in Van Meter.
(BOB FELLER MUSEUM)

record. He had another terrific season in 1951, winning twenty-two games and pitching his third no-hitter against the Tigers on July 1.

When Feller retired at the end of the 1956 season, he had won 266 games and lost 162, and had 2,581 strikeouts. He had pitched three no-hitters and twelve one-hitters. The Cleveland Indians retired his number 19 uniform. Missing almost four years of baseball because of the war probably cost him more than a hundred wins and a thousand strikeouts and pitching records that would have stood for decades.

But the baseball world did not forget his record-setting abilities. Bob Feller was inducted into Baseball's Hall of Fame in 1962, his first year of eligibility. In July 1969 he was selected as the "Greatest Living Right-Hand Pitcher" as part of Professional Baseball's Centennial Celebration.

Feller and his wife, Anne, live in Gates Mills, Ohio, where he continues to be a pitchman for the Cleveland Indians in the public relations department. A bronze statue of Feller pitching, commissioned by the Cleveland Indian organization, greets fans who come to Jacobs Field, the Cleveland ballpark.

But Feller has not forgotten Iowa, and Iowa is not about to forget Feller. On June 10, 1995, the Bob Feller Hometown Exhibit opened in Van Meter, displaying baseball memorabilia and highlights from his career, and Feller often returns to sign autographs and meet the people. (One of the items on display is the bat Babe Ruth was pictured leaning on during his retirement ceremony in June 1948—a bat that belonged to Feller.) The exhibit is open daily, and you can find more information at *www.bobfellermuseum.org*.

Iowans are proud to call Bob Feller one of their own—loyal to his team, his state, and his country.

The Man Who Created the "Chicago Orphans"

Adrian (Cap or Pop) Anson, Hall of Fame baseball player from Marshalltown, played for and managed the Chicago White Stockings from 1876 to 1897. He took his team to Hot Springs, Arkansas, in the spring of 1887 for a preseason game against the St. Louis Browns—this was the beginning of spring training as we now know it.

During his professional career (1871–1901), Anson played every position but pitcher and accumulated 3,041 hits—astounding, considering that for more than twenty years his team played few more than a hundred games per season. He hit .300 or better twenty times, including .421 in 1887, and was the National League champion batter in 1879, 1881, 1887, and 1888. When he retired he held the record for hits, at-bats, doubles, RBIs and runs. The Chicago team adopted the name "Orphans" in his honor upon his retirement in 1901, because the players felt like they had lost a father. (The name was changed to the Chicago Cubs in 1902.) Anson was inducted into the Baseball Hall of Fame in 1939, just three years after George Herman (Babe) Ruth.

World's Highest Paid Athlete

Frank Gotch, the best known athlete of his era, helped make wrestling the popular sport it is today.

Frank Alvin Gotch was born April 27, 1878, in Humboldt. He became the American wrestling champion in 1904 and held the World Freestyle Heavyweight Champion title from 1908 to 1913.

At 205 pounds, the six-foot Gotch was smooth-muscled and known for his blinding speed and famous toehold. He defeated George Hackenschmidt, "the Russian Lion," who was the original World Heavyweight Champion, in 1908 in Chicago. When the Russian complained of his rough tactics, a rematch was scheduled. Thirty-one thousand spectators paid a total of $87,953 to see the rematch at Comisky Park in Chicago in 1911, which Gotch won.

When he accepted $100,000 to appear in three "flickies" (films) in 1915, Frank Gotch became the world's highest paid athlete. Because of his success, the sport of wrestling took off in the Midwest, and many great wrestlers of the next generation came from the region. To this day, many of the best amateur wrestlers come from the Midwest, especially in the college ranks, including the University of Iowa and Iowa State.

You can find Frank A. Gotch Park two miles south of Humboldt, and there is a Frank Gotch display in the Humboldt County Historical Museum located southeast of the junction of Highways 169 and 3 in Dakota City.

Did You Know? The first official National Collegiate Athletic Association (NCAA) wrestling tournament was held in Ames in 1928. Oklahoma Agricultural & Mining (now Oklahoma State) was the winning team. They were coached by former Iowa wrestler, Edward Gallagher. For the next fifty-seven years, a school from either Iowa or Oklahoma won all but three NCAA national championships.

Down (on His Knees), but Not Out

On March 3, 2001, Simpson College senior Nick Ackerman won the NCAA Division III wrestling title in the 174-pound weight class by defeating Nick Slack. Slack, from Augsburg College in Minneapolis, was the defending national champion and had won six matches in a row. But what's most impressive about Ackerman's accomplishment is that he won the title without legs (and without wearing prosthetics).

When Ackerman was eighteen months old, doctors amputated both of his legs below the knees because of a fast-moving, life-threatening form of meningitis. When he was four, he took off his prosthetic legs and jumped off the high-dive board at the Colfax swimming pool. He competed in many sports growing up, and as a high school senior at Colfax-Mingo got a standing ovation when he finished sixth at the state wrestling meet. Dan Gable, the famous Iowa State wrestler and Iowa coach, asked for his autograph—the only time Gable ever remembers asking for an autograph.

In 2001 Ackerman and Iowa State University's undefeated national champion Cael Sanderson were honored as co-winners of the Dan Hodge Trophy, awarded to the nation's best collegiate wrestler.

Ackerman's attitude is "what's the big deal?" But many of us do think it's a big deal. Bryan Poulter, Ackerman's high school coach, posted a sign on the door of the Colfax-Mingo wrestling room that reads: "A young man walked out of here on his knees and placed sixth in the state. How did your practice go?"

Did You Know? Iowa State's Cael Sanderson finished his collegiate wrestling career on March 23, 2002, by winning his 159th consecutive match and his fourth national championship. No one has ever won four NCAA Division I wrestling titles with no defeats. He also was the first four-time winner of the tournament's Most Outstanding Wrestler award. Way to go, Cael!

A Wrestler's Heaven

You can find the world's largest collection of wrestling memorabilia at the International Wrestling Institute and Museum in Newton, covering both amateur and professional levels. The museum features displays on Dan Gable, Rocky Marciano, Frank Gotch, and Verne Gagne. It also contains a decoupage image of Jacob wrestling the angel of the Lord and a life-size mural of Abraham Lincoln as a wrestler. (Lincoln was probably the best wrestler to be elected president.) The museum also hosts an annual Hall of Fame Induction Weekend and Celebrity Golf Tournament. For more information visit *www.wrestlingmuseum.org*.

Did You Know? Nicknamed "the Roland Rocket," Gary Thompson was the first two-sport All-American at Iowa State. He outscored Wilt Chamberlain in a basketball game against Kansas in 1957.

A Premier Track and Field Meet

Drake University athletic director, John L. Griffin, one of the prime movers in the formation of the NCAA, came up with the idea of the Drake Relays in 1910 in order to give his Bulldogs (the Drake team nickname) some early season outdoor competition. It would also give nearby colleges and high school athletes the same opportunity. His idea blossomed into one of the world's premier track and field meets.

The 2003 Drake Relays resulted in the thirty-eighth straight sell-out of the Saturday program in the 18,000-seat Drake Stadium—the longest streak in U.S. Track history. Twelve athletes who held Drake Relays records competed in the ninety-fourth annual Drake Relays held in April 2003. They included Kip Janvrin of Panora, who won his ninth consecutive Drake Relays decathlon title.

Strange . . . but True

Drake University runner Mark Manchester wore a unique uniform when he ran the mile leg of the medley relay in the 1926 Drake Relays. He had forgotten his pants, so he didn't wear any! He wore only his jersey, jock strap, and shoes.

How Girls' Basketball Got Its Start

Girls' high school basketball is believed to have first appeared at Dubuque, in 1898. Dubuque's first games were intercity games played mostly at the YMCA.

Ottumwa was active in girls' basketball from 1900 to 1923, playing surrounding towns, such as Washington, Albia, and Mystic, and interclass games. Muscatine and Davenport were also involved in the sport. By 1920 the Davenport High School *Blackhawk* paper reported, "It is interesting to notice that the girls are becoming more enthusiastic over sports every year. . . . We give our heartiest congratulations to the Girls' Basketball Team."

In the early days, the typical girls' uniforms were pleated black bloomers with white or colored middy blouses and long dark ties, with full-length black stockings. The uniforms were often homemade, so they varied in style and color. In 1925 the Allerton team members had different shoes and stockings, but all wore bright-colored stocking caps with white pompoms.

The first annual Iowa high school girls' basketball tournament was in Des Moines in 1920. It was an invitational tournament held at Drake University, attended by twenty-four teams. Correctionville beat Nevada 11–4 to become the first girls' state champions.

In 1925 the Iowa High School Athletic Association dropped the game, believing that competitive sports before paying crowds was not good for girls. The large city schools were in the vanguard to restrict girls' basketball to interclass games. One speaker said: "I coached girls' basketball once, and my conscience has bothered me ever since for the harm I might have done the girls." Not everybody agreed with the decision, especially not the smaller towns that had participated in the invitational state tournaments between 1920 and 1926.

Superintendent John W. Agans of Mystic retorted: "Gentlemen, if you attempt to do away with girls' basketball in Iowa, you'll be standing in the center of the track when the train runs over [you]." Afterward about twenty-five men, mostly from small towns, met in a corner of the church where the meeting was being held, and decided to begin a new girls' organization, the Iowa Girls High School Athletic Union, which was founded in 1927.

The Iowa Girl

When E. Wayne Cooley became executive director of the Iowa Girls High School Athletic Union (IGHSAU) in 1954 at age thirty-two, basketball was the only sport offered to high school girls in Iowa, and only at smaller schools. He took the job only if the directors would let him expand the program.

Thus began girls' golf, tennis, track and field, cross country, swimming and diving, synchronized swimming, softball, soccer, gymnastics, and field hockey. The Iowa girls thrived and the nation noticed. In 1968 CBS News came to Veteran's Auditorium in Des Moines to broadcast a live report from the Iowa Girls State Basketball Tournament. By 1980 Iowa was the unchallenged leader in high school girls' athletics. IGHSAU is the only organization in the nation solely devoted to interscholastic competition for girls, and more than seventy thousand students participate in sports sponsored by IGHSAU.

Cooley, who originally planned on staying in his post for five years to gain experience before moving on, stayed for forty-eight years, until retiring in 2002. He deserves the credit for expanding and strengthening the IGHSAU and providing opportunities for Iowa girl athletes.

The Iowa Girls High School Athletic Union is the only organization in the nation solely devoted to interscholastic competition for girls. (COURTESY IGHSAU)

Did You Know? By 1947 the Iowa Girls High School Athletic Union had grown so much that it had to employ a full-time secretary—and Iowa continues to be the only state with a girls' athletics organization that requires full-time staff.

Five Players or Six? A Big Decision

Until 1934 Iowa girls' basketball was played in three courts with six players: two forwards, two guards, a running or "side" player, and a jumping center. Two-court ball, with three forwards and three guards, began in 1935. Another big rule change in 1941 allowed a guard to tie up the ball (grab the ball, which forces a "jump ball") when the opponent was in the lane.

Through the years, rules were changed and adapted. In 1982 the

IGHSAU adopted the nation's first use of the three-pointer in girls' high school play, and then the thirty-second clock. But the biggest change in Iowa girls' basketball since 1935 occurred in 1983, when school districts were allowed to determine if they wanted five- or six-player basketball.

The six-player team did allow more girls the opportunity to play, and it was unique. Also it took a lot of skill to be able to do something with the ball when you only had two dribbles (the two-dribble limit was a six-player rule). At the state tournament level you saw a lot of great games.

But colleges play with five players, so switching to this format would mean that girls would no longer have to learn a new style at the college level.

In 1993 the Union voted to end six-player basketball—and a dynasty ended. But tradition dies hard and to this day you can still hear talk of the glory days of Iowa girls' basketball, when the national legend of "the Iowa Girl" seemed to be at its peak.

No More RBIs at ISU

Iowa State University cut its baseball program after the 2002 season. At 109 years, it was the university's oldest sports program. Budget problems forced the cut, and the men's swimming and diving program also died. One bright note on this sad page of ISU history is that the Cyclones won their final home game on Cap Timm Field against number one Nebraska, 5–1.

Did You Know? Jack Fleck from Davenport won the U.S. Open Golf Championship in San Francisco in June 1955 by defeating Ben Hogan in a playoff. The two men were tied at the end of the regular seventy-two holes. It was considered the biggest upset of the year, and Fleck was the first Iowan to ever win golf's most coveted honor.

Stran©e . . . but True

When golfing for the first time at the Laurens Golf and Country Club, you're cautioned to look both ways and up before shooting—because the airport's grass runway is right in the middle of the golf course! Of course there's very little air traffic in Laurens, usually just an occasional crop duster or single-engine plane. Still, you have to be careful. One afternoon an airplane misjudged the runway and landed on a green.

More Great Athletes from Iowa

★ **Nile Kinnick:** An Adel native, Kinnick was an All-America halfback for the University of Iowa football team and won the Heisman trophy in 1939, after leading the Hawkeyes to a record of 6–1–1, including a 7–6 victory over top-ranked Notre Dame. He was average in size and speed, but a great clutch player, punter, and passer, as well as an inspiring leader. Kinnick was the number one male athlete of 1939, professional or amateur (ahead of Joe DiMaggio and Joe Louis), and voted number one position for the 1940 All-Star game. He died on June 2, 1943, at age twenty-four when his naval plane crashed into the Caribbean Sea during a wartime training exercise. The University of Iowa stadium was named after him in 1972.

★ **Dan Gable:** Born October 25, 1948, in Waterloo, Gable was an outstanding high school wrestler at Waterloo West (64–0), and college wrestler at Iowa State (118–1). His only defeat came in the NCAA finals his senior year. He won an Olympic gold medal in 1972 without giving up a single point to any of his six opponents. He was the University of Iowa wrestling coach from 1977 to 1997, compiling a record of 355–21–5. He is a three-time Olympic head coach (1980, 1984, and 2000) and assistant to the athletic director at the University of Iowa.

★ **Kip Janvrin:** In 2001 this Panora native won his first national title at the USA Outdoor Championships, becoming the oldest-ever U.S. decathlon champion. He set a record for most career decathlon wins (thirty-three) and an American record for most career decathlons over eight thousand points (twenty-six). He has been nationally ranked since 1989 and has completed all but two of his career decathlons. In 2003 he won the Drake Relays decathlon for the four-teenth and ninth consecutive time, with 7,789 points. In September 2002 at age thirty-seven he won a twenty-event double decathlon in Turku, Finland, and scored 14,185 points to break the 1992 world record of 13,906 points.

★ **Kurt Warner:** Warner, a 1999 NFL MVP from Cedar Rapids, played high school football at Cedar Rapids Regis and college football at the University of Northern Iowa, where he didn't start until his senior year in 1993. He played Arena League ball for the Iowa Barnstormers from 1995 to 1997 and for Amsterdam in the NFL Europe in 1998. Playing for the St. Louis Rams, in 1999 he threw for forty-one touchdowns (only the second player in NFL history to throw for forty or more touchdowns), had nine 300-yard games, and the fifth highest single-season passer rating of all time with 109.2.

Strange . . . but True

Pheasant, duck, and turkey hunting are all popular sports in Iowa, but Virgil Walters of Exline bagged an elephant on September 23, 1923.

The elephant had escaped from the circus in Lancaster, Missouri, and circus owner Billy Hall had tried in vain to turn him by firing a shotgun full in his face. When the elephant charged Hall, he dived into a ten-foot ditch. The enraged beast kept running. About two hundred people tried to take shots at him in Coal City, where he chased Esper Hart up a tree and shook the tree until Hart fell. Finally Walters brought the elephant down with a 30-30 Enfield army rifle in a field in Iowa.

When the World Rides Across Iowa

On July 22, 1973, *Des Moines Register* columnist John Karras wrote: "Donald Kaul and I are going to ride from Sioux City to Davenport the week of August 26 and we'd like to have as many of you as are able join us along the way." Two hundred fifty bicyclists showed up to start with them. One hundred fourteen of them made the entire 412-mile trip, including Clarence Pickard, age eighty-three, from Indianola, who wore a pith helmet and rode a second-hand ten-speed women's Schwinn Varsity. That first ride was called the Great Six-Day Bicycle Ride Across Iowa.

The ride the following year was called SAGBRAI (Second Annual Great Bike Ride across Iowa) and went 422 miles from Council Bluffs to Dubuque. Two thousand cyclists went along.

The acronym RAGBRAI (*Register's* Annual Great Bike Ride across Iowa) first appeared in the Sunday *Register's* Iowa Living section on January 5, 1975. By 1979 there were six thousand cyclists, and in 1981 Mapleton put up this campground sign: "Welcome to RAGBRAI, Iowa—the only city in the state that can claim as its boundaries the Missouri River on the west and the Mississippi River on the east." RAGBRAI had become a community all its own.

As to pronunciation, Karras always asserted it should be pronounced

The 10,000 bicyclists participating in RAGBRAI stop in Titonka (population 600) in 2001. They put a tractor to a unique use—as a bike end! (COURTESY TITONKA TOPIC, TITONKA)

"ragbray." He and his wife even wrote a book, *RAGBRAI, Everyone Pronounces It Wrong.* Some people call it "ragbrye," possibly because Jim Green of the *Register* included that pronounciation in a 1997 press release.

However you say it, for six days in July Iowa shows people from all over the world just what this state is about.

SPORTS TRIVIA

Q. Boys' and girls' basketball teams from what high school made Iowa history when they both won state championships in Class 1A in 1995?

A. Winfield-Mt. Union/Morning Sun.

Q. Who was the son-in-law of George S. Clarke of Adel, governor of Iowa from 1913 to 1917?

A. Nile Kinnick.

Q. Eventual Heisman trophy winner Nile Kinnick played on an Adel baseball team with what player who would become famous?

A. Bob Feller.

Q. How many states have more golf courses per capita than Iowa?

A. None.

Q. While playing football at the University of Chicago, what Dubuque native became the first Heisman trophy winner?

A. Jay Berwanger.

Q. What multiple-gold-medal-winning Olympian was the first woman to be featured as a Drake Relays contestant in 1961?

A. Wilma Rudolph.

Q. In what year was Des Moines the site of the first professional baseball game to be played at night under permanent lights?

A. 1930.

Q. Olympic gold medals were won in what sport by Fairfield's John E. Jackson in 1912 and Jefferson's Doreen Wilbur in 1972?

A. Archery.

Q. Charley Williams of Independence was the only man to raise and train two horses that hold what record?

A. World stallion trotting record.

Q. University of Iowa swimming coach David A. Armbruster originated what swimming stroke in 1935?

A. Butterfly. (He also developed the flip turn.)

Q. What Iowa college was the first to play in a football bowl game?

A. Drake University, in the Raisin Bowl in 1946.

Q. In what year was Iowa State University's Jack Trice killed during a football game against Minnesota?

A. 1923. (Trice, ISU's first black athlete, died from injuries he received.)

Q. What Holstein native was featured in *Ripley's Believe It or Not!* for scoring 279 points in nine high school football games?

A. Lester (Jack) Eicherly.

Q. What kind of fish is most frequently caught in Iowa?

A. Bluegill.

Q. Born in Iowa in 1938, who was the first woman ever to race at the Indianapolis (Indy) Motor Speedway?

A. Janet Guthrie.

Q. Rocky Marciano, the only undefeated boxing champion, was killed in a plane crash in what town?

A. Newton, on August 31, 1969.

Q. How many Big Ten titles and Rose Bowl appearances did the Hawkeyes earn under football coach Hayden Fry?

A. Three, in 1982, 1986, and 1990.

Q. What Bancroft native pitched for the Brooklyn Dodgers against the New York Yankees in the 1947 World Series?

A. Joe (Lefty) Hatton.

Q. What major league baseball pitcher from Norway threw a three-hit shutout for the Baltimore Orioles in the 1983 World Series?

A. Mike Boddicker.

Q. What Davenport native won the 1947 Heisman trophy at Notre Dame?

A. Johnny Lujack.

Q. What was the largest fish caught on record in Iowa?

A. A 107-pound, 69.5-inch paddle fish caught by Robert Pranschke of Onawa.

10
Arts and Entertainment

American Gothic: A Case of Mistaken Identity

Grant Wood's sister, Nan, modeled for the woman in his painting *American Gothic*. The family dentist, Dr. Byron McKeeby, thirty years her senior, posed as the farmer. Though the public assumed that the couple in the painting were husband and wife, Nan once said, "Grant never saw the picture like that. . . . Grant intended it as a farmer and daughter, not husband and wife."

Nan, whose face was lengthened by her brother so that no one would recognize her, at first was displeased with the painting, thinking that it was not complimentary to her. Grant soon made up for that by having her sit for a portrait of herself.

Nan Wood, a freelance artist herself, was born on a farm near Anamosa to Francis M. and Hattie Weaver Wood. She had three older brothers, Frank, Grant, and John. Although Grant eclipsed her artistic talents, her face is known all over the world—only that of the Mona Lisa is more famous. Her face can be seen at the Art Institute of Chicago, where *American Gothic* is a prized possession. The Art Institute purchased it for $300, after it was shown in an exhibit there shortly after it was painted in 1930. The house Grant used in the background of the painting can still be seen at 301 American Gothic Street in Eldon.

He Came, He Stayed, He Sculpted

In the depth of the Depression, Grant Wood offered Christian Petersen $26.50 per week to work on the Iowa Public Works of Art Project, a New Deal program. So forty-nine-year-old Christian Petersen came to Iowa State College in 1934 to create a sculpture mural as the first artist-in-residence at any college in the nation. The Danish-born Petersen had come to the United States in 1894 at age nine. He had studied at the Rhode Island School of Design and the Art Students League of New York, and become a die-cutter for jewelry manufacturers in New Jersey. Expecting to stay only a few months at Iowa State, he remained for twenty-one years. In 1935 lecture notes he wrote, "A number of years ago, I had the feeling that the center of culture would eventually find itself in the Middlewest. . . . Here I felt folks would be more natural. So judge for yourself. Create an American art, here in the rich soil of the Middlewest, where America has its roots. Here shall be the soil and the seed and the strength of art."

Petersen's first creation at Iowa State College was the *History of Dairying Mural.* A few years later, he was appointed instructor of applied art in home economics. His class, open only to women, became popular, so he soon added more sections and unofficially opened his class to men—making it one of the few classes that were coed.

One of Petersen's best-known works is the *Fountain of the Four Seasons* outside the Memorial Union. The four Osage Indian women were carved from Bedford stone, with Iowa clay used for the terra-cotta panels around the fountain. The high-quality terra-cotta resulted from his collaboration with Paul Cox, head of the ceramic engineering department in the 1930s.

Petersen's twelve major campus public works of art included *The Gentle Doctor,* a sculpture of a veterinarian holding a puppy whose mother is at his feet, which has become an international symbol for veterinary medicine.

Within the last few years, his major works of art on campus have been restored and conserved as part of a $2 million plan by University Museums and its director, Lynette Pohlman, to conserve, catalogue, collect, and display as much of Petersen's work as possible. Initially expecting to find about three hundred pieces, the catalogers ending up finding 1,250. Petersen's wife, Charlotte, and his daughter, Mary, contributed sculptures and more than four hundred of his sketches and drawings.

Grant Wood and Christian Petersen are considered the first regionalist artists in the United States. Although Petersen didn't like being called a regionalist, his work reflects and celebrates Iowa and Iowans. He believed that all people can and should have access to art. Both Wood's and Petersen's works have a simplistic style, but unlike Wood, Petersen did not promote his work and didn't even sign it.

Christian Petersen's sculpture The Gentle Doctor *stands in the courtyard of the School of Veterinary Medicine at Iowa State University.* (PHOTO BY JACK STOCK)

Petersen's humility was a major reason his work was unrecognized by the rest of the world, outside Iowa. Now that is beginning to change. In 2002 the Smithsonian American Art Museum unveiled a new acquisition, Petersen's *Cornhusker*. This sculpture, which Petersen finished along with its companion piece, *4-H Calf*, in 1941 for the Sheldon Munn Hotel in Ames, was missing when Pohlman began her search for the University Museums. It was located in the basement of the Kirkwood Hotel in Des Moines and donated to the university by the hotel owners in 2000.

The model for *Cornhusker* was Marion Link of Story County, the 1940 state corn-husking champion. When Petersen asked Link to model, he agreed on the condition that the face didn't look like him. He didn't want to be recognized and then accused of showing off. *Cornhusker,* with its anonymous face, reflects the humility of both the model and the sculptor.

Petersen retired from the university in 1955 but continued to use his studio in the old Veterinary Quadrangle until his death in 1961 at age seventy-six. His final work can be seen at the Fisher Community Center in Marshalltown: an eight-foot figure of a man holding a child. Petersen had written, "I have carried out an idea. . . . I want to symbolize this generation helping the next generation to see beyond what it has been able to see . . . so the child is looking into the future, having a little more light." What a wonderful last artistic impression.

Carved in Butter

Norma Duffield (Duffy) Lyon came to Iowa State College (now Iowa State University) to become a veterinarian, but became known as the Butter Cow Lady—who turns butter into works of art.

She majored in animal science because women were not accepted in the veterinary program. While she was sculpting a horse and sleigh out of snow for a winter festival, Christian Petersen noticed her artistic talents and she began to study sculpting with him.

Duffy has created the State Fair's life-sized cow sculpted from butter since 1960. The butter cow, which promotes the state's dairy industry, has become a major fair attraction and a cherished tradition. Many other butter sculptures of hers have stood beside her cow in that forty-degree cooler, including Elvis Presley, Dwight and Mamie Eisenhower, the *American Gothic* farmer and daughter, and a recreation of *The Last Supper*. The sculptures last only for the duration of the fair. The butter from the sculptures is saved and reused to make more sculptures for about four years.

An interesting note: Duffy's maiden name is Stong, and her uncle Phil wrote the book *State Fair*, which was made into three movies and a Broadway musical.

Spillville Is Special to Composer and Carvers

Clock carving and composing don't seem to have much in common, but in the town of Spillville they do. Famous composer Antonin Dvořák lived in Spillville with his family during the summer of 1893 while he worked on two pieces of chamber music: the String Quartet in F Major, Opus 96, and

The Bily Clock Museum in Spillville, which features intricately carved clocks, is in the same house where composer Antonin Dvořák lived in the summer of 1893. (COURTESY IOWA TOURISM OFFICE)

the String Quintet in E Flat, Opus 97. He had come to Spillville to get away from New York City for a while, having been told that the area resembled his native Czechoslovakia. He often played old Bohemian hymns on the organ at Mass in St. Wenceslaus Church. The house Dvořák stayed in now also contains the Bily Clock Museum and is open to the public.

The Bily brothers, Joseph and Frank, local resident farmers, spent their winters hand-carving clocks for over forty-five years. They donated their amazing, intricate collection to the town of Spillville upon their deaths, with the condition that it never be moved from the house on Main Street. For information on the Bily Clock Museum/Antonin Dvořák Exhibit, visit *www.spillville.ia.us.*

Czech This Out

Clarabelle Taylor and her husband, Howard, run the Taylor Made Bed & Breakfast House on Main Street in Spillville, across from the Bily Clock

Museum/Antonin Dvořák Exhibit. Howard is one hundred percent Czech. His grandparents on both sides were from Czechoslovakia and he still speaks the language. His mother taught Clarabelle how to make *kolaches,* which she makes practically every day. Here's the recipe.

Kolaches (Czech Pastry)

1 tablespoon instant mashed potatoes

2 teaspoons salt

⅔ cup dry powdered milk

½ cup white sugar

2 cups warm water (105°F)

6 to 7 cups flour

2 tablespoons active dry yeast

2 eggs

1⅓ sticks (10⅔ tablespoons) margarine,

    melted (can use part lard)

2 to 3 cups prepared thick pie filling or cooked filling

    (such as prune, poppy seed, apricot, or cherry)

Mix together the instant mashed potatoes, salt, powdered milk, and sugar. Pour the warm water over this mixture and stir until the powdered milk is dissolved and the potatoes are softened. Add 3 cups of the flour and the yeast. Beat until mixed well and then let set until bubbly. Add the eggs and margarine. Beat in enough of the remainder of the flour until the dough is no longer sticky. Let it rise, punch it down, and pat it onto a bread board. Let the dough rise again, then spread it out into a ½-inch-thick layer. Using a pizza cutter, cut the dough into 2 x 2-inch squares. Put the filling in the center of each square and fold the corners up to meet in the center. Place the pastries on a cookie sheet and let rise until double in size (about 20 to 30 minutes, depending on the room temperature). Bake at 400 to 425°F for 6 to 7 minutes. Makes about 4 dozen.

The Lady Who Lived on a Ladder

Nellie Verne Walker, who was born in 1874, became one of America's foremost female sculptors. She sculpted the statue of James Harlan for Statuary Hall in the Capitol building in Washington, D.C., in 1907; the statue of Chief Keokuk in Keokuk's Rand Park in 1913; and the Polish War Memorial in Chicago in 1927. Walker, who was less than five feet tall, preferred large works of art and so was known as "the lady who lived on a ladder." She was born in Red Oak to Everett Ami Walker and his wife, Rebecca J. Lindsey, and grew up in Moulton. She learned to carve stone at her father's monument works, where he made tombstones. Walker died in 1973.

Ding Becomes Iowa's Darling

Although Jay Norwood Darling wasn't born in Iowa, the cartoonist and environmentalist called the state home and Iowans are proud to call him one of their own. He was born in a Congregational parsonage in Norwood, Michigan, on October 21, 1876. Because of his father's job as a minister, Darling lived in various towns around the Midwest, and he graduated from Beloit College, Wisconsin, in 1900. After graduation he took a job with the *Sioux City Journal* while his father was pastor at the Sioux City Congregational Church. Failing to get a photograph of a citizen for a story he was working on, he instead drew a caricature and showed it to the editor. The editor liked it and printed it on the front page, and before long cartoons signed "Ding" were a regular feature. He had used D'ing, a contraction of the name Darling, on some of these early cartoons, but he later changed it to plain Ding, without the apostrophe. Ding was his college nickname, and had been his father's and older brother's before him. It took Jay to make it famous.

In 1906 Darling became editorial cartoonist for the *Des Moines Register* and began to receive national attention. By 1917 his work was being distributed by the *New York Herald* Syndicate and eventually appeared in 135 newspapers. From 1911 to 1913 he lived in New York, on staff with the New York *Globe*. But he returned to Des Moines, feeling that he was losing vital contact with people and nature. He once wrote, "Out West we have to get our seafood canned. But rather canned seafood and fresh friendships than canned friendships and fresh seafood!"

An avid environmentalist, Darling designed the first federal duck stamp and was instrumental in the establishment of wildlife preservation laws, migratory waterfowl refuges, and soil conservation programs. He served on the Iowa State Conservation Commission, was the founder and first president of the National Wildlife Federation, and was chief of the U.S. Biological Survey from 1934 to 1935. He obtained seventeen million acres for wildlife restoration and ensured that ten million acres of public lands across the United States would be used for game preservation.

Darling believed his cartoons should express the principles of his convictions. His cartoons were seldom bitter, funny but never vulgar, and often critical but optimistic. He was one of the most respected cartoonists in American history and received Pulitzer Prizes for his work in 1923 and 1942. He also received the Theodore Roosevelt Award and the Nash Conservation Award. The Register and Tribune building in Des Moines was designated a historical site because Jay Norwood (Ding) Darling drew there.

Puppet on a String

Remember the Goatherd marionettes in *The Sound of Music?* Bil Baird from Mason City made those and many other wonderful puppets.

William Britton Baird's father, a chemical engineer, gave him a puppet when he was seven, igniting his son's interest in marionettes. Bil, who was born in 1904, graduated from Mason City High School and from the University of Iowa with a major in art and biology. He attended the Chicago Academy of Fine Arts and for five years apprenticed with marionette master Tony Sarg. For three of those years Baird helped produce the large balloons for Macy's Thanksgiving Day parades.

Baird and his wife, Cora, whom he met while working for Orson Wells's Mercury Theater in 1937, created thousands of puppets, including Charlemagne the Lion, Bubbles La Rue, and those Goatherd marionettes.

Bil Baird of Mason City constructed the Goatherd and Goat marionettes for The Sound of Music. (COURTESY THE BIL BAIRD PUPPET COLLECTION, CHARLES H. MACNIDER ART MUSEUM, MASON CITY, IOWA)

The Bairds performed in the Ziegfeld Follies in the 1940s, on television in the 1950s, and at two World's Fairs. They used puppets to encourage children to drink milk and eat vegetables in Latin America and took their puppet show to India, the Soviet Union, and Afghanistan. Baird died in 1987.

A collection of Bil Baird puppets, including the Goatherd marionettes, can be seen at the Charles H. MacNider Museum in Mason City. For more information visit *www.macniderart.org.*

All That Jazz

When Leon Bismarck (Bix) Beiderbecke was two years old, he could play "Yankee Doodle Dandy" on the piano, and at sixteen he learned to play the cornet. By 1924 he was playing with the Wolverine Orchestra and gaining a reputation. He loved to improvise and had a delicate touch and a sweet tone. He was a soloist with Paul Whiteman's Orchestra from 1928 to 1930.

Unfortunately, liquor was a problem for Bix and led to his death at age twenty-eight. He died in New York in 1931 of lobar pneumonia and edema of the brain and is buried in Oakdale Cemetery, Davenport. The Bix Beiderbecke Memorial Jazz Festival is held in Davenport annually.

Friend and mentor Louis (Satchmo) Armstrong once said: "I told Bix to just play and he'd please the cats, but you take a genius and he's never satisfied. . . . If that boy had lived, he'd be the greatest."

And the Band Played On

If you're an Iowan who enjoyed playing in your high school marching band or your town band, you can thank Karl L. King. King was born in 1891 in Ohio and started writing band music at age fourteen. In 1920 he and his bride were invited to guest conduct the Fort Dodge Municipal Band. They accepted the invitation—and never left.

King conducted the Fort Dodge Municipal Band for more than fifty years, until his death in 1971. Through the years he established the American Bandmasters Association and the Iowa Bandmasters Association. He was instrumental (no pun intended) in the passage of the Iowa Band Law, legislation that enabled municipalities to levy a small tax to support a municipal band, and directed the Iowa State Fair Band from 1921 to 1959.

Over the years he published three hundred musical compositions and many marches, which were intended especially for school bands. In 1962 he was elected to the Academy of Wind and Percussion Arts, the highest honor that can be given to a band director. And in 1971, despite having never taught in schools, he was awarded the Edwin Franco Goldman Award from the American School Bandmasters Association.

Fortunately for Iowans, this "King" marched in, kept on marching, and never marched out of his adoptive state. And in Fort Dodge the Karl L. King Marching Band still marches on, giving concerts each Sunday evening during the summer.

Strange . . . but True

Karl L. King's composition "In Old Portugal," which he wrote for famous aerialist Lillian Leitzel, was being played at her performance in Copenhagen on Friday the 13th, when she fell to her death. Leitzal performed on the Roman rings and was most famous for her one-arm rotations (up to 240 at a time). She fell in Copenhagen on February 13, 1931, when the equipment snapped, and she died of her injuries two days later.

From State Fair Blue Ribbons to an Academy Award

When Donnabelle Mullenger was born on January 27, 1921, in Denison, no one suspected that she would one day become a famous and much-loved actress, known as Donna Reed.

When Donnabelle was sixteen she boarded a train for Los Angeles to complete her formal education and pursue her dream of becoming an actress. The American public grew to love her for her sensitive portrayals in films including *It's a Wonderful Life* and *From Here to Eternity,* for which she won an Academy Award for Best Supporting Actress; and for her television series, *The Donna Reed Show*, which aired from 1958 to 1966. In that show she played a mother much like herself—honest, humorous, and nurturing. She was also the producer and director of the show, mastering both lighting and cinematography, while raising four children—Penny, Tony Jr., Tim, and Mary. Reed was proud of being an Iowa farm girl (she won blue ribbons in 4-H at the Iowa State Fair for her biscuits) and often returned to Denison. After her death from cancer at age sixty-five in early 1986, her Oscar was left to the city of Denison. When her family and friends gathered in Denison to honor her, the idea for the Donna Reed Festival and the Donna Reed Foundation for the Performing Arts was born. The first festivals, held in the summers of 1986 and 1987, consisted of Reed films shown at the Ritz Theater; proceeds from ticket sales were used to fund performing arts scholarships for Denison High School graduates.

The foundation soon grew. Formed in 1987 to honor Reed's accomplishments and to support talented individuals pursuing an education and a career in the performing arts, the foundation now provides scholarships, conducts workshops, and promotes cultural activities throughout the year. But the greatest focus of activity occurs each June at the Donna Reed Festival.

The festival features workshops, scholarships, and auditions. The foundation also supports a performing arts center, a full film archive, a museum, and professional studio facilities dedicated to developing new artists. Donna would be proud!

Setting the Story Straight

This story begins in Laurens, population about fifteen hundred, in northwest Pocahontas County, in northwest Iowa. From there, it goes east across Iowa to Mount Zion, Wisconsin—a distance of 253 miles.

Alvin Straight of Laurens, age seventy-three, walked with two canes and no longer had a driver's license due to poor eyesight. In July 1994 he found out that his eighty-year-old brother, Henry, who lives in Mount Zion, Wisconsin, had suffered a stroke. The two had not seen each other in years.

Alvin, wary of public transportation, decided to go to see Henry the only way he knew how to—by driving his lawn mower. He hooked on a trailer packed with food, camp gear, and extra gas and set out. Two days into his journey, his 1966 lawn mower broke down. Back in Laurens, Alvin bought a used John Deere lawn mower and started off again. At five miles per hour, ten hours per day, the trip took him six weeks. A few miles from his brother's place, the second lawn mower broke down and he had to be towed to his brother's house.

The story was featured in newspapers across the country, including the *New York Times,* as well as in magazines and on national television. A John Deere dealer in Texas gave Alvin a new $5,000 mower and put the old one on display back in Texas. In August 1998 filmmaker David Lynch came to Laurens with cast and crew to film *The Straight Story,* a movie about Alvin Straight's unusual journey. The film starred Richard Farnsworth as Alvin and Sissy Spacek as his daughter, Rose. Filmed in Laurens, West Bend, West

Union, Clermont, and Mount Zion, the filming took just about as long as Straight's trip. The *Chicago Tribune* rated the 1999 movie with four stars and the *New York Times* called it "an eloquently, simple, deeply emotional movie."

The moral: A resident of Iowa with a mission can accomplish a lot with a little.

Strange . . . but True

In Crescent, Iowa, you can visit a lawn mower museum called Engines of Yesteryear, run by Fred Archer. He has spent forty years repairing and collecting old mowers and has more than one hundred machines, including a reel mower more than a hundred years old. The most unique mower is a Flymo made in Britain with no wheels—it floats on a cushion of air while it mows.

More Movies Made in Iowa

★ *Penitentiary* (1938)

★ *Union Pacific* (1939)

★ *Cold Turkey* (1971)

★ *F.I.S.T.* (1978)

★ *One in a Million: The Ron LeFlore Story* (1978, for television)

★ *Pennies from Heaven* (1981)

★ *Take This Job and Shove It* (1981)

★ *Children of the Corn* (1984)

★ *Field of Dreams* (1989)

★ *In the Best Interest of the Children* (1992, for television)

★ *Crash Landing: The Rescue of Flight 232* (1992, for television)

★ *The Woman Who Loved Elvis* (1993, for television)

★ *The Bridges of Madison County* (1994)

★ *Twister* (1996)

★ *Cora Unashamed* (1999)

★ *Silverwings* (2000)

★ *Rain* (2000)

King and Bernhardt: One and the Same?

Look up "Sarah Bernhardt" in any encyclopedia and you will read that she was born Rosine Henriette Bernard in Paris on September 25, 1844, the daughter of Judith Van Hard, a Jewish Dutch girl of sixteen. But ever since Sarah King of Rochester, Iowa, ran off to join the carnival, an Iowa legend has claimed that she became Sarah Bernhardt.

Bernhardt was the most famous woman in France for more than fifty years, where her acting abilities and clear-as-a-bell voice became noticed. In her memoirs she wrote that her father was Edouard Bernhardt, a law student of high Belgian birth (other sources say he was French law student Paul Therard), who sent money for her education and paid for her art and sculpting classes when she was a child. At age fifteen she became enamored of the theater and after playing parts in various theaters, became a star while performing at the Comédie Française.

Sarah King's cousin, Mary Finefield Munn, said that Sarah was born on that same day in September but in Rochester, New York, to Mary and Dingsley King. Dingsley was a Jewish mason and plasterer. Mary, Dingsley, and their daughters—four-year-old Sarah and sister Lucy—were on their way to Iowa to visit when Dinglsey died in Ohio. Mary King continued on and being French Canadian, felt right at home in Rochester, Iowa, a French Huguenot settlement. Mary King died in 1851 and Sarah King ran off to join a carnival show in 1860, when she was almost sixteen. The rest of her story is that of Sarah Bernhardt, according to Sarah King's relatives.

So which story is true? In 1904 a heavily veiled woman came to Rochester, picked up bricks from the foundation of the old King house that had burned down some years before, and asked Fred Finefield to point out Mary King's grave. The next morning it was covered in fresh lilies and bricks near the headstone. The woman had come in a hack rented in Iowa City, where Sarah Bernhardt was appearing while on an American tour. Again, some years later, a veiled woman was driven by limousine from Davenport to Rochester and the next morning red roses were found on Mary King's grave. Sarah Bernhardt had been performing at the Burtis Theatre in Davenport on another American tour.

Sarah's cousins saw Bernhardt perform many times in her ten American tours between 1880 and 1918 and noted the strong family resemblance. They believed she adopted an exotic Parisian background to enhance her career.

Bernhardt gave birth to a son, Maurice, when she was twenty. The "Divine Sarah," one of the world's greatest emotional actresses, was one of the first silent movie stars, a sculptress, a painter, a writer, and a producer. She attracted publicity through her outrageous behavior, including having affairs with royalty and keeping a tigress and a lynx as pets. In 1914 her leg was amputated above the knee because her knee, which had been injured in an automobile accident, developed gangrene. So from 1915 to 1918 she was carried on and off the stage, and either leaned against props or sat down to perform.

Was her childhood spent in Iowa? The truth died with Sarah Bernhardt in Paris on March 23, 1923. She died of uremic poisoning following kidney failure and is buried in Le Pere Lachaise Cemetery, in Paris, the city that first embraced her.

The American Beauty

Lillian Russell, the actress and singer who had a legendary affair with railroad magnate, Diamond Jim Brady, was born Nellie Leonard in 1861 in Clinton, on the second floor of the Hotel Clinton. Charles Leonard, her father, was founder and editor of the *Clinton Herald*.

Nellie, an exquisite beauty, loved to sing and, at age eighteen, she went to New York City to pursue a singing career, taking on the name Lillian

Russell. Tony Pastorat introduced her at his casino and this launched her career as "the American Beauty."

The flamboyant Russell loved jewelry and was married four times. Known for her beauty, yet weighing from 145 to 165 pounds, she made plump figures fashionable. She would roll on the floor to try to keep down the size of her hips, and achieved her hourglass figure with tight-laced stays. She also, reportedly, tried to keep her youthful appearance by taking cold showers, eating lots of green onions, and hitting a punching bag.

It was Lillian's voice that President Grover Cleveland heard sing over the first long-distance telephone hookup. She died in 1922.

Entertainers Born in Iowa

★ **Felix Adler:** Born in Clinton in 1895, Adler was the star clown of the Ringling Brothers (also from Iowa) and Barnum & Bailey Circus for almost five decades. From 1919 to 1946 he never missed a performance. He was also known as the "White House Clown" because he was a favorite of the Hoover and Roosevelt grandchildren.

★ **Jack Bailey:** Born John Wesley Bailey III in Hampton in 1907 or 1908, Bailey was best known for hosting *Queen for a Day* from 1945 to 1964, first on radio and then on television. During that time he crowned more than five thousand women and gave away $23 million.

★ **Johnny Carson:** Carson was born in Corning on October 23, 1925. As a toddler his family moved to Clarinda, Red Oak, Avoca, and, finally, to Norfolk, Nebraska, when he was eight. His father worked for the Iowa-Nebraska Light & Power Company. Carson has donated to community projects in Avoca, Corning, Clarinda, and Logan, where his grandfather, Christopher Carson, was mayor from 1944 to 1948.

★ **William Frederick (Buffalo Bill) Cody:** Born in Scott County in 1846, by the age of fourteen Bill was delivering mail for the Pony Express. He earned his nickname by killing more than four thousand buffalo to feed railroad workers in Kansas. He started performing in western shows in 1872 and started his own "Wild West Show" in 1883. He died from uremia, following a kidney disease, in Denver in 1917.

★ **William Clement Frawley:** Born in Burlington in 1887, Frawley will probably always be best remembered as Fred Mertz from the *I Love Lucy* television show. Starting out as a court reporter in Chicago, he eventually found success in Broadway musicals as an Irish tenor and in more than a hundred movies, before being cast as Mertz in 1951. He died in 1966 of a heart attack.

★ **Harriet Nelson:** Harriet Snyder was born in Des Moines in 1909. Her mother was a musical comedy actress and her father was an actor-director. Her maternal grandfather was George McNutt, Des Moines police chief of detectives. Harriet married Oswald Nelson in 1935 after joining his band as a vocalist in 1932. Son David was born in 1936 and Rick in 1940. She starred in *The Adventures of Ozzie and Harriet,* which began on radio in 1944 and then transferred to television in 1952, where it aired for fourteen years. She died in 1994.

★ **Joy Hodges:** Born January 29, 1915, in Des Moines, Hodges launched her career in Chicago after winning a talent contest at the Paramount Theater. Besides singing, she appeared on Broadway, in movies, and on television. She introduced Ronald Reagan to her agent, who then sent him for a screen test. Reagan had interviewed Hodges earlier in Iowa while working for WHO radio, had seen her in 1937 when she was singing at Hollywood's Biltmore Bowl, and had confided his interest in acting.

★ **Cloris Leachman:** Born April 20, 1926, in Des Moines, Leachman started performing at age seven at Drake University Children's Theater. As a teenager, she had three radio shows on KSO and KRNT. She attended

Northwestern University, became Miss Chicago, and after participating in the Miss America pageant in 1946, started a successful career on Broadway. She was the funny Phyllis Lindstrom on the *Mary Tyler Moore Show,* had her own spin-off series from 1975 to 1977, and was on *The Facts of Life.* She won two of her six Emmys playing Phyllis.

★ **Jerry Mathers:** Born June 2, 1948, in Sioux City, Jerry's family moved to California when he was two because his father, Norman, got a job as a school principal. Jerry modeled toddler's clothes for catalogs and did some TV commercials. He later got parts in movies and in 1957 was cast as Theodore (Beaver) Cleaver on the *Leave It to Beaver* television show. That show lasted until 1963 and he still has fans all over the world because of it. Jerry continues to come to Iowa to visit.

★ **Elsa Maxwell:** Born in 1883 in a Keokuk opera house (she claimed), Maxwell became the world's best-known party giver. After supporting herself as a theater pianist, she went into vaudeville and by the end of World War I was organizing parties for European royalty. She invented the scavenger hunt and treasure hunt, which were popular party activities in the 1930s. She was also a songwriter, a columnist, a book writer, a radio show host, a lecturer, and an actress. She died of a heart ailment in 1963.

★ **Glenn Miller:** Born in Clarinda in March 1904, Miller became a composer and arranger as well as a bandleader. The Glenn Miller Orchestra, known for swing music, was at the height of its fame in the late 1930s and early 1940s and had more than forty top ten hits. "Chattanooga Choo Choo," introduced in 1941, spent fourteen weeks on the Hit Parade, sold 1.2 million copies, and was the nation's first gold record. At thirty-eight Miller joined the Army Air Corps and formed the Army Air Force Band. While crossing the English Channel on his way to Paris, his plane disappeared on December 15, 1944. The Glenn Miller Birthplace Home in Clarinda is open to visitors (see *www.glennmiller.org*).

★ **George Reeves:** Born in Woolstock on January 5, 1914, as George Keefer Brewer, George later took his stepfather's surname, Bessolo. He became George Reeves in 1939 when he started his movie career as Stuart, one of the Tarleton twins, in *Gone with the Wind.* He served in the Army in World War II. In 1951 he won the lead role in *The Adventures of Superman,* which ran on television from 1952 to 1957. His death by a gunshot wound to the head in 1959 was ruled a suicide. The 104 episodes of *Superman* continue as reruns.

★ **John Wayne:** Born May 26, 1907, in Winterset, Marion Robert Morrison had his name changed to Marion Michael Morrison when his younger brother was born and given the name Robert. After first moving to Earlham, the Morrisons moved to Lancaster, California, because it was a better climate for Marion's father's lungs. Director Raoul Walsh changed the actor's name in 1930 when he landed his first lead role in *The Big Trail.* Forever after, he was John Wayne and he became one of the biggest attractions in motion picture history, appearing in 250 movies and with a record 142 leading parts. John Wayne died on June 11, 1979, of lung and stomach cancer. His birthplace can be visited in Winterset (see *www.johnwaynebirthplace.org*).

★ **Andy Williams:** Born December 3, 1927, in Wall Lake, Howard Andrew Williams and his sister and three brothers sang in the choir of the Presbyterian Church. When Andy was seven, they moved to Des Moines and later the Williams Brothers Quartette—Dick, Don, Bob, and Andy— began singing on WHO radio's *Sunset Corners Barn Dance Frolic.* The brothers signed a contract with WLS radio in Chicago in 1940, so the family moved to Illinois. Andy's solo career started in 1953 and his television show ran from 1962 to 1971, earning three Emmys. He has had his own theater in Branson, Missouri, since 1992 and in 1998 his birthplace was designated a historic site.

Iowa's Musical Cheerleader

You probably know Meredith Willson, who was born in Mason City in 1902, from his foot-tapping classic musical *The Music Man.*

His parents, John and Rosalie believed they could influence their children's futures by their actions during pregnancy. They wanted their first child to be a writer so they talked about famous authors and works of literature, their second a businessman so they discussed financial matters, and their third a musician so they played music. Dixie, their first child, became a writer of children's stories, radio shows, and screenplays. Their second child, Cedric, became vice president of Texas Industries. And the musical abilities of their third child, Robert Meredith became known worldwide. It doesn't completely prove their theory, but it sure makes you think!

Willson called *The Music Man* "an Iowan's attempt to pay tribute to his home state." Some of his best known songs are: "May the Good Lord Bless and Keep You," "It's Beginning to Look Like Christmas," "Seventy-six Trombones" and "Till There Was You." He died in June 1984 and was buried in Mason City.

A statue of Meredith Willson stands outside the Music Man Square complex in Mason City. (PHOTO BY AUTHOR)

In 1999 an ambitious $10 million project was started, called Music Man Square, to honor Mason City's favorite son. The complex, located next to the Willson home, contains a River City streetscape, a community theater, Reunion Hall, a gift shop, and a museum. When the project is complete, the complex will also contain a conservatory for music education and an exploratorium. (Visit *www.themusicmansquare.org* for more information.)

Willson was a life-long cheerleader for Iowa. He believed in the lyrics he wrote that said, "You ought to give Iowa a try!" (from "Iowa Stubborn," *The Music Man*).

Iowa Stubborn

Oh, there's nothing halfway about
The Iowa way we treat you,
When we treat you,
Which we may not do at all!
There's an Iowa kind,
A kind-a chip-on-the-shoulder attitude,
We've never been without that we recall!

We can be as cold as our falling
Thermometers in December, if you ask about our weather in July.
And we're so by-gone stubborn, we can
Stand touching noses for a week at a time,
And never see eye to eye.

But we'll give you our shirt,
And a back to go with it,
If your crop should happen to die.

So what the heck!
You're welcome!
Glad to have you with us!
Even though we may not ever mention it again!
You really ought to give Iowa,
Hawk-eye, Iowa,
Dubuque, Des Moines, Davenport, Marshalltown,
Mason City, Ke-o-kuk, Ames,
Clear Lake!
You really ought to give Iowa a try!

—"IOWA STUBBORN" FROM MEREDITH WILLSON'S *THE MUSIC MAN*.

Did You Know? Riverside, Iowa, claims to be the future
birthplace of Captain James T. Kirk of the Starship *Enterprise*. Residents say
he will be born there on March 21, 2228, and they host a Riverside Trek Fest
there each year, on the last Friday and Saturday of June, in anticipation.

The Iowa Writers' Workshop

Creativity is awarded a master's degree thanks to Carl Seashore, dean of
the graduate college at the University of Iowa, who in 1922 announced that
students could submit creative work for their theses. Paul Engle took advan-
tage of this opportunity, using his first manuscript as his thesis to receive a
University of Iowa Master of Fine Arts degree.

Engle, who was born October 12, 1908, in Cedar Rapids and had
received his bachelor's degree from Coe College, later took over a series of
conferences for verse writers—which became the Iowa Writers' Workshop.

Engle went on to establish the Translation Workshop and, with his wife,
novelist Hua-ling Nieh, the International Writing Program. For their work with
this program, the Engles were nominated for the Nobel Peace Prize in 1976.

Clark Blaise, who once directed the International Program, described
Engle as "the most influential writer of this century, not for what he wrote,
but for what he did for other writers."

Here are some writers who have attended the Iowa Writers' Workshop,
along with examples of their later work, which gained acclaim.

★ W. P. Kinsella (*Shoeless Joe*, 1982)

★ Jane Smiley (*A Thousand Acres*, 1991)

★ Marjorie Holmes, born in Storm Lake in 1910 (*Two from Galilee*, 1972;
Three from Galilee: The Young Man from Nazareth, 1985; *The Messiah*, 1987)

★ (Mary) Flannery O'Connor ("The Geranium," 1946; *Wise Blood*, 1952)

★ Max A. Collins Jr., (writer of the *Dick Tracy* comic strip from 1977 to
1993; *Road to Perdition*, 1998)

Did You Know? MacKinlay Kantor, born February 4, 1904, in Webster City, won a Pulitzer Prize in 1956 for his book *Andersonville* about the infamous Civil War prison camp. He made his book *Glory for Me* into a movie script, which became the 1946 classic *The Best Years of Our Lives* and won seven Oscars, including best picture. Kantor died in 1977 and his ashes are buried at Graceland Cemetery, Webster City.

The Adventures of James Norman Hall

Born April 22, 1887, at Colfax, James Norman Hall became best known for his stories of the South Pacific. Hall graduated from Grinnell College in 1910, did social work in Boston, and then sailed to the British Isles to tour Scotland by bicycle. During World War I he was in the British Army and then became a pilot for the Lafayette Escadrille, a group of thirty-eight American volunteer pilots who flew and fought for the Allies before the United States entered the war. The Lafayette Escadrille was founded in April 1916 and in February 1918 it was absorbed into the U.S. forces as the 103rd Pursuit Squadron.

After the war, in which Hall was taken prisoner by Germany and later honored as a war hero, he and his friend, Charles Nordhoff, went to Tahiti to spend six months writing. Tahiti became Hall's home for the rest of his life. Both he and Nordhoff married women of partial Tahitian heritage, raised families, and collaborated in writing. Their best-known work is *Mutiny on the Bounty* (1932), which was made into a movie starring Clark Gable and Charles Laughton and won the Oscar for best picture in 1935.

Hall, who came back to Iowa in 1928, 1936, and 1950, said, "My tap roots are in Iowa." He died of a heart ailment and was buried in Tahiti on a hill overlooking Matavai Bay. A plaque near his grave is inscribed with a poem that he wrote as a boy in Iowa.

Washington Calling

In 1970 the first Pulitzer Prize ever given for distinguished commentary was awarded to Marquis William Childs. Born in Clinton in 1903, Childs graduated from the University of Wisconsin in 1923 and received a master's degree from the University of Iowa in 1925. He joined the United Press and then became a feature writer for the *St. Louis Post-Dispatch* in 1926.

In 1934 he began his column "Washington Calling" at his newspaper's Washington bureau. This column was eventually syndicated in about two hundred newspapers including the *Des Moines Register*.

Childs became an expert on politics and a news correspondent in Europe in 1945. He also became a popular speaker and wrote books, including *This Is Democracy* and *Mighty Mississippi: The Biography of a River*. He died in 1990 of a heart ailment.

Advice Columnist Times Two

Twins Esther Pauline and Pauline Esther were born in Sioux City on the fourth of July in 1918 to Abe and Becky Friedman, Russian Jewish immigrants. Esther, nicknamed "Eppie," and Pauline, called "Po-Po," were five feet, two inches tall with black hair and blue eyes when they graduated from Central High School in 1936. They attended Morningside College until their double wedding in 1939. Eppie married Jules Lederer, a salesman from Detroit, and Po-Po married Morton Phillips of Minnesota. The Lederers moved to Chicago in 1954 and a year later Eppie became the new Ann Landers, taking over for the *Chicago Sun-Times* columnist who had died. Less than three months later, in early 1956, Po-Po became advice columnist Abigail Van Buren for the *San Francisco Chronicle*.

At one time the sisters reportedly received fifteen thousand letters a week and had an estimated two hundred million readers. Ann Landers (Eppie) died on June 22, 2002, in Chicago at age eighty-three. Dear Abby (Po-Po) lives in Beverly Hills, and her daughter now writes her column. The twins will forever be linked together as the world's most widely read advice columnists.

A Keokuk Newspaper Gives Mark Twain His Start

Samuel Langhorne Clemens, later known as Mark Twain, lived in Iowa while a young man. He moved to Muscatine in the summer of 1854 to join his older brother Orion, who had purchased the *Muscatine Journal* in 1853. Later, when remembering the sunsets in Muscatine, Twain would write, "I have never seen any, on either side of the ocean, that equaled them. They used the broad smooth river as a canvas, painted on it every imaginable dream of color, from the mottled daintiness and delicacies of the opal, all the way up . . . to blinding purple and crimson conflagrations, which were enchanting to the eye. . . . It is true Sunset Land."

After being away for about a year, Twain returned to Iowa in 1855 and worked for Orion for two years at his Keokuk printing business. At a printers' banquet in Keokuk on January 17, 1856, he gave his first after-dinner talk. The *Keokuk Post* was the first paper to buy his written material. In 1886 he, his wife, Olivia, and their children attended a family reunion in Rand Park in Keokuk on the Fourth of July. And in 1889 he bought a home for his mother, Jane Clemens, then age eighty-two, at 626 High Street in Keokuk.

Mark Twain was born in Missouri, but apparently liked the Iowa shores of the Mississippi pretty well.

Whodunit? We Finally Know!

She is a pretty, athletic, and smart young woman. Her fearlessness and determination, coupled with her power of observation, allow her to fulfill her desire of helping others feel safe. She has been described as a female Robin Hood and she has inspired and captivated three generations of girls. She is a book character and her name is Nancy Drew.

Edward Stratemeyer of the Stratemeyer Syndicate created the name and concept of the female sleuth, Nancy Drew. (The same company published the Bobbsey Twins and Hardy Boys fiction series.) But it was Mildred Augustine Wirt Benson who brought Nancy to life. In 1930 Stratemeyer asked Augustine, then twenty-five, to write the Nancy Drew mysteries. She agreed, signing a secrecy contract saying she wouldn't reveal her identity as the author. She wrote the first book, *The Secret of the Old Clock,* in two months and by the end of that year had written the first four volumes under the pseudonym Carolyn Keene. She received $125 per book and no royalties, and, until 1980, no recognition as the author.

Benson was born on July 10, 1905, in Ladora, Iowa, to Dr. J. L. and Lillian Augustine. She sold her first story at age twelve for $2.50 to *St. Nicholas* magazine and went on to write more than 130 books. She earned a journalism degree from the University of Iowa in 1925 and in 1927 earned a master's degree in journalism, the first awarded there. For a year she worked at the *Clinton Herald,* then moved to Cleveland, Ohio, and later to Toledo, with her husband, Asa Alvin Wirt. He died in 1947 and Mildred married George A. Benson, editor of the *Toledo Times.* She worked for the *Times* from 1944 to 1975, when it ceased publication, and then became a reporter and columnist for the *Toledo Blade.* Although officially retired at the end of 2001, she continued to go into work once a week to write her column "On the Go with Millie." She became ill while at work, was taken to the hospital, and died after going into respiratory arrest on May 28, 2002. Her daughter, Margaret (Peggy) Wirt, survives her.

For fifty years Benson kept her identity as the author of twenty-three Nancy Drew books secret. In 1979 Harriet Stratemeyer Adams sold the rights of the syndicate to Simon & Schuster. In 1980, when Benson testified in a court case involving the publisher and the rights, the world learned of her identity.

Benson wrote volumes 1–7 of the Nancy Drew series (1930–1932), volumes 11–25 (1937–1948), and volume 30 (1951). (Volumes 8, 9, and 10 were written by a man!) She put herself into the character and it shows. When Benson was a swimming instructor, so was Nancy (volume 3), and after Benson took flying lessons and got her pilot's licenses (commercial, private, seaplane, and instrument), Nancy flew planes (volumes 14 and 22).

Four Nancy Drew films were made in 1938 and 1939 and a board game was produced, but Benson never received any royalties. Only her readers— and the publisher—benefited.

ARTS AND ENTERTAINMENT TRIVIA

Q. What did the fathers of George Reeves, John Wayne, and Jean Seberg have in common?

A. They were druggists or pharmacists in Iowa.

Q. What CBS news broadcaster and *60 Minutes* reporter was born in Dakota City in 1923?

A. Harry Reasoner.

Q. What Iowa connection did band conductor Paul Whiteman and author Ernest Hemingway have in common?

A. They both had grandparents in Iowa (Whiteman's near Bedford and Hemingway's near Dyersville).

Q. What famous brother singing duo, with hits such as "Bye Bye Love" and "Cathy's Clown," got their professional start in Shenandoah on radio station KMA?

A. Don and Phil Everly.

Q. What Miss Universe winner was from Ottumwa?

A. Carol Morris, in 1956.

Q. What Arnold's Park native is the only artist to win the Federal Duck Stamp competition five times?

A. Maynard Reece.

Q. What composer, born in Oskaloosa and known as America's Waltz King, wrote "Missouri Waltz," which was adopted as Missouri's state song in 1949?

A. Frederick Knight Logan.

Q. What novel by Fort Dodge native Thomas Heggen became a play and a film starring Henry Fonda?

A. *Mister Roberts.*

Q. What New York fashion designer was born in Des Moines in 1932 as Roy Frowick?

A. Roy Halston.

Q. What Burnside native won a Pulitzer Prize for his national reporting on Jimmy Hoffa in 1958?

A. Clark Raymond Mollenhoff.

Q. Vincent (V. T.) Hamlin, born in Perry in 1900, created what famous comic strip?

A. *Alley Oop.*

Q. James Stevens, born November 25, 1892, in Moravia, published what book of fantastic tales in 1925?

A. *Paul Bunyan.*

Q. What phrase became part of the American vernacular when John Hartzell Spence, founding editor of *Yank*, the World War II newspaper for American troops, put pictures of actresses and models into the newspaper?

A. Pin-up girl.

11
Natural Phenomena

How Big? It Was Jumbo!

The residents of Belle Plaine discovered in 1882 that they were in the midst of an artesian well area. They had dug wells for refrigeration, drinking water, and fire protection. In August 1886 the city hired William Weir to dig a well for the south part of town and the school. Using a two-inch drill he struck water at 193 feet and quit. By the next day the normal flow of water had turned into a rushing torrent.

The townsfolk, concerned, tried to fill it and have it capped, but to no avail. "Jumbo," as the well came to be called, grew to three feet wide. Streets were flooded with water and sand. Two twelve-foot wide ditches were dug from the well to the Iowa River to carry the water. Soon people began to gather to see the wondrous well. One person got too close, fell in, and was shot back out as though by a cannon.

Finally, using hydraulic jacks and huge amounts of sand and cement, Jumbo was closed on October 6, 1887. In its fourteen-month "life" Jumbo spewed up between five hundred and a thousand carloads of sand and an estimated five million gallons of water per day. It had "eaten" 40 carloads of stone, 130 barrels of cement, 77 feet of 16-inch pipe, 60 feet of 5-inch pipe, 162 feet of 18-inch pipe, an iron cone 3 feet in diameter and 25 feet long, and uncounted loads of sand and clay. The site of Jumbo at Eighth Avenue and Eighth Street in Belle Plaine is marked by a plaque on a boulder and is paved over.

Stran©e . . . but True

William Harmon and Norman Reeve built a dam on the Cedar River in 1854 in what is now Waverly. A flour mill was built on the east end of the dam and soon a sawmill was ready for operation. When the water was allowed to flow through the new mill, the clear water came out looking dirty. The foundation was being washed away! Hay, stones, and logs were thrown in to try to stop up the hole, but nothing worked. Finally, Mrs. R. J. Ellsworth suggested that straw beds be used. All agreed and soon eleven straw ticks were gathered and stuffed into the hole. This alleviated the problem and the mill was saved, but it took almost every bed in town!

Therapeutic Mineral Water No Longer Tapped

In the early 1900s the Colfax mineral springs were known all over the world for their therapeutic benefits. Water from the mineral springs was sold throughout the United States in ten-, twenty-, and fifty-gallon jugs. Barrels of it were sent to the White House by order of President Grover Cleveland's physician. Except for two periods of time, once when the pipes running up from the springs were clogged due to earthquake activity, and once when the well was asphalted over for a highway, the mineral water has been available for sale and has been shipped all over the world. But since late 2002 that is no longer the case. The newer well has not dried up, but the finances have.

According to Marilyn Schmitt, who with her husband, Lee, ran the Colfax Mineral Springs Water Company for its stockholders, the costs of digging a new well, relocating the company down the street, meeting increasingly demanding government water-testing requirements, competing with big-name companies, and shipping the water proved to be too much. At this time the mineral water is no longer being pumped. It's there for the drinking, but it will take someone with deeper pockets to make it flow again.

Botanical Rarities on Dead Man's Lake

In the southwest corner of Pilot Knob State Park, three miles east of Forest City, is a small, eight-acre lake called Dead Man's Lake. The most plausible story about how the lake got its name concerns a lone Indian, who stayed behind to live near the lake when his fellow tribesmen moved on. Apparently, he had been unsuccessful at becoming head shaman of the tribe and had decided to quit tribal life. When he died, his tribe buried him there in a cave and sealed up the entrance. The entrance was so well disguised that no one has ever discovered it.

Another theory about the name contends that an early pioneer drove his ox-drawn wagon onto the frozen lake and drowned when the ice gave way.

No matter how the name came to be, the truth is that Dead Man's Lake is a very unusual lake, especially in Iowa. Nearly half of the lake is composed of a floating sphagnum bog, the only one in the state. The lake has no inlet or outlet, and the resultant acidic water has become gradually overgrown with sphagnum, also know as peat moss. The moss has formed a mat on the water, and humus and soil have slowly built up around the vegetation, resulting in a bog that is spongy, yet firm enough to walk on in places. But don't stay in one place too long, as your feet will continue to slowly sink.

Besides sphagnum, the other rare form of life at Dead Man's Lake is the sun dew plant. The sun dew thrives in the sphagnum bog, and the lake is the only place in Iowa where the carnivorous plant can be found. The low-growing sun dew, related by feeding habits to the Venus's-flytrap, eats insects for lunch. At the end of the hair-like red stalks that cover the leaves of the sun dew is a clear, sticky substance that entices and traps unwary insects. After the insects die, the plant digests the remains.

The highly acid water of Dead Man's Lake doesn't support fish but is a habitat requirement for the sun dew, which can be identified by its round, green leaves, about three-eighths of an inch long, with a pink fringe. White flowers appear in mid-summer on three- to ten-inch stems.

If you go looking for the sun dew, be careful on the bog. You might give the locals another story to tell about how the lake got its name!

Water, Water Everywhere

Called the most costly, most devastating flood in U.S. history, the flood of 1993 was considered the greatest natural disaster in Iowa's history. As many as 23 million acres of agricultural and urban land in the Upper Midwest were covered by floodwaters. The entire city of Des Moines was without running water for eleven days and without drinking water for twenty days. Iowa State University's Hilton Coliseum was flooded up to the center court scoreboard. The wet weather that had started early in the year was followed by intense rainstorms in late June and July and led to the unusual duration and magnitude of the flood.

The North Lee County Historical Center in Fort Madison houses the 1993 Flood Museum.

The headlines in the Des Moines Register on July 12, 1993, proclaimed the disastrous effects of the flood. (COPYRIGHT 1993, REPRINTED WITH PERMISSION OF THE DES MOINES REGISTER)

Stran©e . . . but True

The town of Littleport, Iowa, is no more. On May 16, 1999, the Volga River flooded and destroyed the town, and it was not rebuilt. The eighty-eight residents of 1990 had dwindled to just twenty-six people. Mayor J. P. Zapf offered the town on the Internet to any Hollywood studio as "the town you can blow up" for an action movie. Then came September 11, 2001. There were no takers. So in the fall of 2002 the town was razed and most of its residents relocated. Now a barren piece of land between the Volga River and Honey Creek, the area is going to be turned into an informal park for camping.

Don't Like the Weather? Just Wait!

Weather has always been a universal topic of conversation, but nowhere is that more true than Iowa. People like to say, "If you don't like the weather in Iowa, just wait a day." Situated centrally between the Rockies and the Appalachians, air masses channeled down from the north and up from the south tend to collide right over Iowa—and as a result the weather can fluctuate a great deal.

Only Kansas has more tornadoes. Summer days can be hot and humid or rainy and cold. Unpredictable winds can change temperatures fifty degrees within twenty-four hours.

Some state weather averages:

★ Tornadoes per year: 34 (total number is second only to Kansas)

★ Highest temperature: 72.1 degrees, in August

★ Lowest temperature: 17.3 degrees, in January

★ Annual rainfall: 32 inches

★ Annual snowfall: 32 inches

★ Annual temperature: 48 degrees

★ Rainiest month: June

And some state records:

★ Snowfall for one day: 24 inches in Lenox on April 20, 1918

★ Rainfall for one day: 12.99 inches in Larabee on June 24, 1891

★ High temperature: 118 degrees in Keokuk on July 20, 1934

★ Low temperature: −47 degrees in Washta on January 12, 1912

★ Snowiest month: December 2000, 24.7 inches statewide

Did You Know? One of the worst tornadoes in Iowa history hit Camanche on June 30, 1860. Thirty-nine businesses were destroyed, including two churches, and 300 of the 350 homes there were damaged or destroyed. Forty-one people in Camanche died and eighty more were injured. The Camanche tornado killed 125 people in Hardin, Linn, Jones, and Clinton counties.

A Blizzard by Any Other Name

The word "blizzard" has had several meanings, but it came into wide use as a means of describing a violent snowstorm after first appearing in print in the Estherville newspaper in 1870.

The word originally described a heavy blow, and then a volley of musket fire. But O. C. Bates, editor of the Estherville *Northern Vindicator*, used it to describe a storm of wind and snow that cut the town off by drifts on March 14, 1870. He and William Jensen of Estherville are often given credit for coining this use of the word, but both of them might have picked it up from the families of Estherville children tutored by Lephe Wells Coates of Spencer.

Coates, whose husband, Romanzo, was Spencer's first postmaster and a Free Baptist minister, had read the word in her Free Baptist paper, the *Morning Star*, as the name of a man who had a raging temper—Mr. Blizzard. One morning in the winter of 1867–68 she looked out the window and exclaimed, "My, it's a regular Old Man Blizzard of a storm." Her children and the children she tutored that winter adopted the term. This usage of the word became common and is now used everywhere.

Strange . . . but True

According to local sources, Mrs. Samuel Butters, who arrived with her husband in the Prairie City area in 1857, recalled one year when her husband piled corn up as high as the house. The pile was frozen solid by a heavy sleet and rain, forming a natural roof. Mr. Butters then picked a hole in the pile for a door and proceeded to take out enough corn to make a stable for his horses. The "corn barn" stood all winter.

Attack of the Hoppers

Northwestern Iowa was hit hard by the ravages of grasshoppers—actually called Rocky Mountain locusts—from 1873 until 1879, but the devastation in the summers from 1873 to 1875 was especially significant.

Thomas Barry from O'Brien County described the grasshopper invasion this way: "A large black cloud suddenly appeared high in the west from which came an ominous sound. The apparition moved directly toward us, its dark appearance became more and more terrifying, and the sound changed to a deep hum. At first we thought a cyclone was upon us. . . . The cloud broadened out and settled lower as it drew near; the noise became deafening. When it was directly over us it looked like a heavy storm of black flakes, the dark particles singling out and becoming more defined in shape as they descended. We heard the buzzing; we saw the shining wings, the long bodies, the legs.

Rocky Mountain locusts (Caloptenus spretus), *commonly called grasshoppers, hit north-western Iowa hard in the summers from 1873 to 1875.* (DRAWING FROM AN 1877 ENTOMOLO-GIST'S REPORT)

The grasshoppers—the scourge of the prairie—were upon us."

In a few short weeks, the "hoppers" devastated six counties of northwest Iowa as if swept by fire. The noise made by the vast swarms of migratory grasshoppers when they were busily devouring everything in sight was similar to the low crackling and rasping sound of a prairie fire swept along before a brisk wind. When they left, the land resembled a desert, with nothing green remaining. Sometimes they even ate the clothes right off the line. They did leave behind eggs deposited in the soil, to hatch out in the spring.

There were so many grasshoppers that the cattle wouldn't touch the grass and grew thin. Sometimes so many grasshoppers accumulated on the railroad tracks that the oil from their crushed bodies wouldn't allow trains to continue up grades. The rails would have to be sanded for the train to get enough traction to proceed.

The grasshopper invasion, coupled with the financial panic of 1873, caused many in northwest Iowa to leave. But some stuck it out and just as quickly and mysteriously as they had come, the grasshoppers left, disappearing to the northeast, never to return in such numbers again.

Yum, Yum—A Tasty Food Source

Iowa State University has a "Tasty Insect Recipe" website with recipes such as Chocolate-Covered Grasshoppers and Corn Borer Cornbread Muffins. Visit at *www.ent.iastate.edu/misc/insectsasfood.html.* Here's one of the mouth-watering recipes:

Chocolate Chirpie Chip Cookies

$2\frac{1}{4}$ cups flour

1 teaspoon baking soda

1 teaspoon salt

1 cup butter, softened

$\frac{3}{4}$ cup sugar

$\frac{3}{4}$ cup brown sugar

1 teaspoon vanilla

2 eggs

$\frac{1}{2}$ cup dry-roasted crickets

1 12-ounce bag chocolate chips

1 cup chopped nuts

Preheat oven to 375°F. In a small bowl, combine the flour, baking soda, and salt; set aside. In a large bowl, combine the butter, sugar, brown sugar, and vanilla; beat until creamy. Beat in the eggs. Gradually add the flour mixture and insects; mix well. Stir in the chocolate chips and nuts. Drop by rounded measuring teaspoonfuls onto an ungreased cookie sheet. Bake for 8 to 10 minutes. (RECIPE COURTESY OF IOWA STATE UNIVERSITY UNDERGRADUATE ENTOMOLOGY CLUB)

Strange . . . but True

Scientists at Iowa State University have discovered that plain catnip is more effective at repelling mosquitoes than most over-the-counter bug repellents. Bug experts compared the essential oil in catnip with DEET—the main ingredient in most commercial insect repellents—and found catnip was ten times more effective at shooing away mosquitoes. Unfortunately, concentrated catnip has an unpleasant scent that most humans wouldn't want to wear.

Famous Meteorites We Have Known

In mid-August and mid-November you can see meteor showers from Earth. If the meteor falls to Earth, then it is called a meteorite—and Iowa has a few notable ones. Here's a partial list:

★ **Marion Meteorite:** Fell just before 3 P.M. on February 25, 1847, the day that legislation establishing the University of Iowa was signed into law in Iowa City. The largest fragment is on display in the Old Capitol Building, now the University Administration Building.

★ **Amana Meteorite:** Fell just before 10:30 P.M. on February 12, 1875. More than eight hundred pounds of fragments were collected southwest of Homestead in Iowa County.

★ **Estherville Meteorite:** Fell at 5 P.M. on May 10, 1879. This is one of the largest meteorites on record, with fragments weighing 431, 152, and 101 pounds and hundreds of smaller pieces recovered. A monument on State Highway 4, a mile and a half north of Estherville commemorates the event. Pieces can be seen in the Estherville Public Library. The three large chunks were purchased by various museums around the world.

★ **Forest City Meteorite:** Fell late in the afternoon of May 2, 1890, eleven miles northwest of Forest City in Winnebago County. Fragments showered an eight-square-mile area and the fall was seen as far away as Chamberlain, South Dakota, three hundred miles away.

★ **Mapleton Meteorite:** Was discovered July 17, 1939, by farmer Harvey Meevers while cultivating corn on his farm northeast of Mapleton in Monona County. By chance the July issue of *National Geographic* had an article on meteorites and the 108-pound "mass of iron" that Meevers had found was identified. The Field Museum of Natural History in Chicago purchased it.

Peregrine Pair Seeks Insurance

Peregrine falcons are listed as an endangered species in Iowa, and since 1993 a pair of them has been nesting atop the American Republic Insurance Building in downtown Des Moines. The Iowa Department of Natural Resources (DNR) had a video camera trained on the nest with a continuous live feed on the Internet. They hatched at least one chick in 2002 and the DNR plans to have the WebCam set up again in May of 2003.

There were four other peregrine falcon pairs spotted in Iowa last year:

★ Atop the MidAmerican Energy building in Davenport

★ On a cliff near the Lansing power plant

★ On a smokestack at the Louisa Generating Station

★ Atop the US Bank building in Cedar Rapids

Seems to me they all must be people watchers!

Did You Know? There is also a trumpeter swan WebCam which goes online in late May or early June. The swans are located at the Mitchell County Nature Center. Iowa began a trumpeter swan restoration project in 1995. Although the swans were once native to this area, in 1933

there were only sixty-nine of them left, and all of them were at the Red Rock Lakes National Wildlife Refuge in Montana. The initial goal of the Iowa DNR was to have fifteen free-flying nesting pairs of trumpeters in Iowa by the end of summer 2003. In 2002 there were ten pairs reported in the state.

In 1995 Iowa began a trumpeter swan restoration project; there are currently ten nesting pairs in the state. (COURTESY UNION SLOUGH NATIONAL WILDLIFE REFUGE, TITONKA)

Lions and Wolves and Bears—Oh, No!

There had been no definitive sightings of mountain lions in Iowa since 1865 in Appanoose County—until 1995. As more and more lion sightings were reported, Ron Andrews, the state's DNR fur-bearer resource biologist, decided to issue a press release in early August 2001 about the possible reemergence of the mountain lion in Iowa. Just two weeks later, all doubts were put to rest when a car struck and killed a 130-pound lion near Harlan in Shelby County. The mountain lion was mounted and can be seen at the Nature Center at Nishna Bend Recreation Area in Shelby County.

There have been a handful of black bear sightings in northeast Iowa, and gray wolves have been documented as far south as Winona, Minnesota, not far from the Iowa border. But Ron Andrews doubts that Iowa will ever have significant numbers of large predators, even though it is amazing how adaptable they can be.

By the way, just in case you come upon a mountain lion, here are a few tips:

★ Try to maintain your composure, move slowly, and don't run.

★ Make noise.

★ If you're wearing a coat, try to puff up as big as possible.

The most likely reaction of the animal would be to escape into cover in a place far away from where it was spotted. Let's hope so!

Other Iowa Endangered Species

Here are some other endangered species that can be found in Iowa:

★ **Animals**
  • Blue-spotted salamander
  • Mudpuppy
  • Barn owl
  • Lake sturgeon

- Spotted skunk
- Prairie rattlesnake
- Dakota skipper butterfly
- Higgin's-eye pearly mussel

★ **Plants**
- Swamp loosestrife
- Winterberry
- Northern lungwort
- Narrow-leaved milkweed
- Pale false foxglove

Strange . . . but True

An elm tree was planted 1.7 miles northwest of Otley in Marion County in 1876 to commemorate the U.S. centennial. The original elm was killed by Dutch elm disease and replaced. If you go to see it, don't think you've forgotten your fourth-grade botany. It looks like an oak tree because it *is* an oak tree. The elm was replaced with a pin oak, but the original DAR marker still remains and reads "Centennial Elm Tree."

Those Gnaw-ty Beavers!

In October of 2002, a one thousand-gallon manure spill in Chickasaw County was caused by and halted by beavers. It seems that the beavers weren't too happy when their space was invaded by a flexible hose that ran from a hog-finishing operation's manure lagoon, under a bridge, over their creek and up to the manure-spreading equipment.

Apparently, during the night, the beavers, whose dam was thirty feet downstream from the hose, chewed holes in it. Pumping was stopped when manure was noticed in the creek bed below the bridge. Fortunately, the beaver dam contained the spill and the manure was simply pumped out of the beaver's holding pond and onto the fields.

Storm Damage Doesn't Stump Him

Chainsaw carver Brian Ruth created five wood sculptures from storm-damaged trees on the Iowa State Fairgrounds in 1998. One portrays an Iowa farmer, pig at his feet, looking over at his granddaughter who's holding flowers behind her back. Another depicts a mother taking a picture of her child holding a fair ribbon as she rests in her father's arms. There is also a sculpture of an older woman resting on a real bench. (You can sit down beside her—she won't mind.) These permanent works of art have become a real attraction at the fair.

Strange . . . but True

In 1880, a surveyor used his walking stick to mark a section line northwest of Anita. The stick took root, sprouted, and grew in the cen-

ter of the intersection of the county roads bordering the fields being measured at the time. Though the state eventually wanted it removed, the locals insisted that it remain. The cottonwood still stands in the middle of the road, showing no scars from being hit by passing traffic, and proving that you *can* fight "city hall."

The Tree in the Middle of the Road, northwest of Anita, near the Cass and Audubon County line, grew from a surveyor's walking stick stuck in the ground in 1880.
(COURTESY AUDUBON COUNTY ECONOMIC DEVELOPMENT CORPORATION)

NATURAL PHENOMENA TRIVIA

Q. What is the state rock?

A. Geode, designated in 1967.

Q. How many different types of fish are found in Iowa?

A. 149.

Q. Fort Dodge is one of the world's leading makers of products made from what mineral?

A. Gypsum.

Q. How many species of birds are found in Iowa?

A. 227.

Q. What is the state bird?

A. Eastern goldfinch, designated in 1933.

Q. What percentage of Iowa is forest?

A. Four percent.

Q. What is the state flower of Iowa?

A. The wild prairie rose (Rosa pratincola), designated in 1897. (COURTESY IOWA TOURISM OFFICE)

Q. How many state forests does Iowa have?

A. Nine.

Q. On the bluffs of what river is one of only three locations in the world where cliff-dwelling pigeons can be found?

A. Iowa River.

Q. When was the first recorded earthquake in Iowa?

A. January 4, 1843.

Q. How did Blood Run National Historic Site near Larchwood get its name?

A. Iron minerals in the soil create blood-colored runoff when it rains.

Q. What is the state tree?

A. Oak, designated in 1961.

12

Inventions, Records, and Spectacular Firsts

A Father's Determination: A Giant Step for Civil Rights

Like many concerned parents, Susan Clark's father wanted his twelve-year-old to have a good education, and he particularly wanted her to study grammar. But grammar was not offered in young Susan's all-black school in Muscatine in 1867.

The determined Clark then sent his daughter to Grammar School No. 2, which consisted of white students. He was forced to take his case to court and, in 1868, the Iowa Supreme Court ruled that Susan be permitted to attend the all-white school. This was eighty-six years before the Supreme Court, in *Brown* v. *Topeka Board of Education* (1954), ruled that separate educational facilities were inherently unequal and therefore unconstitutional.

Points made in the Clark ruling included

★ The Constitution makes no distinction "as to the right of children between five and twenty-one to attend the common schools."

★ A board could not require "children of Irish parents to attend one school and children of German parents to attend another."

217

★ "If it should so happen that there be . . . poorly clad or ragged children in the district, and public sentiment was opposed to intermingling such with well-dressed youths, it would not be competent . . . to pander such false public sentiment and require the poorly clad children to attend a separate school."

★ To bar Susan "would tend to perpetuate the national differences of our people and stimulate a constant strife, if not war, of races."

This far-reaching decision made Iowa one of the first states to integrate its public school systems. Also in 1868, Iowa amended its constitution to grant voting rights to blacks.

Landmarks in Iowa's Civil Rights

In 1948—seven years before Rosa Parks refused to give up her bus seat to a white man in Montgomery, Alabama—Edna Griffin of Des Moines and two others challenged the Katz drugstore policy of refusing to serve African Americans at its lunch counter in Des Moines.

Discrimination based on race was already unlawful in Iowa, and misdemeanor criminal charges were filed against the manager under an 1882 Iowa statute that made it a crime to refuse service based on race. The Iowa Supreme Court upheld the manager's conviction.

Earlier important landmarks in Iowa's civil rights legacy include

★ The Iowa Territorial Supreme Court ruled in 1839 in the case of Ralph that when a slave becomes an Iowa resident, he or she is free. This was eighteen years before the U.S. Supreme Court ruled in *Dred Scott* v. *Sanford* in 1857 that Negroes are not U.S. citizens and denied Congress the power to prohibit slavery in any federal territory.

★ Iowa's Third Constitutional Convention in 1857 provided two steps toward equality for blacks in Iowa by adding a personal liberty clause to the Bill of Rights and legalizing court testimony from blacks.

The Davenport Doctor Who Fought Diphtheria

Dr. Walter L. Bierring of Davenport was in Paris in 1894, the year a diphtheria antitoxin was developed there. He witnessed an early series of tests using the antitoxin and saw the death rate cut in half.

In the 1890s as many as *nine thousand* diphtheria cases a year were reported in Iowa, and the death rate could be as high as 50 percent. When Bierring got back to Iowa he injected a horse with diphtheria germs. He gradually increased the germ concentration in successive shots, and developed an antitoxin serum from the blood of the now immune horse. He used the serum on twenty-two people in Davenport in the winter of 1894–95 and only one died.

Today we are protected from diphtheria by vaccinations, but back then the antitoxin serum gave life to tens of thousands. Many Iowans owed their lives to the "horse doctor" from Davenport.

This Janitor Found a Cure

Janitor Harvey Lillard was bent over with back pain and had hearing problems from years spent working in a mine. Dr. Daniel David Palmer happened to be studying in the same Davenport building where Lillard worked, and found a bump on his back when he examined him. Palmer suspected a misaligned vertebrae was pinching a nerve going to the ears.

Palmer adjusted Lillard's back, and the excited janitor proclaimed his hearing immediately improved (further adjustments reportedly restored his hearing completely). The practice of what would become chiropractic was born. Two years later, Palmer founded the Palmer School and Cure, later the Palmer Infirmary and Chiropractic Institute in Davenport.

Chiropractic soon became a family tradition. Palmer's son, Bartlett Joshua, received his diploma from the school in 1902 and became the head administrator in 1906. B. J. incorporated and changed the name to Palmer School of Chiropractic in 1907. His wife, Mabel, became a doctor of chiropractic in 1905 and taught at the school for more than thirty years. Their son, David, assumed the presidency of the school in 1961, changing its name to Palmer College of Chiropractic. He died in 1978 and his daughter, Vickie Palmer, now serves as chairman of the Board of Trustees of the Palmer Chiropractic University System, which includes Palmer College of Chiropractic West in San Jose, California.

B.J. Palmer defined chiropractic as "a method of eliminating the cause of disease by adjusting the spinal column without the use of drugs, medicines, or instruments." He said the adjustments "relieve any impingement of the delicate nerve fibers which, by interfering with the free flow of Nature's life-giving force, results in impaired or abnormal functions."

B.J. Palmer had other interests besides chiropractic—he also started radio station WOC in Davenport in 1919. It was the second licensed radio station in the country, a few months behind KDKA in Pittsburgh. In 1930 B.J. bought WHO in Des Moines and in 1949 WOC-TV became Iowa's first commercial TV station.

Did You Know? B.J. Palmer owned the world's largest collection of spinal columns. Many of the specimens can be seen in Lyceum Hall in Davenport.

What's in a Name?

Daniel David Palmer got help in naming his new science involving manipulation of the vertebral column from his friend, Reverend Samuel Weed, who spoke fluent Greek. Weed proposed using *cheir,* the Greek word for "hand," and combining it with *praktikos,* meaning "done." Hence "chiropractic"—done by hand—came into use.

This Iowan Built the First Digital Computer!

John V. Atanasoff built the first electronic digital computer in the basement of the physics building at Iowa State University, with the help of graduate assistant Clifford Berry.

Atanasoff had graduated from the University of Florida in 1925 with a

The Atanasoff-Berry Computer (ABC), the first electronic digital computer, was built in the basement of the physics building at Iowa State University in 1939. (IOWA STATE UNIVERSITY LIBRARY/SPECIAL COLLECTIONS DEPARTMENT)

degree in electrical engineering, received a master's degree in math from Iowa State University in 1926, and then began to teach math there. Trying to figure out a way to quickly solve math problems, Atanasoff convinced the university to hire an assistant, Clifford Berry, and in 1939 they built the first computer. He named it the Atanasoff-Berry Computer or ABC. It pioneered many of the functions that drive modern computers: binary arithmetic, separate memory and computing functions, and an internal clock control.

Then World War II intervened and both men were called into military support services and did not seek a patent. So John Mauchly, a physicist at Ursinus College in Pennsylvania, who had visited Atanasoff and saw his plans and the working model of the first computer, went to work. He made his own version, the Electronic Numerical Integrator and Computer, ENIAC, in a secret deal with the U.S. Army, and eventually became known as "the Father of the Computer."

The truth came to light in 1973 in a court battle between Sperry Rand Corporation and Honeywell involving patent rights. Judge Earl Larson found that Mauchly's computer patent was invalid because his ENIAC was "derived from Atanasoff and that the invention claimed in the Mauchly patent was derived from Atanasoff." But because there had been no original patent application sought, neither Iowa State University nor Atanasoff and Berry ever received any royalties for the device that started us down the information highway.

Strange . . . but True

Wilbur Teeters, University of Iowa dean of pharmacy from 1904 to 1937, kept a souvenir pie—filled with enough strychnine to kill ten people!

A man had asked Teeters to check out the pie. The man's wife had baked it, and he was suspicious because she normally did not make him pies. He wrote to Teeters: "Since she has not been in the habit of baking me pies, I wonder if you would mind finding out what is in this one."

Known as the "poison expert," Teeters frequently testified in murder cases involving poisonings. He once wrote, "A toxicologist's work is never dull. . . . Although it brings me in contact with the sordid side of life, I am always conscious that the people involved represent a very small percentage of humanity. I get comfort, not from the comparatively few that I have helped send to the penitentiary, but from the larger number of troubled souls who are relieved of their fear of being poisoned."

Till the Cows Come Home

Ted Waitt founded Gateway Corporation, one of the world's leading PC manufacturers, in 1985 on his family's cattle farm near Sioux City. He started with a $10,000 loan guaranteed by his grandmother and a rented computer. His rural beginnings are evident on every box the company ships out—covered with black and white cow spots. The distinctive cow-spotted boxes first appeared in 1991 and, according to their website, about ten thousand of them are shipped out daily.

Did You Know? Burlington native Robert Noyce, who was born in 1927, discovered the microchip simultaneously with Jack Kilby of Texas Instruments in 1958. This integrated circuit made the computer revolution possible, enabling computers and other electronic equipment to be faster, more compact, and cheaper. Noyce graduated from Grinnell College in 1949 with a bachelor's degree in physics and math. He received a doctorate in electronics at the Massachusetts Institute of Technology in 1953 and started Intel Corporation in Santa Clara, California, in 1968. He became known as "the Mayor of Silicon Valley." He died of heart failure in 1990.

The Wizard of Wireless

Lee DeForest, born in Council Bluffs in 1873, was granted more than three hundred patents before his death in 1961. He graduated from Yale with a Ph.D. in 1899 and soon after invented an electrolytic decoder to accept wireless transmissions that worked better than the device Marconi had made.

Five years later he was known as "the Wizard of Wireless" because of the many discoveries and improvements he had made in the field. At age thirty-four he perfected the audion or radio tube and soon became known as "the Father of Radio." If that wasn't enough, he then went on to invent a method of adding soundtrack to film and the sound motion picture industry was born. Lee DeForest was truly an inventive genius.

Vail Makes Rail Mail Service Sail

Theodore Vail, who moved with his family to a farm near Waterloo in 1866 when he was twenty-one, became the first president of AT&T.

In Waterloo Vail pitched for a semipro baseball team and then became a railroad station agent. When he reorganized the railway mail service, the excellent service was recognized clear to Washington, D.C., so he was called to head the U.S. railway mail system.

In 1878 Alexander Graham Bell's father-in-law hired Vail as general manager of the new telephone industry, and his organizational skills cata-pulted him into becoming the first president of the American Telegraph and Telephone (AT&T) in 1880. He held that position until 1887 and then came out of retirement in 1907 to take the position once again. He died in 1920, a year after he retired from AT&T the second time.

Did You Know? In 1930 the town of Williams was chosen by Bell Telephone as the first rural community west of the Mississippi to have dial telephones. And incidentally, Iowa has more independent telephone companies than any other state. (We Iowans are an independent bunch!)

Can You Hear Me Now?

Arthur A. Collins, who was born in 1909 and grew up in Cedar Rapids, founded the Collins Radio Company, which became a world leader in quality aviation and space electronic equipment. CBS used a Collins radio to broad-cast from Rear Admiral Richard E. Byrd's second expedition to the South Pole in 1933. Collins Autotune radios allowed Allied pilots during World War II to quickly switch frequencies and make it harder for enemy radio jammers. And, thanks to a Collins radio, we heard Neil Armstrong say on the moon, "That's one small step for man . . . one giant leap for mankind." And all of this started when nine-year-old Art Collins made his first radio from some telephone parts and a Model T Ford spark coil, in a Quaker Oats box.

Away Go Troubles Down the Drain

Mrs. Milt Blanc of Des Moines thought flushing potato peels down the toilet was a good way to get rid of them. She was wrong! One day the skins clogged the drain. Milt called his dad, Sam, for help. Sam brought over a hand auger and after an afternoon's labor he and Milt finally unplugged the peelings from the sewer line. Sam went home convinced that there had to be a better way. He worked on the problem and about three years later, by 1934, he came up with a solution. He hooked up his Maytag washing machine motor to a spiraled cable with cutting augers on the end and set it on small wagon wheels. His wife, Ettie, suggested the name—and the Roto-Rooter was born.

It seemed clogged sewers were a problem all over and Roto-Rooters were in serious demand. Roto-Rooter businesses were started across the country and became one of the first franchise industries. Many of us remember the ad jingle, which was recorded at WLS in Chicago in the early 1950s by Captain Stubby and the Buccaneers: "Call Roto-Rooter, that's the name, and away go troubles down the drain." It has been called the greatest ad campaign ever created.

Sam Blanc invented the original Roto-Rooter machine in 1933.
(COURTESY ROTO-ROOTER CORPORATION)

And to think it all started with a potato-peeling Iowa woman whose husband called his dad in Des Moines for help. Now that's a family operation!

Strange . . . but True

Davenport plumber Scott Baer won the 1998 Roto-Rooter Monster Root Award. The award, the plumbing industry's version of the Oscar, is given annually to the plumber who retrieves the biggest root from a pipe or drain. Baer sucked out a willow tree root that was clogging up a four-inch drainpipe—all seventy-three and a half feet of it. It took three hours to pry out the monster root. Baer said, "It was the tree or me—and I wasn't gonna let it be the tree." Baer received a plaque from Roto-Rooter, and a photo of the prize-winning root is displayed at the Roto-Rooter Hall of Fame in West Des Moines.

He Did It with Mirrors

Thomas Doughty from LeClaire is credited with inventing the first periscope, during the Civil War. While serving on a river monitor boat during the Campaign of the West, he affixed mirrors to a piece of steam pipe so that the captain could peer over the wooded bluffs to observe the movements of the enemy. The device was forgotten, but by World War I a similar device became standard equipment on all submarines. The U.S. Navy attributes the invention of the periscope to Simon Lake, but Iowans prefer the Doughty story.

Did You Know? Noel M. Anderson, born April 12, 1916, on a farm near Cylinder, invented the frost-proof water hydrant.

Button, Button, Who's Got the Button?

When button maker John F. Boepple cut his foot on a mussel in the Mississippi near Muscatine, he didn't think of food, he thought of fashion—pearl buttons to be exact. Boepple had made buttons from bone and horn when he lived in Germany, and he had brought his tools when he immigrated to America in 1887. The mussel he cut his foot on inspired him to start making buttons out of mussel shells in Muscatine in 1891, and thus began the pearl button industry in Iowa.

William P. Molis, superintendent of the waterworks in Muscatine, helped Boepple finance his factory in 1897. When plumbers Nick, Tom, and Pat Barry came to work at the factory, they invented automatic saws and drills specifically for button making, which replaced the foot treadle lathe and hand machines. Muscatine was reported to be the only town in the world where button-making machinery was manufactured—and it was machinery invented by Iowans! Eastern merchants liked the Muscatine pearl buttons and the business took off.

Others became interested in this new industry and more button factories were started. Hundreds of men became mussel diggers and Muscatine became known as "the Pearl Button Capital of the World." In 1916, a peak year, the industry paid out $2.5 million in wages. By 1929 fifty-two factories yielded $6 million worth of product. Many button factories didn't make it through the Depression, but in 1956, seven Muscatine plants produced 500 million pearl buttons, 95 percent of all those produced in the United States.

The zipper, plastic buttons, and eventual scarcity of mussels changed all that. The last pearl button factory in Muscatine stopped producing pearl buttons in 1966. Buttons are still made in Muscatine, and although pearl is no longer used, the city is still known as "the Pearl of the Mississippi." The Pearl Button Museum in Muscatine preserves the history of the factories and workers employed in the industry from 1891 to 1947.

All it took was a German immigrant and a misstep in the Mississippi to create an entire industry and put a city in Iowa on the world map.

Stran©e . . . but True

An eight-year-old platform rocker belonging to the Floyd Holladays of Muscatine started rocking "all by itself" in March 1950. Offers for television programs came, and in May the rocker was taken to New York where it "rocked vigorously" for a large audience. But by August 25, according to the *Wireless Flash News,* the Holladays announced that "for all practical purposes" the chair had stopped rocking.

Washing Machines in the Off-Season

Once the home of nine washing machine companies, Newton is recognized as "the Washing Machine Capital of the World," and is still home to Maytag.

Frederick Louis (F.L.) Maytag became "the Washing Machine King." Born in 1857, at age twenty-four he took a job with a Newton farm implement dealer and by 1890 had started the Maytag Company. Initially it made farm machinery, but in 1907 it began manufacturing and marketing washing machines during the winter when farm equipment sales were slow.

Maytag chief engineer Howard Snyder designed the 1907 Maytag hand-power washer. He added an electric motor in 1911 and steadily made other improvements until his most successful invention, the gyrofoam washer, was marketed in 1922. By the following year Maytag stopped selling farm equipment altogether. In October 1954 Maytag introduced its new automatic washer by allowing Newton housewives to wash their clothes free in fifty machines set up in the courthouse square. By the 1960s the Maytag Company was the largest manufacturer of domestic laundry equipment in the world.

In 2001 Maytag purchased Amana's appliance operations for $325 million. Maytag currently ranks third in U.S. major appliance sales, behind only Whirlpool and General Electric. The Maytag Historical Museum is located in the Jasper County Historical Museum in Newton. On display are many Maytag products, including washing machines, World War II aircraft parts, a vacuum cleaner, a lawn mower, and a Maytag toy racing car.

Stran©e . . . but True

A Maytag washing machine that had been running continuously, day and night, at an appliance store in St. Cloud, Minnesota, since April 10, 1992, finally quit in January 1996. The Maytag Company believes that washer holds the record for longest continuous washing. Now that's dependability!

Maytag Is Also Famous for Blue Cheese!

Elmer H. Maytag, son of F.L., didn't follow in his father's footsteps. Instead he leaned toward farming and put together a nationally famous herd of Holstein-Friesian cows.

Elmer began his herd in 1919, and by the 1930s the Maytag Holsteins were gaining awards and recognition all over North America. Fred Maytag II, Elmer's son, took over the herd in 1940 and sought for an additional way to use the high-quality milk. He set up an agreement with Iowa State University to use its new process for making blue cheese, and in 1941 the first wheels of Maytag Blue Cheese were made.

Maytag Blue Cheese quickly became acclaimed by cheese experts and food editors as the finest American blue. It is now widely recognized as one of the five finest cheeses in the world. More than three decades later, the cheese is still made the same way. The small handmade batches are aged six months, twice as long as ordinary blue cheese, and every wheel is guaranteed. Visitors are welcome at the cheese shop that overlooks the cheese plant and Maytag Dairy Farms in Newton.

The Real McCaugheys

Like many couples with infertility problems, Kenny and Bobbi McCaughey (pronounced "ma-coy") sought medical help. But for them that help unexpectedly resulted in the birth of live septuplets—the first ever in the world—on November 19, 1997. The McCaughey babies were unusual not only because there were so many of them, but also because the parents chose to try to have all seven. The doctors had advised them to keep only two or three of the fertilized eggs, but the McCaugheys' strong Christian beliefs would not allow them to terminate any.

The pregnancy was not easy and the babies had to be delivered early, but all survived. The proud parents named the four boys and three girls Kenneth, Nathan, Brandon, Joel, Alexis, Natalie, and Kelsey, and they came home to join their big sister, Mikayla. The septuplets turned five in 2002 and are thriving. Alexis has hypotonic quadriplegia, which causes muscle weakness in her legs, and Nathan has spastic diplegia, which causes rigidity in his legs. But both continue to improve and are becoming more mobile every day. At first the family had seventy volunteers helping weekly, but it is more on its own now.

The event was major news around the world, and the family was given many gifts, including a new house. But things have quieted down since that first year, as quiet as it can be with eight young children. On Mother's Day 2001 Bobbi started writing a weekly journal entry for *americanbaby.com*. One entry was a list of suggestions for moms of multiples. Bobbi advised: take lots of pictures, accept whatever help is offered, take care of yourself, ignore negative people, and take each day as it comes. Good advice for all parents!

Seven Siblings Times Fifty—A Lot of Wedded Bliss!

In December 1989 George and June Sundblad of Sioux Rapids celebrated their fiftieth wedding anniversary—making George the seventh of his siblings to celebrate such an anniversary! George and his four brothers and two sisters, who grew up on a farm near Larabee, all had had fiftieth wedding anniversaries. The other siblings and their spouses were Karl and Julia Sundblad of Albert City, Walter and June Sundblad of Albert City, Elmer and Dorothy Sundblad of Albert City, Oscar and Nillie Sundblad of Sioux Rapids, Florence and Vernal Anderson of Marathon, and Esther and Clarence Larson of Laurens.

First Powered Tractor Built in Froelich by Froelich

John Froelich was born in Giard, Iowa, in 1849. In 1892, while living in Froelich, Iowa (named for his father), he built the first gasoline tractor that could propel itself backward and forward. He harnessed a Van Duzen gasoline engine on a Robinson running gear equipped with a self-manufactured traction arrangement. Froelich sold his invention to the Waterloo Gas Traction Engine Company in 1893. The firm was unable to make the tractor practical, however.

Birthplace of the Farm Tractor

Two engineering students, Charles W. Hart, of Charles City, Iowa, and Charles H. Parr of Wisconsin met at the University of Wisconsin in 1892. Their friendship and mutual interest in gasoline engine research led to the establishment of the Hart-Parr Gasoline Traction Engine Company in

In 1900 in Charles City, Charles Hart (LEFT) *and Charles Parr* (RIGHT) *founded the world's first commercially successful farm gas traction engine company. The company's ads introduced the word "tractor."* (COURTESY FLOYD COUNTY HISTORICAL SOCIETY)

Charles City in 1900. That same winter their company became the world's first successful producer of farm gas traction engines. While this was the twelfth prototype tractor designed and built in the world, the Hart-Parr No. 1 was the first commercially successful farm tractor and Charles City became known as the birthplace of the tractor industry. The company was bought out in 1929, and stopped making tractors in Charles City in 1988.

Some other notable firsts attributed to Hart-Parr include

★ First tractor factory

★ First tractor advertisement

★ First oil-cooled engine

★ First valve-in-head engine

★ First multispeed transmission

★ First electric hydraulic system

★ First successful kerosene-burning tractor engine

★ First foreign tractor business

★ First live independent PTO (power take-off)

Hart-Parr No. 3, a Model 18-30 built in 1903 and sold to George Mitchell of rural Charles City, can be seen in the Smithsonian Institute in Washington, D.C. "Old Reliable," a 1913 Model 30-60 Hart-Parr tractor, is on display at the Floyd County Historical Museum in Charles City.

"Old Reliable," a 1913 Model 30-60 Hart-Parr tractor, can be seen at the Floyd County Historical Museum in Charles City. (COURTESY FLOYD COUNTY HISTORICAL SOCIETY)

Did You Know? In the early twentieth century the Hart-Parr factory got its electrical power by belting ten tractors at once to the generators and putting them under full load. The testing broke in the engines, and the electricity generated provided power for the shop's equipment. Each tractor engine had to produce well over its rated horsepower for at least eight hours, or it was rejected and torn apart for inspection.

Stran©e . . . but True

Eight antique Farmall tractors from the town of Nemaha (population 120) in Sac County perform square dances every year—yep, you read that right. Driven by eight men, with four of them dressed as women, the tractors "dance" to music called by a square dance caller in the Farmall Tractor Promenade. The driver "couples" wear matching colors: red, yellow, blue, and green. The four drivers portraying women drive six-horsepower C Farmalls, and the other four drive twenty-five-horsepower H Farmalls. The idea was hatched in January 1998 as a way to draw people to Nemaha's centennial celebration and the tractors haven't stopped dancing. Promenade your partner and do-si-do!

Iowans at Their Best

The state's highest citizen award is the Iowa Award, given "to encourage and recognize the outstanding service of Iowans in the fields of science, medicine, law, religion, social welfare, education, agriculture, industry, government, and other public service" and to recognize the "merit of their accomplishments in Iowa and throughout the United States." It was created by the Iowa Centennial Memorial Foundation, which was established by Governor Robert D. Blue and the Iowa Legislature in 1948. The Iowa Award is given about every five years and is financed by the foundation's trust fund. Recipients include

★ 1951: President Herbert Hoover (engineer, humanitarian, author, and president of the United States)

★ 1955: Jay N. Darling (cartoonist, conservationist, Pulitzer Prize winner)

★ 1961: Dr. Frank Spedding (educator, chemist, worked on the first atomic bomb)

★ 1961: Dr. James Van Allen (educator, physicist, involved in rocket space exploration)

★ 1966: Henry A. Wallace (secretary of agriculture, vice president of the United States)

★ 1970: Mamie Eisenhower (first lady, wife of President Dwight D. Eisenhower)

★ 1975: Dr. Karl King (composer, bandmaster)

★ 1978: Dr. Norman Borlaug (crop geneticist, worked to end world hunger, Nobel Peace Prize winner)

★ 1980: Monsignor Luigi Liguitti (director of National Catholic Rural Life Conference)

★ 1984: George Gallup (founder of the Gallup Poll)

★ 1988: Meredith Willson (composer, musician)

★ 1992: Carrie Lane Chapman Catt (leader in suffrage movement, worked for world peace)

★ 1996: Simon Estes (international opera singer)

Shenandoah Sidewalk Stars

When Shenandoah renovated its downtown in 1999, it decided to honor famous Iowans by creating a Walk of Fame. Tile plaques surrounded by gray tiles are embedded in the sidewalks on both sides of Shenandoah's main street, Sheridan Avenue. Each plaque includes the person's name, the reason for his or her fame, and a maroon-colored map of Iowa with a star indicating where he or she lived.

The walk was dedicated in September 2001, and by September 2002 it had 90 tiles with 107 names. Some tiles contain more than one name, such as the five Sullivan brothers from Waterloo. Some other names on the walk are Herbert Hoover and Ronald Reagan, Olympic wrestler Dan Gable, nurserymen Earl May and Henry Fields, actress Donna Reed, and artist Grant Wood. Fifty more blank plaques await names and will be placed within a half block of Sheridan Avenue.

Did You Know? Professor Frank D. Paine chose the name VEISHEA in 1922 for the Iowa State University celebration by using the first letters of the five divisions of the college: Veterinary, Engineering, Industrial Science, Home Economics, and Agriculture. One weekend every spring, the celebration showcases the services and academic programs of the university through exhibits, demonstrations, and a parade.

Bet You Couldn't Eat This in One Sitting

Alyssa Armbrecht, a food science and chemical engineering major from Rockwell City, as committee chair of the annual VEISHEA celebration at Iowa State University supervised a record-breaking event on April 20, 2001—the building of the world's biggest Rice Krispie Treat, weighing 2,480 pounds.

The effort was in honor of Mildred Day, who graduated from Iowa State University in 1928 with a degree in home economics. Day had created the prototype for the Rice Krispie Treat as a fundraiser for the Camp Fire Girls in the 1930s while working at Kellogg's. It was introduced to the public in the 1940s.

What ingredients were needed for the giant Rice Krispie Treat? The giant shopping list included

★ 1,460 pounds of Hy-Vee marshmallows

★ 220 pounds of Land O' Lakes butter

★ 820 pounds of Kellogg's Rice Krispies

The mammoth snack took eight hours to make, was towed to the university Physical Plant to be weighed and verified, was a "float" in the VEISHEA parade, and was then cut up in pieces that sold for a dollar each. The proceeds were donated to Ames Youth & Shelter Services.

Mildred would have been pleased!

This Fellow Didn't Believe It!

Wayne Harbour of Bedford was obsessed with proving that the events cited in *Ripley's Believe It or Not!* were not true. For twenty-six years this postmaster wrote a letter a day about at least one claim in the daily cartoon. By 1970 he had sent 22,708 letters but apparently had not proven one of his contradictions to Ripley's claims. His letters are in Ripley's collection.

It Happened in Iowa—Believe It or Not!

Iowa has its share of world records. Here are some entries from *Ripley's Believe It or Not!* and the *Guinness Book of World Records*.

RIPLEY'S

★ **Tallest cornstalk:** Don Radda of Washington, Iowa, grew a cornstalk measuring 31 feet, 3 inches in 1946.

★ **Tallest structure of free-standing playing cards:** Brian Berg of Spirit Lake built a card structure 14 feet, 8 inches tall, when he was eighteen years old in 1992. Since then he graduated from Iowa State University with a degree in architecture, and in 1999 he built a tower of cards just shy of 26 feet. At 131 card-stories high, it was a new record and took 91,800 cards to build. The house was built in the lobby of the casino at Potsdamer Platz in Berlin, Germany.

★ **Longest operation:** In 1979 James Boydston of Des Moines underwent an operation on his arteries that started on June 15 and ended 47 hours later on June 17.

★ **Oldest to graduate college:** Myrtle Thomas of Iowa received her college diploma from the University of Nebraska at Omaha at the age of 100 in 2001.

★ **Largest collection of oil rags:** As of 1997 Ed Haberman of Tama has more than 1,300 oil rags collected from service stations around the United States.

GUINNESS WORLD RECORDS

★ **Largest ice cream sandwich:** Hy-Vee, Inc. in conjunction with Wells Blue Bunny, Metz Baking Company, and Giese Sheet Metal made an ice-cream sandwich weighing 2,460 pounds at Dubuque on February 27, 1998.

★ **Most boards broken by hand in one hour:** Greg Ryman broke 2,897 boards in one hour at Prairie Life Health and Fitness in Des Moines on March 16, 2002.

★ **Steepest tightrope walk:** Javier Gomez of Bettendorf completed a 61.5-foot tightrope walk, with an average slope of 33 degrees without a balancing pole on July 12, 1999, in Bettendorf.

★ **Largest commercially available pizza:** Paul Revere's Pizza in Mount Pleasant bakes and delivers a pizza with a 4-foot diameter and an area of 1,814 square inches. The record was set and confirmed on May 1, 2001.

★ **Most yards gained passing in a Super Bowl game:** Kurt Warner threw 414 yards for the St. Louis Rams in Super Bowl XXXIV in Atlanta, Georgia, on January 30, 2000. Warner was born in Burlington and graduated from Cedar Rapids Regis High School.

Firsts from Iowa

Here are some national and world "firsts" that Iowans can be proud of.

★ **First home microwave oven:** Amana produced the Radarange, the world's first 115-volt countertop microwave unit for home use, in 1967.

★ **First fast-food franchise:** Fred Angell, a Muscatine butcher, established America's first fast-food franchise, Maid-Rite, in 1926 in order to sell his new sandwich of the same name. He was also the first to use drive-up and walk-up windows as a convenience to customers.

★ **First U.S. state-financed extension service:** The Agricultural and Home Economics Extension Service was established at Iowa State University in

1906. It also had the first Agricultural Experimental Station, the first educationally owned television station (WOI), the first experimental kitchen, and the first statistical laboratory.

★ **First appendicitis operation:** In 1885 Dr. William Grant of Davenport performed the world's first appendicitis operation on Mary Gartside, age twenty-two.

★ **First women admitted along with men:** The first class enrolled at the University of Iowa in 1856 had eighty-three men and forty-one women, making it the first state institution of higher learning to admit women using the same standards as for men. The University of Iowa also established the first state-supported School of Religion.

★ **First gold dental crowns:** Dr. B. F. Philbrook of Denison was the world's first dentist to cast gold dental crowns, using an alloy of gold. He reported it in the *Iowa Dental Journal,* but it was more than a decade before other dentists started to use his process. With minor variations, tooth crowns are still made that way today.

★ **First computerized newsroom:** The *Quad-City Times* of Davenport was the world's first all-electronic, computerized newsroom.

★ **First woman dentist:** Lucy Hobbs Taylor of McGregor was accepted as a member of the Iowa State Dental Society in 1865, and earned her dental degree in 1866, a world first.

★ **First woman Republican chair:** Mary Louise Smith of Eagle Grove was chosen as the National Committee chair of the Republican Party in 1974. She served until 1977.

★ **First woman notary public:** Emily Calkins Stebbins of New Hampton became the nation's first woman notary public in 1865.

★ **First woman superintendent of schools:** Phoebe Sudlow of Davenport was hired as superintendent of Davenport schools on June 19, 1874, a national first.

★ **First gas pump:** John Tokheim of Humboldt County built the world's first pump for pumping gasoline from a tank in 1898. His pump was purchased by Standard Oil.

Iowa Rule Book

One Iowa resident came up with this list of rules and guidelines to be handed to visitors entering the state. Don't let the mocking tone fool you—it's all in good fun and Iowans actually welcome all visitors with great hospitality.

★ That slope-shouldered farm boy did more work before breakfast than you'll do all week at the gym. Give him your respect—he sure deserves it.

★ It's called a gravel road. No matter how slowly you drive, you're going to get dust on your BMW. We have a four-wheel drive because we need it. Drive one or get out of the way.

★ We all started hunting and fishing when we were nine years old. Yeah, we saw *Bambi*—we got over it.

★ Any references to "corn fed" when talking about our women will get your butt kicked . . . by our women.

★ Go ahead and bring your $600 Orvis Fly Rod. Don't cry to us if a flat-head breaks it off at the handle. We have a name for that thirteen-inch trout you fish for—bait.

★ If that cell phone rings while a bunch of mallards are making their final approach, we may shoot it.

★ The Hawkeyes and the Cyclones are as important here as the Lakers and the Knicks . . . and a dang sight more fun to watch.

★ No, there's no "Vegetarian Special" on the menu. You can order the Chef's Salad and pick off the ham and turkey.

★ So you have a $60,000 car? We have a $2.5 million combine that we drive two weeks every year.

★ We have one stoplight in town. We stop when it's red. We may even stop when it's yellow.

★ Yeah, we eat catfish, carp, and turtle. You can find sushi and caviar at the bait shop.

★ They are hogs. That's what they smell like. Get over it.

★ The "Opener" refers to the first day of pheasant season. It's a religious holiday.

★ Yeah, we have sweet tea. It comes in a glass with two packets of sugar and a long spoon.

★ Yeah, every person in every pickup waves. It's called being friendly.

★ One last thought—the "s" on the end of Des Moines is silent.

 # INVENTIONS AND RECORDS TRIVIA

Q. As the world's largest manufacturer of ice cream in one location, Well's Dairy, Inc. and its Blue Bunny branded items, has made what town "the Ice Cream Capital of the World"?

A. LeMars.

Q. What year was Des Moines the site of the first complete college football game to be played at night on a hundred-yard field?

A. 1900. (On October 5 Drake University beat Grinnell College, 6–0.)

Q. What chemist, who was born in Burlington in 1896, invented nylon while working at DuPont in 1935 and was one of three scientists who discovered neoprene, the first successful synthetic rubber, in 1931?

A. Wallace Carothers.

Q. Christian K. Nelson of Onawa invented what ice cream novelty?

A. Eskimo Pies.

Q. Iowans read more books per capita than how many other states?

A. Forty-nine.

Q. Dr. Robert Millikan, born in Maquoketa in 1868, was the first American to win the Nobel Prize in what field?

A. Physics.

Q. The first women's suffrage parade was held in what town in 1908?

A. Boone.

Q. What Cedar Rapids physician developed x-ray treatment for cancer?

A. Arthur Erskine.

Q. William (Shorty) Paul, team physician for the Iowa Hawkeyes until his death in 1977, was recognized as the developer of what two pharmaceutical products?

A. Bufferin and Rolaids.

Q. Who grew the thirty-eight-foot beard now at the Smithsonian Institution?

A. Hans Langseth of Northwood cultivated the beard for almost fifty years, until his death in 1927. (He was buried but the beard was not! When the well-preserved beard was found in an attic chest, it was donated to the Smithsonian.)

Q. What is the most crooked street in the world?

A. Snake Alley in Burlington, which has one continuous curve. (COURTESY IOWA TOURISM OFFICE)

Q. John Naughton, who was born in 1915 near Parnell, created what new device for the dental profession?

A. The reclining dental chair (the original Den-Tal-Ez chair is part of the collections of the National Museum of American History, Smithsonian Institution, Washington, D.C.).

13
Matters of Grave Concern

The Telltale Tombstone

In the early 1900s Heinrich and Olga Schultz, who owned a small farm near Washta, hired a mysterious stranger as a farmhand, despite the warnings of their friends and neighbors. The trusting couple gave Will Florence food, board, and a small salary.

Florence revealed little about himself, other than that he had come from Texas and was recovering from some health problems.

After hearing that the local bank was about to fail, Schultz went into Washta and withdrew most of his money, planning to return it when the bank crisis had passed. That was the last time he was seen alive.

Three days later, a friend, concerned about the old couple, went to the house to find Heinrich and Olga dead on the kitchen floor. They had been killed with an ax. The house was a wreck and Will Florence had vanished.

Arrested a few days later in Nebraska, Florence was returned to Washta. The local prosecutor was convinced of his guilt, but Florence was released because of a lack of evidence. He vanished again. Shortly after, a strange tale began about a face that was beginning to emerge on the tombstone of the Schultzes. Many believed it was the murderer's face. Those who knew him swore it was the face of Will Florence.

Was it the power of suggestion or was the gravestone actually changing? A marble dealer was brought in to examine the stone. He explained that the "atmospheric influences of the rust and veins in the marble" were causing the changes and predicted that the face would grow plainer. It did.

After much prodding two police detectives agreed to take a closer look at the stone and at the case. They uncovered new evidence that solidly implicated Will Florence in the murder. A warrant was issued for his arrest, but he was never found. The man had disappeared, but many believe his likeness had appeared on the tombstone of Heinrich and Olga Schultz. Was he the murderer? If so, it's a case of the telltale tombstone!

Strange . . . but True

According to the county history book [*And So They Came . . . to Bloomfield Township* by the Bloomfield Township Historical Society (Winneshiek County: 1980)], Billy Merical and his wife were walking along the railroad track north of Castalia when they were hit by a train. Mr. Merical was killed but Mrs. Merical got caught up in the cowcatcher on the front of the train and was carried several miles. When the train finally stopped, the engineer asked her, "What is your name?" She replied, "It's Merical." The engineer said, "I know it's a miracle, but what is your name?"

The Spirited Community of True Inspiration

A religious group calling themselves the Community of True Inspiration established the Amana Colonies in 1854 west of Iowa City—and some ghostly tales are associated with the seven colonies.

One tale concerns the area known as Indian Dam, built by a Sauk tribe more than three hundred years ago. Located north of Homestead on the Iowa River, Indian Dam is said to be haunted by the restless spirits of the Sauks, and on full-moon nights the sound of drums and Indian chants can be heard there.

Another tale is told of a pale blue light that can be seen over the grave of

Mary Wright in the Sprague Cemetery, just west of Homestead. Mary died at the tender age of six in 1854. The light supposedly appears during the final minute of every year and has been seen ever since Mary's death—a unique New Year's Eve occurrence.

Yet another ghostly Amana haunt can be found on a sharp bend in the road between Middle and High Amana. Called Geist Ecke or "Ghost Corner," it is believed to be haunted by a variety of frightening spirits. Through the years many have reported witnessing white, filmy apparitions at this curve in the road.

Home At Last

A B-25J Mitchell light bomber took off on a mission from a U.S. air-base in Tacloban, Leyte, in the Philippines, on January 9, 1945. It never came back. What happened to the plane and its crew, including copilot Neil Davis, was a complete mystery.

Then, in 1999, a call came from the Office of Mortuary Affairs in Washington, D.C., telling Bill Nesmith of Omaha, "I think we may have found your uncle." The plane wreckage had been found in 1992 on a mountain slope in a remote area of Sibuyan Island. Identification of the remains was made possible from a DNA sample given by Davis's nephew, Bill.

On Saturday, February 24, 2001, the ashes of Army Second Lieutenant Neil B. Davis were buried with full military honors in Rose Hill Cemetery in Shenandoah, ending part of the fifty-six-year mystery. When Davis's headstone had been erected after his disappearance, it had been inscribed, "Lost somewhere in the Pacific in World War II." Now that "somewhere" is known and a native son has come home.

Did You Know? The daughter, granddaughter, and great-granddaughter of Betsy Ross, the maker of the first American flag, all lived at 718 Avenue F in Fort Madison. Betsy Ross's granddaughter is buried in a Keokuk cemetery.

Legend Has It . . .

According to local lore, an entire covered wagon was buried with the people still in it on a hill in LeClaire in the late 1800s. The occupants supposedly died of cholera. At the time of the burial, the area was rural farmland, but now the Glendale Cemetery is there. However, even today the locals won't bury anyone else on that hill.

The Several Resting Places of Sergeant Floyd

The Sergeant Floyd Monument, on a bluff overlooking the Missouri River just south of Sioux City, was designated a National Historic Landmark in 1960 by the U.S. Government, the first such designation in the country.

This hundred-foot-tall white stone obelisk commemorates Sergeant Charles Floyd, the only member of the 1804 Lewis and Clark Expedition to die on the journey. Floyd, a relative of William Clark, died August 20, 1804, of what historians believe was appendicitis. He was the first American soldier to give his life in the service of his country west of the Mississippi River.

Expedition journals state: "We buried him to the top of a high round hill overlooking the river and country just below a small river without a name to which we name and call Floyd's River, the bluffs, Sergeant Floyd's Bluffs. We buried him with all the honors of War, and fixed a cedar post at his head with his name, title and Day of the month and year."

Because erosion had caused the grave to slide down the bluff, in 1857 Sioux City residents retrieved the skull and other bones and buried them about two hundred yards east of the original site. In 1895, because of concern that cattle were trampling the grave, residents reburied the remains at a new site marked with a marble slab.

Finally, in 1900, the remains of Floyd were permanently interred beneath the present stone monument. The 278-ton obelisk is located just off Highway 75 near Glenn Avenue and is open to the public.

Strange . . . but True

A Monumental Mistake

The Sergeant Floyd Monument has been mistakenly identified as the Washington Monument more than once by reputable sources.

On July 6, 1950, the *Sioux City Journal* ran a Fourth of July page of patriotic pictures prepared by the Associated Press. A photo of the Floyd Monument was misidentified as the Washington Monument. Not only did Sioux Citians recognize the monument and the people in the photo, they knew who had taken the photograph and when it was taken, as they made clear in their letters to the newspaper.

Apparently when the photograph was sent to the Library of Congress for copyright deposit, it was labeled incorrectly and a caption card was made with the incorrect label. Again in 1986, in the August-September issue of *Modern Maturity* magazine, the

The Sergeant Floyd Monument (LEFT), the first designated National Historic Landmark in the country, was built in 1900 and stands 100 feet tall. (COURTESY COUNCIL BLUFFS CONVENTION & VISITORS BUREAU) The Washington Monument (RIGHT) is 555 feet tall. Its construction began in 1848 and it was finished in 1884. (LIBRARY OF CONGRESS)

same photo was used and labeled as the Washington Monument.

The late Louise Zerschling, a *Sioux City Journal* reporter who discovered the 1986 error, quoted a reader as saying, "I know the Washington Monument is high, but I didn't realize you could see the Missouri River from the top."

The Black Angel of Iowa City

In 1911 Teresa Dolezal Feldevert commissioned a nine-foot bronze angel statue with outstretched wings as a monument in Iowa City's Oakland Cemetery for her husband, Nicholas, who had died in 1911, and her teenaged son, Eddie Dolezal, who had died of meningitis at eighteen in 1891. Created by Mario Korbel of Chicago, the angel arrived in Iowa City on November 21, 1912. But for some reason, as the bronze memorial weathered, it darkened to a foreboding black color. Despite attempts to restore the gleaming bronze, the black remains, and according to legend, grows a little blacker every Halloween.

Probably as a result of this unusual black coloring, tales of death and curses became associated with the statue. Stories have been recounted of apparitions spotted in the cemetery and strange sights and sounds around the monument. Some people say that looking directly into the mysterious eerie eyes of the angel at midnight will result in a fatal curse. Others claim that the curse only occurs if the person actually touches the statue.

The story of the curse remains unproven. Is the Black Angel of Oakland Cemetery really cursed? You can check it out, if you dare! The statue is located on Lot #1 in Block #24.

The Black Angel of Council Bluffs

Commissioned in 1917 and completed in 1919, the Black Angel of Council Bluffs is the Ruth Anne Dodge Memorial, created by Daniel Chester French, the sculptor responsible for the statue of Abraham Lincoln in the Lincoln Memorial in Washington, D.C. This solid bronze sculpture represents a winged angel standing in the prow of a boat, one arm outstretched and the other holding a vessel from which flows a stream of water.

Ruth Anne Dodge, wife of noted railroad engineer and Civil War General, Grenville M. Dodge, died in 1916 and this memorial was commissioned by her daughters. The sculpture depicts a dream sequence experienced by Mrs. Dodge on the three nights preceding her death. Her vision involved a beautiful young woman in the prow of a boat as it approached a rocky shore through a mist. The woman, whom Mrs. Dodge thought to be an angel, carried a small bowl under one arm and extended the other toward Mrs. Dodge in an invitation to drink from the water flowing from the bowl. The angel spoke twice, saying, "Drink, I bring you both a promise and a blessing." On the third night's visit, according to her daughter Anne's account, Mrs. Dodge took the drink and felt "transformed into a new and glorious being." She died soon after.

The monument, dedicated in 1920, carries these inscriptions:

> "Blessed are the Pure in Heart, for they shall see God." Matt. 5:8

> "And he showed me a pure river of the water of life; clear and crystal, proceeding out of the throne of God and of the Lamb." Rev. 22:1

> "Let him that is athirst come and whosoever will, let him take of the water of life freely." Rev. 22:17

The memorial is a valuable work of art and has been placed on the Register of National Historic Places. It is located at Lafayette and N. Second Streets in Council Bluffs.

The Black Angel of Council Bluffs is the Ruth Anne Dodge Memorial, located at Lafayette and N. Second Streets. (COURTESY COUNCIL BLUFFS CONVENTION & VISITORS BUREAU)

Runaway Hearse

Around 1915 Louis Smith farmed and ran a livery barn in Marble Rock, and he also drove the horses for funerals. For such occasions, he kept a matched set of black horses along with heavy nets and tassels for decoration. Once when leaving a funeral at the Dunkard Church just south of Marble Rock, he turned the horses too sharply on the hillside and the hearse overturned on top of him.

The mourners rushed to open the overturned casket and discovered no damage to their Aunt Lizzie's body. The relatives remarked that their aunt had always been afraid of a runaway and now, after death, she'd been involved in one.

After checking on the dead body, somebody finally did turn the hearse back over and check on Mr. Smith. Fortunately the only thing hurt was his pride. He got back onto his seat and the cortege proceeded to the cemetery.

Strange . . . but True

The first deaths recorded in Marble Rock were J. J. Ridell and S. C. Ridell, killed by lightning while in bed on the night of June 19, 1885.

Urns for Diehard Sports Fans

Canuck's Sportsman's Memorials in Des Moines will put the ashes of your deceased loved one inside just about any sports object you choose. Did your loved one like to bowl or watch football? How about a memorial bowling ball or football? Was hunting or fishing more his kind of sport? Ashes have been placed in duck decoys, shotgun shells, and fishing lures. Ice hockey sticks and golf clubs have even been used to hold the ashes of deceased sports fans.

According to *Wireless Flash News,* owner Jay Knudsen knows his sports-oriented items are a little strange, but he feels they allow people "more choices than the same old morbid stuff."

Stran©e . . . but True

Mourning a Mule

The *LeMars Sentinel* carried this mule obituary on February 13, 1903:

"Jennie," perhaps the oldest mule in northwestern Iowa, died at the home of her owner, Bert Van Pelt, west of Orange City on Friday of last week at the age of forty-one years. Jennie first saw the light of day in Marion County, Iowa, and with her mate drew a load of household furniture from Pella to Sioux County in '69; this train of wagon teams being the very first settlers of the colony. Jennie also bore the distinction of being one of the four-mule teams which drew the county safe and records from Calliope in '72, when the boys relocated the county seat without ceremony or ballot. Jennie's mates, on this famous trip, preceded her to muledom by several years. In her late illness she was nursed like a child and her death was almost equally mourned.

Mules meant a great deal to early Iowans. The state even has a mule cemetery, located at the 1844 Nelson Homestead Pioneer Farm and Museum, northeast of Oskaloosa. The two mules buried there, Becky and Jennie, served in the artillery in the Civil War.

Noteworthy DAR Grave Markers

In Iowa, you'll find markers of interest put up by the Daughters of the American Revolution (DAR). Marked graves include

★ Jane Brown Moore (1807–1886): great-great-grandmother of Richard M. Nixon, and one of Iowa's pioneer women; buried in the Indianola Cemetery south of town in the "Old City Section" on Row 7 in the south end

★ **Eli Hoover** (1820–1892): grandfather of President Herbert C. Hoover; buried in the Hubbard Cemetery in southwest Hardin County

★ **Chief Wapello** (1787–1814): a leader of the Sauk and Fox tribes; buried, at his request, beside his good friend General Joseph M. Street (first Indian agent; died 1840) at Agency, east of Ottumwa, in Wapello County

The tombstone of Eli Hoover, grandfather of President Herbert C. Hoover, is in the Hubbard Cemetery in southwest Hardin County. (COURTESY CITY OF HUBBARD, IOWA)

No Matter Where I Go . . .

James Grant was born in North Carolina and came to Davenport in 1838. He was a successful attorney and served as Speaker of the Iowa House of Representatives in 1852. He had been a district judge, and after retiring from the law, he went to the Massachusetts Institute of Technology to study mining engineering. He then went to California where, at age sixty-nine, he managed a gold mine.

In 1885, at age seventy-three, he wrote: "No matter where I go, whether . . . in the mountains of Colorado or the vine clad hills of California, my mind is ever going back to Iowa, its bar and its Judges and its people. . . . Iowa is my home and if I die away from that I suppose somebody will bring me there."

He was right. When he died in Oakland, California, in 1891, he was brought back to the land he loved and buried in Oakdale Cemetery in Davenport.

Notable People Buried in Iowa

Here is just a sampling of the many notable people who have found their final resting place in Iowa. For more names, visit *www.iowa-counties.com/ etcetera/notables_buried.htm.*

- ★ Don Ameche: Resurrection Catholic Cemetery, Dubuque

- ★ Bix Beiderbecke: Oakdale Cemetery, Davenport

- ★ Amelia Jenks Bloomer: Fairview Cemetery, Council Bluffs

- ★ Herbert and Lou Henry Hoover: Hoover Historical Site, West Branch

- ★ Harry Reasoner: Union Cemetery, Humboldt

- ★ Taimah (Tama): Taimah Memorial, Burlington

- ★ Henry A. Wallace: Glendale Cemetery, Des Moines

- ★ Henry C. Wallace: Woodland Cemetery, Des Moines

- ★ War Eagle: War Eagle Memorial, Sioux City

- ★ Meredith Willson: Elmwood Cemetery, Mason City

- ★ Grant Wood: Riverside Cemetery, Anamosa

GRAVEYARD TRIVIA

Q. Which of the original twelve national cemeteries designated by Congress at the same time as Arlington is in Iowa?

A. Keokuk National Cemetery.

Q. Bancroft's Greenwood Cemetery is the final resting place of Reverend Ozias A. Littlefield, the founder of what church?

A. The Little Brown Church, Nashua.

Q. What town has a cemetery with a monument for each war, beginning with the Civil War and concluding with Desert Storm?

A. Carroll.

Q. In August 1898 Belmond's Lizzie Bartholomew became the first woman to do what?

A. Be licensed as a funeral director.

Q. Near what town was Old Whitey buried (the famous war horse that once belonged to Zachary Taylor, twelfth president of the United States and general during the Mexican War)?

A. Mount Pleasant.

Q. On what historic day were trees, still alive today, planted at Main and First Streets in Maynard?

A. The day President Abraham Lincoln was assassinated: April 14, 1865.

Virtual Iowa

The following is a list of selected websites pertaining to Iowa. Although this is not a comprehensive list, it should give you a good start on your virtual trip of Iowa. Many more websites can be found through links from the official Iowa Tourism website (which includes links to all major cities and towns) and the State of Iowa web page. You can also type a few key words into your favorite search engine and go from there.

Comprehensive Sites with Links

General: *www.iowa.com*

    www.netins.net/showcase

    www.iowa-counties.com

Art: *www.culturalaffairs.org/iac*

Historical & Genealogical Societies: *www.obitlinkspage.com/hs/ia.htm*

Iowa Division of Tourism: *www.traveliowa.com*

    Central Iowa: *www.iowatourism.org*

    Eastern Iowa: *www.easterniowatourism.org*

    Western Iowa: *www.traveliowa.org*

    Tour Iowa Online: *www.touriowa.com*

Museums and historic sites: *www.iowamuseums.org*

    www.iowaartists.org/museums.htm

    www.collectics.com/museums_iowa.html

    www.silosnsmokestacks.org/associates/information.htm

Nature:

    National wildlife refuges: *www.midwest.fws.gov/maps/iowa.htm*

    Nature centers: *www.traveliowa.com/thingstodo/attractions*

        (keyword = nature center)

Outdoor recreation:

    Association of County Conservation Boards: *www.ecity.net/iaccb*

Iowa Association of Campground Owners: *www.gocampingamerica.com*

Iowa Department of Natural Resources: *www.state.ia.us/government/dnr*

Sports: *www.iowa-counties.com/sports*

State of Iowa: *www.state.ia.us/*

Maps, weather, etc.: *www.iowa.statesite.com*

Unique attractions: *www.roadsideamerica.com/map/ia.html*

Agriculture

Iowa Barn Foundation: *www.iowabarnfoundation.org*

Iowa Farm Bureau: *www.ifbf.org*

Iowa Farmer Today: *www.iowafarmer.com*

Iowa State Fair: *www.iowastatefair.org*

ISU Extension Service: *www.exnet.iastate.edu*

Amusement Parks

Adventureland: *www.adventurelandpark.com*

Arnold's Park: *www.arnoldspark.com*

Historic Sites

Brucemore: *www.brucemore.org*

Fort Des Moines: *www.fortdesmoines.org*

Fort Madison: *www.fort-madison.net/oldfort*

Grotto of the Redemption: *www.nw-cybermall.com/grotto.htm*

Little Brown Church: *www.littlebrownchurch.org*

Terrace Hill: *www.terracehill.org*

Villisca: *www.villiscaiowa.com*

History

Achievers: *www.iowahallofpride.com*

Aviation: *www.flyingmuseum.com*

www.iawings.com/publications/history.htm

Billy Sunday: *www.looking4trailhitters.com*

General Jack Pershing: *www.visitadaircounty.com*

Iowa Lincoln Highway Association: *www.lincolnhighwayassoc.org/iowa*

Iowa Mormon Trails: *www.lisco.com/iowamormontr*

Lewis and Clark Trail: *www.lewisandclarktrail.com*

Railroads: *www.dot.state.ia.us/rail/railhistory.htm*

Roto-Rooter: *www.rotorooter.com*

State: *www.iowa-counties.com/historical/iowahistory.htm*

State Historical Society: *www.iowahistory.org*

Transportation: *www.dot.state.ia.us/histbook.pdf*

Underground Railroad:
  www.maquoketa.k12.ia.us/Briggs/UGRR/iowa_ugrr_links.html

Humanities

Art: *www.legionarts.org*

Jay Norwood Darling: *www.dingdarlingsociety.org*

Film: *www.state.ia.us/ided/film*

Donna Reed: *www.donnareed.org*

Humanities Iowa: *www.uiowa.edu/~humiowa*

Music: *www.iowarocknroll.com*

Bix Beiderbecke: *www.bixsociety.org*

Karl King: *www.s-hamilton.k12.ia.us/KarlKing*

Glenn Miller: *www.glennmiller.org*

Major Cities

Ames: *www.ames.ia.us*

Bettendorf: *www.bettendorf.lib.ia/us*

Cedar Falls: *www.cedarfalls.org*

Cedar Rapids: *www.cedar-rapids.com*

Council Bluffs: *www.councilbluffsiowa.com*

Davenport: *www.cityofdavenportiowa.com*

Des Moines: *www.desmoinesia.com*

Iowa City: *www.iowacity.com*

Sioux City: *www.downtownsiouxcity.com*

Waterloo: *www.waterloocvb.org*

West Des Moines: *www.wdmchamber.org*

Museums

Amana: *www.amanaheritage.org*

Anamosa State Prison: *www.members.aol.com/aspmuseum*

Art: *www.macniderart.org*

Christian Petersen: *www.museums.iastate.edu/PetersenFrames.htm*

Grant Wood: *www.crma.org/collection/wood/wood.htm*

Bily Clocks/Dvořák: *www.spillville.ia.us*

Bob Feller: *www.bobfeller.org*

Danish: *www.dkmuseum.org*

Floyd County: *www.catt.org/fchs.html*

Herbert Hoover Presidential Museum and Library: *www.hoover.archives.gov*

Living History Farms: *www.livinghistoryfarms.org*

Maytag: *www.jascomuseum.com*

Norwegian: *www.vesterheim.org*

Pearl Button: *www.pearlbuttoncapital.com*

State Historical: *www.iowahistory.org/museum*

Toy: *www.dyersville.org/museum.htm*

Wrestling: *www.wrestlingmuseum.org*

Science and Nature

Atanasoff-Berry Computer: *www.cs.iastate.edu/jva/jva-archive.shtml*

Loess Hills: *www.loesshillstours.com*

Wildflower photographs: *www.primefocus-iowa.com/wildflowers.html*

Sports

Drake Relays: *www.drakerelays.org*

Golf: *www.golfguideweb.com/iowa/iowa.html*

High school: *www.iahsaa.org* & *www.ighsau.org*

Hunting and fishing: *www.iowaoutdoors.org*

Iowa Intercollegiate Athletic Conference: *www.iowaconference.com*

RAGBRAI: *www.ragbrai.org*

Skiing and snowboarding:
www.unitedstatesoutdoors.com/ia/skiingsnowboarding/slopes.html

Tourist Attractions

Amana Colonies: *www.amanacolonies.com*

Amish: *www.kalonaiowa.org/village/index.html*

Boone: *www.scenic-valleyrr.com*

Elkhorn: *www.danishwindmill.com*

Field of Dreams: *www.fieldofdreamsmoviesite.com* or
www.leftandcenterfod.com

Iowa State Fair: *www.iowastatefair.org*

Madison County: *www.madisoncounty.com*

Mason City: *www.themusicmansquare.org*

Okoboji: *www.vacationokoboji.com*

Orange City: *www.orangecityiowa.com*

Pella: *www.pella.org*

Winterset: *www.johnwaynebirthplace.org*

Trails

Bike trails and maps: *www.msp.dot.state.ia.us/trans_data/mrsid/bikemap.html*

Iowa Natural Heritage Foundation: *www.inhf.org*

Iowa Trails: *www.iowatrails.org*

Universities

Drake: *www.drake.edu*

Iowa State: *www.iastate.edu*

University of Iowa: *www.uiowa.edu*

University of Northern Iowa: *www.uni.edu*

Index